POLITICAL MEMORY AND THE AESTHETICS OF CARE

STANFORD UNIVERSITY PRESS
Stanford, California

Printed in the United States of America on acid-free, archival-quality paper

ISBN: 978-1-5036-2932-5 (cloth)
ISBN: 978-1-5036-3012-3 (paperback)
ISBN: 978-1-5036-3013-0 (ebook)

Library of Congress Control Number: 2021945965

Cover design: Rob Ehle

Cover image: Elina Krima | Pexels

Typeset by Kevin Barrett Kane in 10/14 Adobe Garamond Pro

Cultural Memory
in
the
Present

Hent de Vries, Editor

POLITICAL MEMORY AND
THE AESTHETICS OF CARE

The Art of Complicity and Resistance

Mihaela Mihai

Stanford University Press
Stanford, California

Contents

Acknowledgments

This book emerged out of a project funded by the European Research Council (Starting Grant no. 637709). Within this project, I had the opportunity to work with an excellent group of early career researchers. Maša Mrovlje, Diana Popa, Mauro Greco, and Gisli Vogler were helpful teammates and wonderful intellectual interlocutors and I thank them for their companionship.

Several scholars read the full manuscript and offered lavish feedback. Danielle Celermajer, Camil Ungureanu, Bronwyn Leebaw, Maša Mrovlje, and Mathias Thaler patiently helped me improve the text—I humbly thank them for their time and effort. Margaret Atack commented extensively on the French chapter, Sakiru Adebayo offered insightful suggestions on the South African case study—I am deeply grateful to both.

Individual chapters were presented at several universities—Cambridge, Oxford, Warwick, Sydney, Monash (Prato), Southampton, and York—and as part of the annual meetings of the American Political Science Association (Boston), the European Consortium for Social Research (Joint Sessions in Pisa and General Conference in Oslo), and the Association for Political Thought (Oxford). On these occasions and in conversation over the years, I had lots to learn from Mónica Brito-Vieira, Pumla Gobodo-Madikizela, Andrew Schaap, Tracy Strong, Maria Alina Asavei, Moira Gatens, Paul Gready, Toby Kelly, Lars Waldorf, Emily Beausoleil, Mihaela

Czobor-Lupp, Bogdan Popa, Verena Erlenbusch-Anderson, Vikki Bell, Jonathan Havercroft, Radhika Govinda, Bryan Nichols, Medria Connolly, Millicent Churcher, Cynthia Milton, and Barbara Boswell.

The large research group in political theory at Edinburgh provided an excellent academic community, alongside the newly founded Centre for Ethics and Critical Research. Christina Boswell, Janet Calvert, Christine Bell, Fiona Mackay, and Jonathan Spencer provided invaluable professional mentorship—for which I thank them.

I am grateful to Hent de Vries for considering my work for the series Cultural Memory in the Present. At Stanford University Press, Erica Wetter and Faith Wilson Stein were exemplars of professionalism. The anonymous reviewers offered insightful, detailed, and constructive suggestions—all remaining errors are, of course, mine. Susan Karani shepherded the project to publication with great care and commitment. Plaegian Alexander provided excellent copyediting, and Jill Poeggel helped compile the index. Stephanie Adams did a great job at promoting the project.

My friends—Nur, Sossie, Adham, Kerri, Cris, Maya, Lola, Karlo, Vass, Toby, Nida, Faye, Nicola, Nehal, and Farah—helped sustain the energy that such a long project requires. Moreover, this book would not have been possible without the unwavering trust and unconditional support I received from my extended family—I thank Ina, Gabi, Gigi, Geli, Hakan, Heinzi, and Isabella for their kindness, hospitality, and generosity. Above all, Mathias was always there to listen and read.

The idea of the caring refusenik was first sketched in my 2019 "The Caring Refusenik: A Portrait," *Constellations* 26 (1): 148–162, https://doi.org/10.1111/1467-8675.12384. An earlier version of my socio-ontological sketch was published in "Understanding Complicity: Memory, Hope and the Imagination" *Critical Review of Social and Political Philosophy* 22 (5): 504–522, https://doi.org/10.1080/13698230.2019.1565692, adapted by permission of the publisher Taylor & Francis, www.tandfonline.com. The aesthetic mechanisms I discuss in chapter 2 were first articulated in 2018 in "Epistemic Marginalisation and the Seductive Power of Art," *Contemporary Political Theory*, 17 (4): 395–416, https://doi.org/10.1057/s41296-017-0186-z, adapted by permission from Springer. An earlier version of the analysis of *Lacombe, Lucien* appeared in 2019 in "The 'Affairs' of Political Memory: Hermeneutical Dissidence from National Myth-Making,"

Angelaki 24 (4): 52–69, https://doi.org/10.1080/0969725X.2019.1635825, reprinted by permission of Taylor & Francis www.tandfonline.com. A section of my reconstruction of Bourdieu's work appeared in my 2016 article "Theorizing Change: Between Reflective Judgment and the Inertia of Political Habitus," *European Journal of Political Theory*, 15 (1): 22–42, reprinted by permission of SAGE Publications. Lastly, my take on the limits of the heroic model was outlined in 2020 in "The Hero's Silences: Vulnerability, Complicity, Ambivalence," *Critical Review of Social and Political Philosophy*, online first, https://doi.org/10.1080/13698230.2020.179 6332, adapted by permission of Taylor & Francis, www.tandfonline.com.

Introduction

ON A SUNDAY AFTERNOON, in a French town, two friends, Bérenger and Jean, sit and chat on a café patio. Bérenger is a misfit, who cannot "get used to life" and who resorts to alcohol to alleviate his *spleen*, while Jean is the perfectly adjusted citizen. He loves his job, is cultured, and takes pride in his integrity and rationality. As various townsfolk go about their daily business in the two friends' vicinity, unexpectedly, a rhinoceros gallops by, raising a cloud of dust and momentarily alarming everyone. After a minute of shock and awe, things slowly fall back into place. Everybody returns to what they were doing before this bizarre apparition, when suddenly another animal passes by, trampling a cat. Although this second incident triggers general outrage, and a clerk suggests that the authorities should intervene, the conversation gradually derails into a dreamlike, obsessive exchange, full of clichés, over the correct species of the animal: was this an Asian or African rhinoceros?

This is the opening scene of *Rhinoceros* (1959), a play by French-Romanian playwright Eugène Ionesco (1909–94). As it progresses, we understand that humans are turning into rhinoceros. More and more people get green skin and grow horns, and Ionesco intimates that the transformation is not entirely outside one's control: it is nothing like an accident but more like a choice one makes from within one's social situation.

Personal ambition, class mobility, political commitments, certain modes of thought, a corrupt sense of solidarity, and cowardice gradually push various people to embrace the transformations: rhinoceros begin to appear beautiful, strong, noble, and harmless. If you are not a rhinoceros yourself, you only need get out of their way when they crisscross the town in herds at great speed. Everyone has a friend, a colleague, or a relative among the rhinoceros—which makes it difficult to take a joint position on their destructive presence: social allegiances and identities feed rhinoceration and render it normal. Complicity and accommodation emerge as relational phenomena, underpinned by the destruction of a plural space of meaningful dialogue and the replacement of speech by animal roars. As Bérenger realizes in act 2: "Everyone's in the same boat!"[1]

Whereas most residents get used to these massive animals galloping around, Bérenger grows fearful, anxiously observing his friends either turn into rhinoceros or become excessively tolerant toward them. He is berated for his intransigent insistence on the distinctions between "normal" and "abnormal" and "speech" and "trumpeting" and his refusal to adjust to the situation and "be happy in spite of everything." His urgent desire to "do something about it" is insufferable and so is his feeling of responsibility: "Sometimes one does harm without meaning to, or rather one allows it to go unchecked" (act 3). He "spoils everything" with his "bad conscience"; he is a "neurotic with no sense of humour." He is afraid yet stubbornly repeats that he will not accept the situation, that communication is impossible with the animals because their guttural noises are meaningless and their trumpeting silences dialogue.

He is told "rhinoceritis" is a temporary epidemic and that those transformed "will get over it." Crucially for this project, Bérenger remarks: "But it's bound to have certain after-effects! An organic upheaval like that can't help but have . . ." (act 3). By the end, he is the last human in town. He experiences intense ambivalence and despair: he tries to convince himself that the animals are indeed beautiful and unsuccessfully attempts to imitate their trumpeting. Eventually, he "snaps out of it." His lonely cry "I'm not capitulating!" ends the play.

Rhinoceros captures a society's ideological contamination and gradual slide into complicitous accommodation to systemically violent regimes, characteristic of the twentieth century's authoritarianisms. It offers an account of how a society's plural space of meaning and the relationships underpinning it are destroyed, gradually replacing political conversations with incomprehensible noises—a reference to the intolerant proclamations of authoritarian ideologies. Nobody is perfectly immune, and, most importantly, such transformations have aftereffects that make clear and sharp discontinuity with the past impossible. However, even though everyone but Bérenger becomes a rhinoceros, Ionesco hints at how certain class, professional, and interpersonal aspects of subjectivity render some individuals more vulnerable than others: while there is a relative uniformity of result, the timing of when and the reasons why people get "infected" are different, depending on who they are and where they are located within the social fabric.

Rhinoceros is autobiographical: Ionesco was born to a Romanian father and a French-Jewish mother, whose family converted to Calvinism to avoid French anti-Semitism. He emigrated to Paris in 1942, when a military dictatorship ruled Romania and fought the war on Germany's side. Before leaving, Ionesco witnessed the increasing popularity of the extreme-Right party, the Iron Guard, whose nationalistic hallucinations infected part of the intelligentsia to which he belonged.[2] The play is a direct comment on being seduced by exclusionary and violent ideologies and becoming a perpetrator of, an accomplice with, or a bystander to political regimes underpinned by exclusionary, violent visions. Slowly but surely, large parts of the population slide into conformism and accommodation to systemic violence in a climate of monovocal, deafening trumpeting. Later in his life, Ionesco hinted that the play spoke to the twentieth century's extremes of the Left as well. He referred to the French under the German occupation, but also French intellectuals' fascination with Stalin (Quinney 2007). Moreover, and very interestingly, at some point in the play Bérenger provocatively wonders if the epidemic originated "in the colonies" (act 3)—thus pointing toward imperial ideologies of domination.

Ionesco's play constitutes a good starting point for thinking through the complexity of complicity with systemic violence and resistance to it. First, it provides lucid reflection on violence's societal underpinnings, the breakdown of communication and meaning, and their replacement with oppressive mystifications. It skillfully reveals how widespread complicity with violence is mediated by ideology ("trumpeting"), power structures, institutions, intersectional positionality, and forms of sociality that normalize wrongdoing. Routinized, unreflective patterns of complicity or series of complicitous acts turn structural violence into a resilient "ecology" (Celermajer 2018). Individuals' social embeddedness renders them vulnerable to their world's ideological hijacking—that is, to the colonization of their political and hermeneutical space by rhinoceros. Through rhinoceritis, abuses against certain groups become permissible, part of the everyday repertoire of social interaction (Crawford 2007; Z. Miller 2008; Pankhurst 2008; Afxentiou, Dunford, and Neu 2017), allowing violations to go on unhindered for long periods, often transgenerationally.

This picture is in stark contrast to the idea of complicity that usually dominates public and certain academic debates about systemic violence, ideas that are dominated by a legalistic paradigm, which individualizes guilt and focuses on discrete acts of violence. The relational and structural nature of complicity is foregrounded in the play—in Bérenger's words, "Everyone's in the same boat!"—in ways that highlight the high levels of social implication by a variety of groups. However, more often than not, postrhinoceration master narratives of refounding and reconciliation strategically obscure the uncomfortable fact of generalized complicity, purging it from a "people's" or a "nation's" past because of a much desired "fresh start" or a "clean slate." This desire triumphs despite the fact that, as Robert Meister (2011, vii–viii) put it, "Political transitions are not just new beginnings; they are also what I call 'survivor stories' that reflect a non-neutral judgment on the history that preceded them. In this respect, they are always about what the past will have been now that 'we' have changed."

Second, the play provides us with an account of resistance that eschews the exceptional, masculinist, moral, patriotic, resolute, and courageous "hero elect," a model that generally overdetermines national mythologies—discursively, institutionally, and aesthetically. Ionesco sketches the portrait of an unlikely resister: Bérenger is far from being an exemplary, virtuous, and upright citizen, who unwaveringly fights injustice in the service of the community. Prior to the rhinoceros' arrival, it is Jean who appears to fit the hero script. Bérenger is a maladjusted, scruffy man, a social failure, a drunkard. And yet, while Jean succumbs to the epidemic, it is Bérenger who resists it against all odds. It is Bérenger the marginal, the man who sees through the artificiality and repressive elements of comfortable, bourgeois, provincial life, who understands the animals' advent for the catastrophic event that it is. His location outside the boundaries of respectability provides him with a good position and the necessary resources to avoid infection. He is alienated—emotionally and epistemically—from both rhinoceros and humans: he can understand neither the animals' trumpeting nor his friends' willingness to do away with morality and meaning. He correctly senses, moreover, that such radical changes are bound to have aftermaths. He is the last man standing, trapped in his home, surrounded by hundreds of rhinoceros who stare at him through the windows.

However, throughout, Bérenger has moments of hesitation: he tries to join the chorus of rhinoceros and waivers in his refusal, petrified with fear. His state of mind evolves in response to the interactions he has with his colleagues, friends, and the woman he loves. At the height of his despair, he even attempts to persuade himself of the rhinoceros' beauty and nobility. Therefore, how should we think of heroic resistance when Bérenger himself is no stranger to ambivalence and cowardice? How can we make space for resisters' silences, hesitations, and even complicities in the community's political master narratives? How can we enrich our political imagination about what counts as resistance given that the Bérengers of this world never make it in mythologized accounts of valor?

These two themes foregrounded in the play—pervasive complicity and impure resistance—make the object of a double erasure in many communities' political memory and its aesthetics. The complexity, relationality, and temporality of complicity that Ionesco captures dramatically is rarely—if ever—tackled institutionally in the aftermath of violence. Widespread complicity with violence is one of the thorniest challenges for memory-making projects, almost always pushed under the historical carpet. In obscuring it, national refoundation mythmakers operate a first erasure. To the extent that institutional measures are taken to deal with participation in violence, a victim–perpetrator dyad structures them.[3] As we shall see in the case studies included in the second half of this book, a legalistic, individualizing imaginary has historically dominated these measures with highly constricting consequences: both the scale of public involvement in violence and the complex social determinants at play have been obscured. This first erasure thus has an absolving effect but, most importantly for this project, it leaves untouched the social underpinnings of violence: naturalized ideas, relationships, practices, forms of sociality, institutions, and socialized affective registers. This misdiagnosing of the past enables the continuation of certain systemic exclusions and violent habits. I suggest that this continuation can be grasped *both* ideationally, because intolerant political visions are reproduced over time, *and* formally, because institutionalized practices of imposing certain visions of the past in an absolutist and intransigent manner on the community's space of meaning—its colonization—are firmly located within a rhinocerotic mode of doing politics. Ionesco thus warns us about the enduring repercussions of widespread involvement with violence and its aftereffects: hegemonic memory tropes are deployed—trumpeted—to occlude shameful episodes and aspects of the nation's past and to silence dissenting memories of "what happened." Bérenger's cautioning his fellow citizens about the epidemic's sequelae could not be more appropriate because what Meister calls "the intertemporal aspect of justice as a struggle against the ongoing effects of bad history" (2010, x) is rendered impossible by this first erasure. Needless to say, it does not operate only ideationally but gets reflected in concrete, material patterns of exclusion and violence in the present.

Simultaneously, a second erasure is at play: mythmakers usually fabricate and celebrate the category of the "hero elect"—unwavering, singular, usually male resisters, whom the community should worship and honor for generations to come. This canonization—which, as we shall see, features aesthetic elements—purifies all resisters of their vulnerabilities and uproots them from the very relationalities and structures that make their actions possible, while concurrently occluding the contributions of those who cannot be easily subsumed under this predominantly masculinist, exceptionalist blueprint. Resisters' moments of cowardice, betrayal, and ambivalence, their silences and complicities, and their flaws of character but also the violence and abuses they commit in their struggle are purged from inventories of honor. This erasure is enabled by the way in which national myths normally capture political violence in antagonistic, dichotomic terms, of "us" versus "them," reducing history's cast of characters to "perpetrators," "victims," and "heroes," to the exclusion of those who do not neatly fit any of these reductive roles.

The effect of this second erasure is complex. First, the community's political imagination contracts in terms of what they can conceive of as possibilities and modalities of resistance. This image of the hero elect crowds out the multiple historical experiences of resistance, which depart from this idealized vision and which might, however, serve as more plausible, more tangible, and thus more inspiring exemplars: the fearing, wavering, impure Bérengers of the world rarely count as embodiments of national bravery. The absolute hero colonizes political memory, thus impoverishing collective visions of political agency and contestatory politics, devaluing and potentially disabling alternative practices of resistance and critique. A "metaphysics of purity" (Shotwell 2016, 16)—that focuses on separability, exceptionality, standing *outside* and *above* the community—is operative here, simultaneously disavowing human relationality and misrecognizing effective action by tainted and not-so-nobly motivated resisters. Second, the second erasure purges the struggle of all its sins and allows revolutionary excesses, betrayals, and violations to remain unchallenged. Because of their dogmatic obduracy, such mythological visions maintain the community's hermeneutical space closed and thus facilitate the reproduction of not only the habits of trumpeting but also the very practices and relationships—economic, political, and cultural—that led to violence in the first place.

This book does not deny the existence of exemplars of virtue, commitment, and courage, whose sacrifices have served to reinvigorate and sustain political struggles in moments of doubt or despair. Nor does it seek to dilute resistance to such an extent that problematic equivalences are established between life-threatening acts of courage and minor gestures of dissent. In inviting the reader to embrace the ambivalent, wavering, sometimes cowardly or complicit aspects of resistance and to honestly reckon with resisters' own violence and cruelties, I aim to dislocate strong demarcation lines between the good and the bad, to reveal the relationality that underpins even the most exemplary practices of resistance, and to excavate figures which, though imperfect, have contributed to antirepressive struggles and, exactly because their shortcomings, can inspire others to resist. Moreover, as the historical analyses included here will confirm, the heroes who do make it in communities' pantheons are often defined along strict ethnic, racial, and gendered lines, which gives us yet another reason to be cautious about their sanctification.

These two, interrelated erasures lie at the center of this book. I approach them driven not by a punitive or moralizing impulse but by a desire to understand and problematize their mechanisms and effects and to unearth and recover what they bury in the depth of oblivion: socially complex and temporally dynamic practices of involvement with violence across a large spectrum of actors, as well as alternative, messier resistances.[4] As I hope to show throughout the book, the impetus of this project is to offer a nuanced cartography of the "in-between" that can help us better grapple with the protean shadows of the past in the present. Such a cartography is, I suggest, a stepping-stone for thinking through the shape that a politics of solidarity might take in the aftermath and the obstacles it might face.

The decision to start this book with a reconstruction of Ionesco's play is meant to redeem one other key argument I hope to make—namely, that the epistemic-political value of artistic engagements with the thorny issues of complicity and resistance can play an important part in political efforts to undercut resilient patterns of habitual "trumpeting." Rejecting both romanticized views of art's revolutionary potential and elitist celebrations of the avant-garde and formal innovation, the book proposes that, by virtue of specific characteristics, certain artworks might help untie memory knots (Sanyal 2015; Milton 2014) and thus open the space of meaning to more complex accounts of historical agency, both complicit and resistant. I argue that such artworks can problematize the double erasure at the center of most national mythmaking by enabling readers and spectators to travel into the world of both the complicit and the resisting and, in the process, have their affective and intellectual investment in reductive national mythology undermined. Encounters with certain literary and cinematographic works open up the possibility of inhabiting imperfectly, without mastery, the muddy waters of systemic violence, giving us an insight into the forces at play and how they both constrain and enable action. Alison Landsberg (2004) coined the term "prosthetic memory" to refer to engagements with artistic works—including highly popular forms—that get the viewer to see the world from a different point of view, that is, a different embodied positionality and emotional horizon. Critically elaborating on Landsberg's idea of prosthesis and thematizing the mediated nature and hedonic charge of artworks, I argue that certain works can *seductively sabotage* our attachments to dominant—comfortable and reductive—narratives about the past. In this project, I look in particular at film and literature for their status as established art forms in the countries of interest included in the second half of the book—France during the German occupation, Romania during its Communist dictatorship and South Africa under apartheid—in terms of the strength of their tradition, their reach, and their popularity. I do not dispute that other forms of art can be just as useful for troubling the double erasure,[5] but I focus on these forms for the sake of illuminating the case studies of interest here, where literature and cinema enjoy long and rich histories. I suggest that literature and cinema can create what José Medina calls "epistemic friction" (Medina 2013b) between shared, entrenched, exclusionary mnemonic habits, on the one hand, and alternative visions of historical temporality, on the other. As I show in the chapters that follow, their power to unmoor the ideational, emotional, and sensorial anchors of political memory makes them valuable tools in interrupting self-serving, reductionist, and redemptive hegemonic narratives about past violence.

Creatively building on the literature in care ethics, I then read certain artists' work of seductive sabotage as a work of *mnemonic care* for the health of the hermeneutical space of memory—one that is delivered aesthetically. Artists who target problematic erasures and the investments they instigate and who are committed to muddying the waters of selective political remembering, to highlighting the ambiguity and viscosity of the in-between, and to pointing to the resilience of violent sequelae can be thought of as carers and nurturers of inclusive political and hermeneutical relationships. The openness, plurivocality, and "kaleidoscopicity" (Medina 2013b) of processes of memory-making—as opposed to their colonization by intolerant trumpeting—constitute important objects of hermeneutical care, which involves the sustained and risky labor of rejecting and combating certain occluding master narratives and their entrepreneurs. I suggest that artists aiming to patiently, self-reflectively, and consistently pluralize a community's space of meaning by aesthetically short-circuiting socialized attachments to the double erasure can best be understood as *caring refuseniks* of national historical mystifications.

These theoretical arguments will be rendered concrete through the analysis of three cases that showcase a variety of contexts of political action, marked by authoritarianism, military occupation, colonialism, and white supremacy. My case selection is driven by certain thematic concerns, which I outline below, but the theoretical framework I advance in this book can illuminate a variety of other cases of systemic violence. The duration and temporal dynamism of the violent orders included here varies, influencing the scope and intensity of actors' expectations. As the chapters in the second half of the book show, notwithstanding certain specificities that I will highlight in each context, very similar social dynamics and axes of identity influence how individuals navigate the spectrum of involvement. Moreover, all three countries experienced the double erasure this project focuses on. Lastly, in all three, the past is a privileged object of artistic production, enough time having lapsed to allow such production to flourish.

Historical and anthropological accounts of the nature of violence constitute the background against which visions of complicity and resistance from films and novels are discussed for each case. This book does not subscribe to an unreflective idea of the possibility of a complete and objective history that should underpin official memory: historical narratives are always imbued with ideology. Yet this does not imply that all perspectives on the past are equally true or equally conducive to inclusive politics. I rely on rigorous works that muster evidence to question certain aspects of national mythologies and pluralize the voices heard in the public space. Forgetting and omissions are inevitable and, some would argue, even necessary at the level of political memory-making. Not all forms of forgetting and not all omissions are equivalent, however, and it is the critical theorist's mission to carefully judge which ones contribute to the reproduction of patterns of domination and marginalization. The political stakes are high: social imaginaries inform and are informed by constellations of power and the material configuration of a society—and that invites careful scrutiny. This book focuses on a specific double erasure, one that, via reductionism at the level of narrative and intransigent, univocal absolutism at the level of modality has important deleterious effects on the quality of the relationships and the institutions that a community can cultivate in the wake of violence.

The inclusion of historical and anthropological material is also meant to show how similar sociopolitical imperatives—of "fresh starts" and "clean slates"—led to the double erasure. Moreover, historians and anthropologists share with artists the labor of caringly refusing national mystifications and, in all three cases, books produced within these disciplines have kickstarted significant public debates. Yet, due to the aesthetic characteristics I introduced above—the capacity to provide a powerful prosthetic experience and to seductively sabotage exclusionary investments—cinema and literature are privileged here as media of political transformation.

In choosing the specific artworks for each case, I was guided by several criteria. Thematically, I looked for works that not only vindicated my theoretical arguments in variable and powerful ways but also enriched and extended them. Formally, I included both challenging and accessible works: while it tends to be the case that uncomplicated, didactic works have a stronger effect on the public, how impactful a work ends up being is also a function of the kind of public it faces, as well as the context where it is produced and consumed. Some of the works discussed here had a great deal of visibility via the economy of prestigious awards and prizes; others enjoyed commercial success. Still others are by lesser-known artists—and they have been purposefully included to balance my thematic and formal criteria with a concern for the ethics and politics of knowledge production in the affluent western academia, where this book is produced. While some canonized figures and their highly impactful works are examined here, I also showcase emerging or marginalized voices, in an effort to give a more encompassing vision of the artistic field in each country. Some of the novels covered in this book have not been translated into English or other languages that would give them international circulation, and some of the films have never been shown or only shown in art schools outside their country of origin.[6] While some are the object of an extensive secondary literature—with which I engage—others have been neglected by exegetes. Certainly imperfect in accomplishing its political and ethical ambitions, the lineup proposed here will ideally facilitate exciting cross-cultural encounters and make a small dent in rigid hierarchies of artistic esteem. Moreover, in engaging with these particular texts and films, I aimed to live up to an ethos of hermeneutical care myself, seeking to foreground works that expand, without overdetermining or exhausting, an understanding of "what happened." The hope is that this book itself can be partly read as a caring attempt to foreground lesser-known works and artists who have painstakingly and patiently troubled their communities' mnemonic waters, often from the periphery of national and global cultural fields.

Methodologically, this is an interdisciplinary, critical-hermeneutical exercise, reflecting on *how* we need to think about complicity and resistance and the public memory thereof. Throughout, the book moves back and forth between theory and the empirical case studies, with a view to cross-pollinating them in a productive and mutually illuminating manner. In this sense, at no point is theory privileged over the historical and artistic material: the conclusions to all empirical chapters reflect on how the theoretical frame is enriched, extended, and rendered more sophisticated by the specificities of the case studies. Moreover, I cross arbitrary disciplinary frontiers in search of concepts, evidence, and illustrations. Insights from critical theory, history, cultural studies, the philosophy and sociology of art, feminist thought, and literary studies are brought to bear on this project's driving questions. Such crossings are risky because they involve giving up any idea of comprehensiveness or mastery. For example, in relation to the cases, I do not purport to contribute to the exciting debates about form in literature and film studies. While I do, to an important extent, discuss the formal characteristics of the works included here, Koleka Putuma's definition of "storytelling" as "How my people remember. How my people archive. How we inherit the world." (2017, 11) sits at the center of this project: it is through stories that communities organize their memories of violence, archive their wounds, celebrate their redeemers, and project themselves into the future—discursively and materially—and it is via an analysis of these stories that we can both identify the bodies marked for exclusion from official mnemonic regimes and estimate the cost of those exclusions to present relationships and politics.

Nor do I aim to offer a comprehensive engagement with the artistic production about past violence in each of my three case studies. Instead, I seek to offer a persuasive argument about how we should think about complicity and resistance, how official narratives fall short, and where we might look for counternarratives. The goal is to throw into sharper relief the complexity and temporal dynamism of implicatedness. To put it differently, the book aspires to provide an account of how most people are neither principal perpetrators nor outstanding heroes nor innocent victims, but always somewhere in the middle, responding to reality from within their own social island and temporal horizon, in more complicit or more resistant ways.

The structure of the book reflects the logic of the argument. The first two chapters constitute the theoretical core of the project. Chapter 1 provides some necessary ground-clearing. It begins by unpacking the double erasure at the center of redemptive historical mythmaking. While many scholars are concerned with the punishment of the guilty, the recognition of victims' voices, and the celebration of the great, I zoom in on imposed forgetting about widespread complicity in past violence, which risks reproducing that very violence over time. Moreover, I also propose to examine the granularity of resistance—resisters' ambivalent and complex motivations, violent abuses, cowardice, and complicities—usually occluded from master narratives and their centering of superlative heroes. To reiterate, the point here is to foreground stories of impure resistance, which may be more accurate and hence more plausible and more effective models for future political engagement.

A particular set of socio-ontological assumptions informs official narratives about the past, assumptions that appear to help communities draw that much-desired sharp line between the guilty, the innocent, and the brave but that end up constricting both the sense of the challenges that need facing and the imagination necessary to tackle them. These assumptions, I argue, emerge from an individualistic, sovereign understanding of agency and responsibility, an understanding that partially emanates from law's empire and trespasses into the realm of political and historical judgment, overdetermining political actors' and scholars' imagination. Conceptualizing responsibility in highly individualized, intentional, and temporally static ways, these problematic views reduce history's cast of characters to perpetrators, victims, and heroes, limiting the account we get of past violence, involvement *in* and resistance *to* it, its dynamics, and the agents involved. As I show in chapter 1, unfortunately, these assumptions are not exclusive to official narrative-making and institutionalized national doxas: certain academic literatures' imaginaries—in political philosophy, transitional justice, and memory studies—are colonized by individualistic accounts of responsibility that distort our understanding of violent histories and erase agents and practices that do not fit neatly under perpetratorship, victimhood, or heroism.

The first theoretical chapter seeks to reveal the much more complex picture that obtains if we look at the past and its continuation into the present through a structurally attuned, relational, and temporally dynamic lens. Through this lens, complicity and resistance no longer appear as a dichotomy but as a continuum of positions individuals can occupy in the in-between that grows in the penumbra of state-sanctioned, exclusionary political institutions and ideologies. In critical conversations with several social and political theorists, I argue that these positions can only be accounted for by a reflection, first, on how being socialized in an exclusionary political common sense normalizes widespread violence and, second, on how a variety of axes of distinction—such as class, gender, racialization, or religion—mediate the effect of the common sense on differently positioned individuals. Thus, complicity and resistance can only be understood in relation to a political community's doxa and its heterogeneous social positionalities, which both influence the nature of relationalities an agent is enmeshed in at a certain point in time.

It is important to note that one's position on the spectrum of involvement is not fixed. Understanding patterns as opposed to acts of complicity requires an examination of the interplay between memory, imagination, and hope and of the horizons of expectations that they open, constrained both by changes in the context and in an individual's location on the social map. Individuals' situated hopes and fears and their temporally dynamic sense of their own agency determines how they navigate the muddy waters of systemic wrongdoing, individually and with others.

This temporally dynamic, structurally sensitive cartography of the spectrum of involvement loses the precision displayed by both national mythologies and individualizing, temporally static academic approaches to systemic violence. I propose that the losses in moral and political clarity that this messier picture produces are compensated for by what we gain in terms of understanding and grappling with the complexity of our social reality and the multiple ways in which it can engender violence. Adhering to the alternative—relationally, structurally, and temporally sensitive—ontology proposed here also helps us better estimate the political costs involved in institutionalizing the double erasure at the level of official memory. To the extent that we are more aware of the positionalities and relationships that fuel complicity with systemic violence and those that nurture practices of resistance against it, we will be better able to work politically on averting future violence, whatever new forms it might take.[7]

So how can we tackle the messy aftermaths of violence, given the emotional, cognitive, and embodied anchoring of exclusionary ideas not only in institutions but also in people's minds, emotions, and bodies? How can we trouble the double erasure that prevents a more thorough and more honest reckoning with the past? Who can help pluralize the space of meaning-making, given the official shoring up of reductive official narratives?

Relying on insights from social epistemology, memory studies, and the philosophy and sociology of art, chapter 2 proposes that certain artworks can seductively sabotage reductive narratives about what happened by prosthetically enabling audiences to see the world of systemic violence in its complexity, from different points of view, and as it changes over time. Such works can trigger productive forms of perceptual hesitation and disrupt the automatism of socialized memory, opening a space for remembering differently, imagining alternative forms of relationality, and hoping for better futures. I suggest that, due to their hedonic elements and mediated nature, artworks are better positioned than historical and anthropological accounts of the past to interrupt cognitive and emotional investments in reductive mythmaking about the past. In terms of their content, I foreground artworks that illuminate and problematize the double erasure at the center of this book and that provide a more nuanced, temporally sensitive picture of the spectrum of involvement, of its inhabitants' subjectivities and their position-takings. Artworks that feature "unlikely" resisters as well as resisters' ambivalent motivations, silences, cowardice, betrayals, and violence might expand communities' resistant imaginaries and help cultivate lucidity about the costs of opposing a repressive order. Films and novels that thematize the public yearning for a heroic past and for obscuring widespread complicity—that reveal memory's artificiality and its vulnerability to self-serving machinations and distortions—are also valuable for clarifying what is at stake in the double erasure.

Last but not least, the chapter makes the case that, beyond such artworks' effect on their immediate readers and viewers, as interventions into the hermeneutical space of the nation, they can be read as instantiations of an aesthetic labor of care for the health of that very space. Leaning on feminist theorizing in care ethics, I argue that artists who, through their work, chip away at dominant mythologies by uncovering their blind spots care for memory via aesthetic means. I propose to conceptualize the refusal of "grands récits" that operate the double erasure discussed in chapter 1 as the expression of a commitment to nurture, sustain, and protect the plurality and openness of the hermeneutical space of memory. The artists who take responsibility for the epistemic environment they share with others provide what Gayatri Chakravorty Spivak (2013) calls "patient epistemological care," which presupposes a dedicated effort to eradicate "monocultures of the mind," counteract the reproduction of intolerant trumpeting, and nurture the flourishing of honest and complex visions.

Chapters 3 to 5 offer a series of empirical and interpretive analyses that seek to demonstrate the utility of the theoretical framework introduced in the first part of the book but also enrich it in light of the insights emerging from each context. Chapter 3, dedicated to France under the German occupation, begins with a historical reconstruction of the context's key elements, highlighting moments that shrunk or expanded agents' horizons of hope. I introduce a series of positions on the spectrum of involvement, complicit and resistant, and outline the main parameters of the official politics of memory as it changed over time, with a view to tracing the occlusions at work in it.

This historical preface prepares the ground for a discussion of several works that target the French version of the double erasure. First, I propose an examination of *gestapistes*[8] and *legionnaires*[9]—of men who joined the repressive institutions of Vichy and the occupier. I discuss a novel and a film that—in focusing on some of the most reviled collaborators—were received as assaults on the pieties of postwar memory making. Louis Malle's 1974 *Lacombe, Lucien* and Jacques Laurent's *Le petit canard* from 1954 are analyzed for their revealing the complex positionalities from within which people glide into and move within the spectrum of complicity. In

particular, I zoom in on how their classed and gendered habitus constitute individuals' horizons of hope and the decisions they make against
the background of an anti-Semitic, conservative doxa, a repressive political order, and its institutions. Moreover, both works cast doubt on the
moral intransigence of the legal purges that marked the end of the war
by revealing the complex situatedness and ambivalence of all human
actions, which make difficult any cut-and-dried assessment of individualized responsibility.

The section that follows takes us into treason territory. Patrick Modiano's 1969 *La ronde de nuit* and Brigitte Friang's *Comme un verger avant
l'hiver* (1978) foreground a double agent and a traitor, respectively. Modiano's protagonist, the Swinging Troubadour, is caught between two camps:
a morally righteous yet calculating cell of resisters and a scrupleless yet
compassionate bunch of criminals recruited by the French police to do
their dirty political work. In foregrounding a double agent anguished by
the inability to identify with either of the two worlds claiming his allegiance, Modiano points to the implausibility and reductionism of the cast
of characters that national mythologies often consecrate: moral heroes and
monstruous wrongdoers. Friang's novel, in contrast, powerfully reveals
resisters' investment in heroic mythology and their own participation in
forms of monovocal trumpeting: it shows how institutionalized silences
about the underbelly of resistance help keep a glorious image in place,
ensuring a variety of privileges for resistance veterans. Moreover, in foregrounding a devout woman resister, the book challenges the emphasis
of virile salvific violence that postwar French mythologies consecrated.

In the last section, I look into artworks that dispute a form of complicity that the French were all too keen to address—moralistically and
abusively—namely, the so-called "sentimental" or "horizontal" collaboration. I investigate the social constitution of a form of collaboration that
aligned with and ensured the reproduction of the patriarchal national
order—including the consecration of its patriotic manly heroes by both
the Right and the Left of the postwar political spectrum—and discuss
two illuminating, nonreductive visions of romantic encounters across
enemy lines: Marguerite Duras's *La douleur* from 1985—in particular,
the section titled *Ter le milicien*—and *Hiroshima, mon amour*, a 1959 film
directed by Alain Resnais on a script by Duras.

Symmetrically to chapter 3, chapter 4 begins by outlining the horizons of hope and despair that framed how various categories of Romanians navigated the authoritarian Communist order that lasted over four decades. I highlight several specific forms of complicity and resistance and then move on to a discussion of the past's mystifications by key memory entrepreneurs after 1989, aiming to contour the shape that the double erasure took in this context. Then, as in the French case study, I introduce several films and novels that proposed unassimilable visions of the past.

I begin with a novel and a film created in the 1980s, for their highlighting the impossibility of remaining morally and politically uncontaminated given the long-term closing of the horizon of hope. They both foreground temporality and the role hope and fear play in how individuals navigate the muddy waters of complicity over time. Complicity is presented as interstitial and anchored in a series of practices, relationships, attitudes, and institutions. The novel *Plicul negru* (*The Black Envelope*) was written by Norman Manea and published in a heavily censored version in 1986[10] and integrally only in 1996. I analyze the uncensored version both for its shedding light on the complex in-between and for its bringing to the fore the continuities between subsequent forms of systemic violence— Fascist and Communist—without, however, demonizing the "ordinary beasts in the swamp called the present." Alongside this novel I explore Dan Pița's film *Concurs* (*Orienteering*), from 1982, as an allegory that problematizes "percepticide"[11]—a complicitous practice of unhearing and unseeing things that might place a burden of responsibility on hearers and seers. Pița reveals percepticide's catastrophic effects when it is practiced on a large social scale, against the background of quotidian surveillance and authoritarian harassment.

The following section tackles the fragile underpinnings of hope and human relationships' erosion by fear and proximate instances of betrayal. I select two novels by Herta Müller, the 2009 Nobel Laureate for literature, and read her work as yet another contribution meant to caringly disrupt the monocultural political memory assiduously cultivated in Romania after 1989. *Heute wär ich mir lieber nicht begegnet* (*The Appointment*; *Astăzi mai bine nu m-aş fi întâlnit cu mine însămi* [1997]) principally deals with a lover's betrayal, while *Herztier* (*The Land of Green Plums*; *Animalul inimii* [1994]), with a cherished friend's. These works foreground the relationality of hope and the crucial role of proximate relationships in scaffolding resisters in adversity—thereby subverting the image of sovereign heroes that nations tend to canonize. Simultaneously, the novels show how fear corrodes these relationships just as they become more important in nurturing the individual. Interestingly for this project, both books thwart any temptation to pass harsh judgments on even this most painful type of betrayal: in revealing hatred's failure to completely replace love, Müller seduces the reader away from reductive, self-righteous, punitive fantasies.

Last but not least, I look at two films that tackle the artificiality of political memory and its mystification for the needs of the present. *Medalia de onoare* (*The Medal of Honor*) (2009) by Călin Peter Netzer reflects on the pliability of both individual and collective memory: as we shall see, its protagonist brings together the figure of the traitor and of the fabricated hero-elect in ways that can productively disorient the viewer's moral and mnemonic compass. In contrast, *A fost sau n-a fost* (*12:08 East of Bucharest*) (2006) by Corneliu Porumboiu focuses on a provincial community's investment in a political illusion, that of their own participation in the revolutionary events that led to the end of communism on December 22, 1989. Porumboiu refuses the trap of glorious revisionism and injects a dose of healthy honesty by including multiple contradictory voices and perspectives on the past. Thus, both films threaten intransigent, heroic narratives and open up the hermeneutical space to alternative, though less consoling, truths.

As in the previous two chapters, I begin the chapter on South Africa with a reconstruction of the main modalities of inhabiting and refusing the hierarchical racial order of the apartheid state. In doing so, I mark watershed moments and try to provide a dynamic cartography of the spectrum of involvement—both resistant and complicit. I then move on to a discussion of the official story of "rainbowism" and its supporting male martyrologies, joining the critics who have identified the various erasures it institutionalized. The second half of the chapter discusses several artworks that, I suggest, have the capacity to seduce readers and viewers away from the official narratives parsed out by the convenient operations of the political-mnemonic scalpel.

The first subsection is dedicated to unassimilable events, practices, actors, and voices concealed by the double erasure. Zoë Wicomb's *David's*

Story from 2001 tackles women's resistance and the sexual violence committed against them in armed resistance's training camps. Through a variety of narrative and stylistic devices, Wicomb highlights the incompatibility between the sacralized struggle and its patented male heroes, on the one hand, and the erasure of women fighters, their experiences, and their voices, on the other. In the hands of a woman narrator, David's story becomes one that recognizes women's knowledges, actions, and suffering, knocking the male armed fighter off his pedestal. I then read *Bitter Fruit* by Achmat Dangor—also published in 2001—as an account of what must be denied in the new political dispensation for rainbowism's martyrs to remain unscathed and firmly established within the national narrative of forgiveness and reconciliation. A former resister fighter, Silas, is struggling to reconcile his public image as a virile, tough Umkhonto weSizwe (MK)[12] operative and African National Congress (ANC) politician with his wife's rape by the apartheid police. His triple investment—in his own virility, past heroism, and successful political career—sits uneasily with the fact of the rape, which is also erased by the Truth and Reconciliation Commission's (TRC's) emphasis on male gendered victims and perpetrators.

The two works discussed next help us reflect on the functioning of a regulative ideal of masculinist heroism, both at the level of the everyday practice of resistance and at the level of political memory. *The Innocents* (1994) by Tatamkhulu Afrika sheds light on the costs this ideal imposes on those who internalize it and relentlessly aspire to live up to it, as well as on their relationships with others. In choosing as protagonists three young Muslim men who long to be recognized as trustworthy allies in the antiapartheid political struggle while simultaneously staying true to their religious commitments, Afrika highlights the tensions the ideal triggers when it clashes with other dimensions of identity—affecting both those who uphold it and those who fail to do so. Meanwhile, John Kani's film *Nothing but the Truth* (2008) sheds light on how this ideal colonizes the hermeneutical space of memory in ways that, first, turns real, messy, and impure political biographies into hagiographies and, second, renders other, less heroic forms of resistance invisible. The film also thematizes hermeneutical care for the space of meaning in the wake of white supremacist apartheid as central to the task of refounding the community on more equitable bases.

The chapter ends with the analysis of a novel and a film, both set in Johannesburg and both using the city's material texture to reflect on the afterlives of apartheid. Moreover, both vindicate the ontological sketch introduced in the first part of the book, as well as Bérenger's warnings about violence's sequelae. Published in 2001, Ivan Vladislavić's *Restless Supermarket* draws the portrait of a rhinoceros—a retired proofreader, Aubry Tearle—whose reveries in 1993 betray a deep nostalgia for a glorified, colonial past that never was. Vladislavić masterfully shows the recalcitrance of colonial doxas and the habitus they underpin, as well as the obstacles they pose for democratic refoundings. The novel is juxtaposed with Ralph Ziman's *Gangster's Paradise: Jerusalema* (2008), which problematizes a different type of aftermath: the generalized disappointment about the betrayal of the revolution. In the gangster film genre, *Ziman* undermines any unwarranted dreams of "clean slates" by tackling naturalistically the indisputable reality of ongoing systemic poverty, racial segregation, and disproportionate white affluence, all reproduced beyond the "new dawn" of 1993.

Lastly, the concluding chapter summarizes the book's key findings, sketches the broader theoretical and ethical implications of the main arguments, and reflects on the paths not taken—methodologically and theoretically. Moreover, it kick-starts a conversation about the role of responsible and responsive theorizing about systemic violence and its social and relational underpinnings. More precisely, it invites scholars of political violence and its memory to carefully—and caringly—consider the ethical and political dimensions of putting pen to paper on such complex matters.

With this map in place, let us now turn to the task of conceptual ground-clearing.

1   Tracing the Double Erasure

RECKONING WITH THE PAST IS A COMPLEX, multidirectional[1] hermeneutical exercise, involving both memory and the imagination: it includes
sifting through and interpreting events, practices, and actions such that the
past can be read in relation to the present and the future. Certain *grands
récits* colonize a community's mnemonic space, closing it off and making
it difficult for different visions of "what happened" to be expressed and
contested publicly. The ideological hijacking of memory makes the object
of a complex and insightful literature (Norval 1998; Schaap 2004; 2008;
Moon 2006; Booth 2008; Hirsch 2013; Brendese 2013; Khoury 2017; Bull
and Hansen 2016; Winters 2016). Social epistemologists (Pohlhaus 2012;
Origgi 2012; Dotson 2011, 2012, 2014; Medina 2013b; Alcoff 2015) have
analyzed the complex social, political, and economic inequalities behind
the exclusion of certain narratives about the past from collective meaning-
making processes. Moreover, feminist (Lugones 1987; Alcoff 2000), critical
race (Mills 1998, 2007, 2014; Collins 2000), anti-, post- and decolonial
theorists (Fanon 2008; Mohanty 2003; Spivak 2013) have warned about the
reproduction of oppression and marginalization through the selective silencing of certain voices and accounts of the past from the vision of "History"
that gets cultivated transgenerationally. This extensive body of work draws
the connection between the blind spots in official history and their role in

stabilizing exclusionary imaginaries and institutions—along lines of gender, class, racialization, sexuality, religion—in the present of the communities involved.[2] As P. J. Brendese (2013, 11) argued, we need to be vigilant over how "legacies of forgetting allow certain identities stigmatized as unequal to remain unquestioned, and thereby perpetuate inequalities of power and racial resentments."

I follow in these thinkers' footsteps and focus on a particular aspect of the ideological overdetermination of memory. While most of the literature rightly zooms in on the exclusion of victims' voices and their hermeneutical sources from the official record and on the devastating effect this has on them and their communities, I focus on how official visions of a violent recent past often operate a different yet connected double erasure.

First, in limiting their cast of characters to (certain) perpetrators, victims, and heroic resisters, they conceal the in-between area of widespread complicity with systemic violence that Ionesco captured so well in his play. Post-Vichy France, South Africa after the official end of apartheid, and Romania after 1989—the cases examined in this book—are just some of the many contexts where the imposition of the official story left the in-between untouched. Conveniently palatable accounts were manufactured and publicly sanctioned in view of sustaining a redemptive view of history and outlining a luminous blueprint for the future. This was made possible only to the extent that the deep structural and relational underpinnings of violence were rendered invisible and the "nation" or the "people" was absolved of historical responsibility. What is more, in their absolutist intransigence, such visions maintained the community's hermeneutical space closed, reproducing the very widespread practices and relationships of exclusion—economic, political, cultural—that led to violence in the first place. In Benedik's (2018, 2) terms, the memory institutionalized in these spaces was "non-committal" in the sense that it decoupled present and past policies: the reproduction of structurally embedded exclusion and suffering thus remained politically misrecognized.

Second, a certain type of hero colonizes the space of political memory, obscuring the ambivalence and ambiguity that, to various degrees, mark any form of political action, heroic action included. Resisters' cowardice, compromises, silences, betrayals, and violence constitute obstacles to national mythologies of discontinuity and are therefore duly relegated to forgetting. This second erasure thus diminishes collective visions of political contestation, devaluing and potentially disabling effective practices of impure resistance and critique.

This first theoretical chapter traces this occluding process, revealing how the hermeneutical space of public memory gets occupied by certain "controlling images" (Hill Collins 2009) of history's main protagonists and thematizing the costs of such an "occupation." To the typical vision of political agency enshrined in national myths—but also in academic and institutional discourses, such as some transitional justice and political-philosophical approaches—it opposes a social ontology that aims to shed light on the complexity and temporal dynamism of the spectrum of involvement stretching between perpetrators and resisters. The chapter emphasizes the political importance of identifying and reflecting on the positionalities and relationalities that make complicity with violence possible, as well as on the difficulty of applying strict moral grids, given how rooted human actions are within a community's common sense. Building critically on insights from social and political theory, I trace the cognitive, affective, and sensorial anchoring of political common senses that make violence against different others permissible. Throughout, the ecological character of violence is foregrounded: law, religion, economy, sciences, humanities, arts—all have historically contributed to the stabilization of transgenerational patterns of dehumanization, in which many are implicated. Official political memory and its institutionalization structure individuals' understanding of the present and the future, shaping their perception of one another, emboldening or thwarting their hopes, and defining the scope of their political imagination. To the extent that master narratives about the community, firmly inscribed in citizens' minds and bodies, leave untouched the structural sources—ideational and material—of complicity, violence will, one way or another, seep into the present. It is only by embracing a holistic approach to violence that we can begin to grasp the challenges resilient rhinoceration poses and imagine effective ways to tackle it. And that, as we shall see, requires that we give up on fantasies of "clean slates" and that we make memory committal.

The first section of the chapter captures this double mnemonic mystification in public, but also academic discourses about the past, isolating the reasons behind it: the need for clear-cut distinctions that would, first, enable a discourse of strict discontinuity between the past of violence and the present of peace, truth, and equality; and, second, secure a safe level of stability and public support for the successor regime. The second section problematizes the social ontology underpinning both political and academic discourses about past violence and proposes an alternative account. Building on social- and political-theoretical accounts of human relationality, positionality, and temporality, it tries to reveal what is usually excised from the official story and at what cost. On the basis of this alternative ontology, I then go on to sketch a map of the spectrum of involvement in systemic violence, using examples from the case studies of interest to this book. This map subverts the dominant cast of characters usually at work in both political and academic dialogues about the past, showing the multiple and ever-changing positions individuals occupy in the social field. Once this cartography of action is outlined, chapter 2 moves on to formulating a proposal about how we can best illuminate it, epistemically and politically.

THE DOUBLE ERASURE

Because of their recognizing only (some) victims, perpetrators, and heroic resisters, officially sanctioned accounts of past violence are painfully limited in their capacity to paint a rich picture of violence. Examples abound. The world-famous South African TRC valued the healing potential of encounters between victims and perpetrators, mostly neglecting the murky in-between. Nelson Mandela and the leaders of the ANC were canonized as saintly heroes (Unterhalter 2000; Gqola 2016) while discussions of the systemic nature of apartheid—political, economic, and cultural—were sidelined and rendered largely inaudible by the TRC (Leebaw 2011) and its strategic celebration of "the rainbow nation." In a climate where the language of reconciliation was imposed as the only language for "moving forward" and where public forgiveness emerged as a test of victims' good character, contesting the TRC's vision of historical agency involved assuming the risk of being labeled a "spoiler" of the peace project. The South African case is not exceptional. In post–World War II France, we find the imbrication and mutual reinforcement of rationalizing myths of *résistencialisme* (a term coined by Henry Rousso (1987) to describe the Gaullist myth of a unified, unwavering resistance whose icon was Jean

Moulin) and individual practices of *résistentialisme*—that is, the insincere, post-factum invention of individual resistant biographies, denounced as hypocritical by the political Right after the war (Desgranges 1948). For a long period, the stability of both phenomena prevented a robust public opening of the hermeneutical space of political memory and a meaningful reckoning with the enduring, widespread French anti-Semitism and racism that predated the war and that did not disappear with it. Last but not least, the post-1989 official account of Communist authoritarianism in Romania portrayed the entire population as the helpless, terrified, uniform victim of a megalomaniac tyrant, whose spectacular and illegal trial left largely intact a complex political apparatus and generalized accommodationism. A small group of heroes—some of them self-canonized, many with murky, unacknowledged biographies—were consecrated in the nation's registers of valor.

These examples illustrate how hermeneutical erasure works. Selective habits of historical remembering reflect various groups' unequal access to processes of meaning-making, which is itself a function of these groups' relative social, economic, and political capital within the community. Successor elites' politically motivated search for moral "fresh starts" and for robust public support often leads to certain perpetrators, victims, and heroic resisters ideologically overdetermining the public's imaginary of "what happened." As we shall see in the second half of this book, to the extent that "collaborators" and "traitors" are discussed, a highly gendered and racialized language of moral degeneracy and perfidy dominates, uprooting such figures from the complex relationships and positionalities from within which they acted. While a rich literature aims to complexify the images of the perpetrator and the victim,[3] I here hope to show how the search for moral clarity leads, first, to widespread complicity being curated out of political memory.[4] A *need not to know* (Medina 2013b, 215) by the beneficiaries of these skewed visions—those who cannot fully claim either victimhood or heroism, those who stood by, turned their eyes away, or even enabled or benefited from violence, as well as the political elites who need to refound the polity—sustains these official omissions: knowing and acknowledging complicity would destabilize the collective identity that redemptive accounts of history need in order to establish a sense of entitlement to the future. The historical carpet is thus drawn over widespread involvement *with* and accommodation *to* systemic violence, over historically continuous traditions of exclusion and violence, leaving the hegemonic self-understanding, as well as the distribution of power and privilege it justifies, untouched. The costs of such maneuvers are disconcerting: while the discomfort and (real) destabilizing potential associated with confronting these unsavory elements is avoided, violent habits of thought, behaviors, and institutions get perpetuated.

Political-memory entrepreneurs are not solely responsible for this erasure. Many researchers working in legal studies and legal theory have helped entrench the conceptual narrowing of complicity: to the extent that they tackle complicity, they seek to provide a universal set of sharp analytical tools for differentiating between levels of *individual* complicity in wrongdoing, aiming to support legal reasoning and the ascription of guilt.[5] Scholars disagree about the conditions for counting somebody complicit: debates focus on the type and role of intent, the existence of a causal contribution, and the degree of autonomy necessary, among others.[6] These distinctions are useful for the purpose of parsing out individual liability, yet the legal imaginary remains limited in its capacity to capture sociologically and address politically—as opposed to punitively—the structural and relational nature of violence. The concepts in the legal toolbox are too blunt to even begin to map the vast in-between of bystanders, enablers, indirect beneficiaries of violence, and morally dissociated onlookers.[7] Therefore, most of the middle ground remains, from the legal viewpoint, uncharted. Moreover, adopting a time-slice approach to violence, the legal imaginary abstracts individuals and their acts from their complex intersectional positioning and relationships that make widespread complicity possible, effective, and enduring over time.

Because of its historical embeddedness within law, transitional justice, both as a research field and as an internationalized institutional practice, has often adopted this moralistic and individualizing account of violence over more holistic and structural engagements with the relationality and temporality of violence. While more structurally attuned accounts have been proposed recently, because of its intellectual and institutional origin in law and human-rights discourses and its unquestioned belief in the transformative power of legal processes, the field remains less sensitive to the social and cultural underpinnings of violence.[8] To this reductive view of agency in relation to systemic violence, this book proposes a spectral, temporally dynamic, relational view. Before I outline this alternative account—which I believe sheds light on both practices of complicity and resistance and their complex situatedness—let me briefly discuss the second, interrelated erasure.

An individualistic and moralistic framework also informs ideas of resistance in the public imaginary of most communities with violent pasts. The heroes consecrated in national pantheons are those exceptional individuals who speak up, contest the violent leaders and their henchmen, agitate against the authorities, and take up arms (Zerubavel 2006; Rousso 1987). The hero elect is usually gendered male and has impeccable credentials: he lives up to higher principles by not cowering; his courage expresses moral integrity, commitment, and fortitude in the service of truth, justice, and patriotism. The heroes who enjoy almost sacrosanct status in public consciousness are perceived to have made a conscious decision to choose struggle and to have unwaveringly assumed the risks of pursuing a cause. They are usually thought to display a pure, virtuous character and to sacrifice themselves for the common good (Klapp 1949, 1954, 1964; Campbell 2004; Franco, Blau, and Zimbardo 2011) National mythmaking therefore celebrates them, and future generations are instilled with a sense of pride and awe at their supernatural self-mastery, endurance, and unequivocal dedication and sacrifice (Cohen 2000; Zerubavel 2010).

Heroism and its instantiations have been the object of several literatures, including in history, cultural studies, social psychology, and literary studies (Klapp 1948, 1949, 1954, 1964; Campbell 2004; Franco and Zimbardo 2006; Walker, Frimer, and Dunlop 2010; Zimbardo, Breckenridge, and Moghaddam 2013). Scholars in these varied fields converge on several elements that constitute heroism in public perception. These elements are compiled inductively, by studying national grand narratives as well as large *n* surveys probing citizens' ideas of what counts as a hero. Overlapping typologies emerge from these two sources, highlighting the effect of political socialization on people's imagination. Most include references to martial heroes, saints/martyrs, civil heroes, and political resisters.[9]

Heroic acts are generally seen to result from voluntary, solitary, existential choices, motivated by a noble reason—to serve someone in need or a community. Heroic integrity goes beyond what is normally expected. The hero acts in defense of a worthy cause, incurring great risks. Physical risk is central, though not equally dramatic and immediate for all categories of heroes. The hero displays a great capacity to transcend fear and act decisively and courageously (Franco, Blau, and Zimbardo 2011). Finally, heroic action often places heroes outside their communities, in opposition to the "lesser creatures": even though they have ample opportunities to avoid the sacrifice, they decide to act and assume the danger. This vision of "heroism-as-greatness" dominating public perception conceives of the hero as having "specific, demanding, and exceptional traits that tend to be static and available to only a small subset of the population" (Peabody and Jenkins 2017, 11). Therefore, sometimes, the hero's acts can be seen as a reproach to those who cannot rise to the occasion. In the context of political struggles, the hero is understood to commit to sustained political work, notwithstanding adverse conditions and dangers to their physical and psychological integrity, but also to the integrity of their relatives and friends. Nelson Mandela, Oliver Tambo, Jean Moulin, Philippe Lecrerc de Hauteclocque, Corneliu Coposu, Doina Cornea, and Monica Lovinescu are just some examples of elect heroes canonized in the political communities discussed in this book, whose public perception is shaped by the profile introduced above.

This regulatory, glowing image is thus stabilized in the community's hermeneutical space while its reproduction over time is ensured institutionally. I argue that it eclipses the hesitations and ambivalent motivations that mark all resistance, as well as resisters' own complex positionality and embeddedness within social constellations and the afferent relationalities they inform. Resistance does not emerge ex nihilo, and it often involves compromises, cowardice, and violence. Echoing Michael Rothberg, this book agrees that the "analysis of implication refuses a moralization of politics by remaining skeptical of assertions of purity" (2019, 49) and instead seeks to recuperate less pure and therefore more credible, more tangible, and potentially more motivating exemplars. The suspicion—and hope—is that more grounded, ambivalent, and more relational narratives of resistance can more lucidly and accurately recognize the costs of resistance work. Seeing the hero not as an unattainable, Herculean giant of moral integrity but as often lonely, hesitating, and fearful, sometimes cowardly and sometimes complicit, might reveal what is truly at stake in assuming the risks of resistance. There is also something to be said about the disheartening effect of impossible exemplars, invulnerable, detached, and steadfast. If what it takes is an exceptional hero, many will feel wanting: instead of inspiration, paralysis or despondency might ensue. As Susan Sontag put it: "Some lives are exemplary, others not; and of exemplary lives, there are those which invite us to imitate them, and those which we regard from a distance with a mixture of revulsion, pity, and reverence" (1963). Equally important, more discriminate stories of the violent side of resistance can warn us about the inescapable possibility of reproducing violence in the name of resisting it (Mrovlje 2017).

The double erasure introduced above—of both systemic complicity and the less savory aspects of resistance—is underpinned by the same reductive, individualizing social ontology that denies that "we are inescapably entwined and entangled with others, even when we cannot track or directly perceive this entanglement" (Shotwell 2016, 8). In the case of complicity, this ontology has its roots in western individualistic ideas of responsibility, and their institutionalization in legal, human rights, transitional justice, and democratization discourses. In the case of heroism, in a masculinist model of autonomy and exceptional valor that can be found in a variety of cultural horizons and that is perpetually reinforced by the culture industry and other political entrepreneurs. It is an ontology that conveniently sustains the collective longing for impossible "fresh starts" in the wake of systemic violence. It also helps deflect collective responsibility for tackling violent aftermaths: in focusing on individual attributions of guilt, suffering, and virtue, communities avoid the discomfort of looking deeper down into the social heart of violence.

To this impoverishing—and politically self-serving—view of human action, I oppose a power-structured, positional, relational, temporally dynamic account that will make space for those who do not appear in the national inventories of either infamy or valor. In revealing the spectrum of involvement spanning between perpetrators and heroes, my main goal is neither to denounce nor to praise. This book also resists the temptation of escaping into implausible futures; instead, it undertakes a painful excavation work that invites—to repurpose Donna Haraway's (2016) injunction for this project's goals—a "staying with the trouble" that can nurture committal practices of both memory- and future-making.

AN ALTERNATIVE SOCIAL-ONTOLOGICAL SKETCH

Several coordinates structure the social ontology that I propose as most suitable for grappling with the complexity, internal heterogeneity, and temporal dynamism of the vast social space that opens up between perpetrators and heroes. This section draws on various strands in social and political theory to sketch this ontology, with a view to disabling facile judgments about historical agency. It will also hopefully demystify resistance, grounding it in a way that both sheds light on the skeletons in its closets *and* makes solidarity with impure resisters imaginable. Lastly, it highlights the role of official occluding master narratives in reproducing the structural conditions that make systemic violence always a possibility.

Complicity, just like resistance, does not happen out of time and out of place. Individuals' subjectification through the internalization of certain ideas about the social world that they then help reproduce—the common sense of their community—needs accounting for in thinking through the social, cultural, and political sources of violence and the forms of relationality that make it possible. Individuals are intersubjectively constituted and positioned in a social world at the intersection of several axes of distinction, entrenched in hegemonic discursive orders and the materiality of institutions and practices.[10] To sketch the contours of this structurally attuned ontology, I turn first to Pierre Bourdieu, who offered one of the most sophisticated accounts of socialization, of its cognitive, emotional, and embodied elements—an account that avoids the reductionism of both objectivist and subjectivist approaches to the study of social reality. Given this project's skepticism regarding individualizing, voluntarist frameworks of analyzing both complicity and resistance and its rejection of overdeterministic, homogenizing visions of the in-between, Bourdieu emerges as a good theoretical ally for this enterprise. Moreover, his work also foregrounds the central role of the state in processes of articulating a political common sense that informs socialization and produces the many well-adjusted members of a political community. Bourdieu's conceptual toolkit is particularly useful for explaining the stability of mnemonic master narratives—their erasures included—through an analysis of their embeddedness in the materiality of the public space, in institutions, minds, emotions, and bodies. However, as we shall see, I depart from his account of social change so as to recognize the work of sustained mnemonic care announced in the introduction.

For Bourdieu, "The conditionings associated with a particular class of conditions of existence produce the *habitus*, systems of durable, transposable dispositions, structured structures predisposed to function as structuring structures, that is, as principles which generate and organize practices and representations that can be objectively adapted to their outcomes without presupposing a conscious aiming at ends or an express mastery of the operations necessary in order to attain them" (1990, 53). In other words, the world presents us with *fields* defined as sets of possibilities and impossibilities, opportunities and obstacles, which in time generate dispositions that allow us to adapt to external constraints and live meaningful social lives. Fields are social spaces where individuals seek to influence the distribution of various forms of capital—for example, wealth in the economic field or knowledge and degrees in the cultural field. Our habitus is a set of durable dispositions, which are the product of past experience and which constitute the foundation of all our future perceptions, evaluations, thoughts, and actions. As such, the habitus ensures the "appropriateness" or the "fit" between our actions and appraisals, on the one hand, and the objective social world—the fields—within which we live, on the other.

By limiting the range of possible futures that individuals can pursue, the habitus helps reproduce the very conditions whose product it is. In other words, in internalizing the limits that objective structures set for their plans, individuals help reproduce those very structures. The habitus is a self-generative force behind which there is no master puppeteer and that works cognitively, affectively, linguistically, and sensorially: it consists of both more abstract mental habits, schemes of perception, classification, appreciation, feeling, and action and a bodily *hexis*—that is, the tendency to move and use one's body in a certain way, including posture and accent. When successfully socialized, individuals navigate the social world adhering to systems of classification that appear *natural* to them, comfortably inhabiting the position they occupy in the social structure and the relationships that it opens up as "appropriate." Similar social conditions give rise to collective habitus (1977)—nationality, class, racialization, and gender being some of the clearest axes of distinction, which we will see at play in both practices of complicity and resistance.

As the unconscious "second nature," the habitus grounds a practical sense, a sense that emerges without any calculation or conscious reference to a norm. In Bourdieu's (1990, 59) words, "The practices of the members of the same group or, in a differentiated society, of the same class, are always more and better harmonized than the agents know or wish." Given that public institutions still hold a privileged position in inculcating norms within the population, the national habitus is a powerful structure (2000, 175). The state—mainly through the educational system, the bureaucracy, public museums and holidays, investiture ceremonies and memorialization rituals—serves as a *metafield* that conditions and makes possible all other fields (2012): it produces and stabilizes the cognitive and perceptual frames through which the social world is perceived, incorporated, and thereby reproduced. The state's own authority depends on the successful internalization of these categories in citizens' mental structures, representations, and embodiment, who then unconsciously activate and reproduce these categories in their daily interactions.[11]

When internalized, embodied structures correspond to the objective structures, individuals unconsciously feel "at home" and know how to "play the social game." That is to say, they have a *practical sense*: they successfully navigate reality by undisputedly adhering to systems of classification. Improvisation, creation, innovation—all emerge by reference to the societal common sense—what Bourdieu calls *doxa*, that is, the truths taken for granted in a society, including official truths about its history and its agents: "Common sense is a stock of self-evidences shared by all, which, within the limits of a social universe, ensures a primordial consensus on the meaning of the world, a set of tacitly accepted commonplaces, which make confrontation, dialogue, competition, and even conflict possible, and among which a special place must be reserved for the principles of classification, such as the major oppositions structuring the perception of the world" (Bourdieu 2000, 198). Thus, no one acts out of time, out of discourse, out of a power-structured material space and a common sense that shapes our vision of ourselves and our relationships as part of a community with a history. Particularizing Bourdieu's general conception of social practice to answer the questions at the center of this book, we can safely argue that resisters and accomplices alike will act from within a constellation of power, a set of structures and a network of relationships that constitute them, vulnerable to different degrees, never self-sufficient, simultaneously enabled and constrained by their habitus, their practical sense, and the common sense of their community. Depending on individuals' locations at the intersection of various axes of distinction and the number of communities of meaning they can tap into, they will occupy various positions on the spectrum of involvement with systemic violence. One's position enables certain relationships and precludes others, opens certain vistas on social reality and forecloses others. It influences the horizon of expectations regarding one's own agency and others', their level of social trust, the scope of their political imagination, as well as the content and intensity of their hopes and fears.

Most importantly, this position is not fixed but changes over time, reflecting changes in both the context and the agents themselves. Individuals' sense of time, their capacity to build on the past to imagine a future and to invest emotionally in that future are interrelated aspects of their socially embedded experience, which have repercussions on how they navigate the muddy waters of systemic wrongdoing, in more complicit or more resistant ways. This highlights the need to think about the temporality of action—that is, the ways in which the past and the future are brought together in the habitus. To better capture the always situated interplay between memory, imagination, and hope, I supplement Bourdieu's reflections on subjectification with insights from the work of social psychologists and philosophers who examined the relationship between these faculties and action, both at the individual and collective levels.

As temporal creatures, we build on past experiences—captured in our memories—to project ourselves into a hoped-for future, which we know to be uncertain and not fully within our control. The faculty of imagination intervenes in the twin process of building a coherent narrative of our past (Keightley and Pickering 2012) and of experimenting with strategies and potential trajectories into the future we hope for (Bovens 1999). Thus, hope mediates our relationship with our future, always in light of our past, though not straightforwardly or manifestly. In hoping, we explore imaginatively what we might achieve through our actions, notwithstanding our limitations, our fears, and the negative evidence available.[12]

We continue to have hope as long as we believe in the possibility of a future (Fletcher 1999). Ongoing processes of temporal orientation do not happen in a vacuum, however: hope is always situated within a concrete horizon. Socially embedded memories and experiences influence hope, both in terms of the objects it latches onto and its intensity. Memories are themselves underpinned by ongoing processes of intersubjective self-constitution and the range of experiences our habitus makes possible. The kind and range of objects the imagination conjures in hoping will depend on the kind and range of these experiences—that is, on our habitus. That is to say, our relational positionality impacts the scope of our imagination—that is, the type and number of things we fear and hope for.[13] Visions of the future will be informed by past experiences that constitute the self, by the types of sociality individuals live within and cultivate, by the narrative frames the doxa makes available for filtering experience, and the levels of social trust they enjoy: situated memory and experience provide the imagination with an anchorage and delimit the content and strength of their aspirations.

Given the centrality of relationality in human experience and identity constitution, hope does not have this effect on agency only self-referentially: our hopes about others can facilitate their engaging in various forms of action. Our hopes about others' actions encourage and sustain *them* in their endeavor to live up to our expectations. Thus, our hope provides a scaffold for others (McGeer 2008). Conversely, *their* hopes about us sustain *us*. Because of this dynamizing tendency, hope feeds trust and solidarity. Consequently, there is a strong connection between hope and the very possibility of collective action (Pettit 2004), whatever its goals. However, to thrive, hope needs a responsive world that at least partially supports our efforts (McGeer 2004). Otherwise, its dynamic tendencies fail to nurture individuals' and collectives' sense of agency.[14] As we shall see in the second half of the book, a variety of relationships nurture and support accomplices and resisters alike.

In hoping, we take "an agential interest in the world" (McGeer 2008, 246)—that is, in our own but also in others' future. Losing hope can be dramatic—through war, famine, and genocide—or gradual, through the slow erosion of the capacity to imagine a future, as is the case of political repression, resilient poverty, social marginalization, or encroaching dehumanization. Speaking about the specific case of racialized oppression under white supremacy, Steve Biko (1987, 29) highlighted its effect on hope: "completely defeated," Black people become "convinced of the futility of resistance" and "throw away any hopes that change may ever come." Similarly, feminist theorists rightly argued, "some people's capacities for hope are threatened and damaged by the social, political, and economic circumstances in which they live" (Stockdale 2019, 29) since "not all lives are so thickly or uniformly threaded with hopes. In some lives, at some times, the threads fray to breaking, are cut by violence, or are snapped by deprivation" (Urban Walker 2006, 40–41). When a future is not imaginable, whether because of physical or social death, hope becomes impossible: "To find oneself utterly unable to imagine a desirable, possible future, is to lose the basis for taking an interest in one's own agency" (Calhoun 2008, 29).

Zooming in again on this book's guiding questions, the socially structured and relationally embedded horizon of hope will determine the actions—*both* resistant *and* complicit—individuals engage in within the spectrum of involvement. As the case studies included here demonstrate, hope grows and contracts, rendering certain forms of action more appropriate or more attractive than others. In both hoping and despairing, however, individuals and groups rely on past experiences congealed in their habitus, mediated via their community's doxa, deploying its resources to navigate the present, which sometimes opens up new and unpredictable possibilities. Before mapping the spectrum of involvement in more detail so as to render concrete these rather abstract proposals, I turn to teasing out some key implications of this social ontology in relation to my project's objectives.

First, in order to comprehend the complex dynamics of both complicity and resistance, we must account for the agents' positionality—their habitus—a function of processes of subjectification that influence their experiences, their sedimentation in memory and embodiment, their hopes for the future, and the role they ascribe to their own agency in bringing about that future. Visions of the future will vary in their hopefulness and thus in their motivational power, but all will be affected by the historical context, some in enabling, others in constraining ways. No context is experienced uniformly: gender, racialization, class, ethnicity, and religion—among others—structure that experience and condition the disposition of various groups of individuals on the spectrum. In other words, individuals' ideological, racialized, gendered, classed habitus will inform how they navigate the in-between, in more or less complicit ways.

Second, public, "official" memory is a crucial part of the national doxa, which shapes individuals' assumptions of where the boundaries of the community lie, of who their political allies and enemies are, and of who is a legitimate object of exclusion and violence. They contain both celebratory and denunciatory elements and serve as frameworks for political perception and action. Political societies aim to socialize their members into their mnemonic traditions (Zerubavel 2012), which nurture certain collective aspirations and stymie others. Erasures in the mnemonic traditions correspond to erasures in the national common sense, reflected in the way individuals and groups relate to each other in the present. The "socio-mental topography of the past" (1) features politically self-serving lacunae. Given the stability—though not immutability—of this topography, the challenge is to find ways of disrupting its doxastic power, its exclusionary and absolutist dimensions, that is, its functioning as an unproblematized common sense, as well as the automatism of the perceptions, attitudes, emotions, and actions it underprops.

Which brings us to the third point: the common sense's embodied, affective anchoring in individuals' and collectives' habitus below the radar of consciousness makes the institutions and relationships it underpins not as permeable to rational, argumentative critique as one might think. With Bourdieu, I suspect awareness raising has limited efficacy when we consider that the stability of a community's common sense—including its historical mythology—is reproduced by institutions and individual patterns of behavior. To grasp its resilience, one need only remember the recent scandals triggered by political attempts to reconsider western affluent democracies' colonial pasts and their racialized reverberation into the present, materially and symbolically. Affectively rooted, official visions of who "we" are as a community and of what happened in our past inform the ways in which we behave toward each other, the state, and other groups, within and without the national borders. In a community where the doxa is racialized, ethnicized, classed, and gendered—racialized, ethnicized, classed, and gendered relations thrive.

Consequently, any attempt to think politically (rather than punitively) about past violence and its perpetuation into the present must rely on a moderately skeptical account of the possibility of reflexivity. The analysis of a social, political, and cultural context can help us understand that collaborators, beneficiaries of violence, and bystanders—as well as resisters—often have complex motives for (in)action, some of which are not even fully evident to themselves. Persistent collective percepticide and passivity toward the suffering of certain social categories is enabled by internalized dehumanizing doxas that often elide reflexive intent or scrutiny. As Pumla Gobodo-Madikizela (2020) argued, socialization processes underpinned by an institutionalized "diet of hate" are difficult to neutralize. Scholars of the in-between must therefore remain sensitive to how power relations shape both the contexts and the agents operating in those contexts and carefully trace the inextricable connection between, on the one hand, the structural underpinnings of systemic violence and, on the other, the erasures of widespread involvement with violence within present practices of memorialization. That is to say, we need to pay attention *both* to the complex background against which practices and patterns (rather than spontaneous, individual acts) of complicity with violence emerge, sometimes in uncoordinated but mutually reinforcing fashion[15] *and* the nonaccidental erasures of these practices and patterns from national mythologies. Similarly, the critical analysis of misremembered impure resistances and canonized, unencumbered, mostly masculine heroes needs to be connected to an analysis of gendered, racialized, and classed structures of value and citizenship in the present, which tend to be routinely naturalized and invisibilized. These are not to be treated in isolation for, as I hope to have shown already, they are intimately connected, the expression of long traditions of imagining the "nation," its "virtues," and its others.

This rather grim picture is not meant to invite lamentation or resignation. On the contrary: fourth, this book argues that, faced with the weight of the official past and its mystifications, the critical scholar must identify the fissures in the national doxa and recuperate the heretic, counterhegemonic common senses that have historically challenged it. Bourdieu argued that one could modify social reality by changing the agents' representation of it and, in this sense, words do "wreak

havoc"—especially in moments of structural crisis, such as war, revolution, or economic collapse.[16] Hierarchical relations and mnemonic
mystifications are vulnerable to the destructive effect of counternarratives, which expose and disenchant, and this vulnerability is heightened
when new vocabularies enter a competition to articulate new, unheard-of
possibilities. While agreeing with Bourdieu's argument about the value
of alternative languages that can reconfigure reality during structural
crises, I aim to recuperate the patient and sustained labor of mnemonic
care, performed aesthetically by artists but also politically and scien-
tifically by activists, historians, and social scientists,[17] a labor that has
historically led to meaningful political change. Indeed, crises are crucial
opportunities, for they show the limits of our inherited and cherished
categories. However, these same categories give in to sustained, gradual
efforts to transform them: no doxa is so totalizing so as completely prevent the development of alternative common senses that can progressively
erode and modify it from the margins. As Charles Mills (2014) argued,
socio-mental representations of temporality can differ, depending on the
interests of the particular mnemonic subgroups that they are attached to.
The dissonant memories that challenge hegemonic traditions are usually
downplayed in favor of progressive and redemptive views of history,
but they do feed alternative communities of remembrance. "Segregated
temporalities" mark societies where the hegemonic common sense seeks
to insulate itself against marginalized communities' insistence on *the
unforgettable* (Brendese 2013), in an attempt to render indiscernible the
historical excisions operated by the mnemonic community's "social scalpel" (Zerubavel 2012, 96). Bourdieu is right in pointing out that some
scalpels are sharper than others—the state's possibly being the sharpest.
And yet, as the analysis of our case studies reveals, the excised is narrated
in various forms within memory counterpublics, and it informs patient
practices of mnemonic care—aesthetic, political, academic. To quote
Joseph R. Winters (2016, 6), "These dissonant attachments—to traumatic
events, unfinished struggles, neglected histories, and the recalcitrant
dimensions of that past and present that resist closure and the eagerness
to 'move forward'—are necessary to challenge current configurations of
power, especially since the effectiveness of power depends partly on its
ability to produce forgetful subjects."

"Segregated temporalities," "dissonant attachments," investments in "the unforgettable"—all constitute important sources for mnemonic care-work, be it aesthetic, political, scientific, which seeks to interrupt the automatism of socialized memory. As we shall see in the following chapters, it goes beyond awareness raising and engages communities simultaneously at the cognitive, emotional, and sensorial levels.

To conclude this section, systemic violence has aftereffects that need sustained attention to become less threatening to the world between us. To echo Alexis Shotwell (2016, 8), "We need to shape better practices of responsibility and memory for our placement in relation to the past, our implication in the present, and our potential creation of different futures." Chapter 2 theorizes the power of certain artistic engagements with the past in destabilizing the double erasure by triggering moments of hesitation in reified habits and practices of remembering. Before moving on to this next step, however, I introduce a rough map of the spectrum of involvement with violence. Examples from the three case studies will serve as brief illustrations, with the bulk of the historical analysis to follow in the second half of the book.

A ROUGH CARTOGRAPHY OF INVOLVEMENT

Within violent orders, willing collaborators—those who join the regime's various institutions, informers, propagandists, or *délateurs*[18]—face a promising future as various hoped-for benefits feed their moral disengagement from the victims. Normative commitment to dehumanizing political doxas often reaches the peak of zealotry: fed by histories of racist or ethnic exclusion, the political common sense is curated to enable the swift identification of the community's—the "nation's," the "people's"—enemies. Collaborators' political convictions thus tap into a common imaginary, filtered through their socioeconomic status, gender, religious beliefs, and personal ambition. For example, French anti-Semitism, Afrikaner white supremacism, and Romanian Communist nationalism rendered systemic violence against large groups of people unproblematic. Naturally, cynical opportunism also flourishes—the spectrum of complicity features a variety of entry points—but, as we shall see, it tends to be underpinned by internalized exclusionary practical senses. Physical and economic safety, career boosts, and access to scarce material goods are just some of the perks of willing collaboration.[19] Collaborators who occupy high-ranking official positions are often prosecuted as traitors by successor regimes, as we can see in all the three cases included in this project. However, the legal processing of their acts depoliticizes them and disembeds them from their complex sociality and positionalities.

Various futures are imaginable for bystanders who do not directly collaborate, depending on the length of their historical memory; their social, economic, and political capital; their sense of their own agency; their capacity to navigate circumstances; as well as the availability of opportunities for maintaining or forming new relationships of trust.[20] *Attentisme* (Rousso 1997)—waiting to see how things develop before occupying the most advantageous position—is often initially embraced, at least partially a reflection of the habitus's inertial quality. Passive, strategic compliance enables ordinary citizens to muddle through everyday hardships. To the extent that change becomes unimaginable, people adjust their hopes and actions. For example, by 1939 many French citizens, still traumatized by the losses of World War I, welcomed the German occupation out of a relief that the military engagement ended swiftly, but also out of a long-standing commitment to pacifism. For many, the defeat was a durable solution to the historical enmity between France and Germany—against a background of entrenched, historical anti-Semitism that morally dissociated them from the horrific plight of "undesirable" categories. By the 1960s, Romanians stopped believing in the possibility of any meaningful political change, given the stability of the Cold War geopolitical order and the growing power of the party-state. While many enjoyed the social mobility brought about by the new regime, others engaged in various adjustment strategies, trying to lead meaningful lives via collusion and compromises with what appeared to be an immutable system. In apartheid South Africa, over time, many progressive, English-speaking whites gradually resigned themselves to the enduring electoral success of nationalist Afrikaners. They disengaged from politics, withdrew into their own privileged cultural enclaves and the private sphere, or chose exile. In doing so, they enabled and reaped some of the material benefits of white supremacist violence, while comfortably feeding on the illusion of their moral superiority over Afrikaners.

Some bystanders navigate along the spectrum, becoming collaborators or even perpetrators, especially if they become invested in the repressive doxa—its vision of the future and of the "obstacles" that need removing on the way. During long periods of institutionalized political violence, in the absence of a credible temporal horizon for change, bystanders turn collaborators in order to fulfil professional or personal ambitions within their lifetime, even though they may not be politically committed. Under such circumstances, solidarity in resistance remains improbable. For example, to understand the effect of hopelessness in authoritarian Romania in the 1980s, we would have to "borrow the psyche of someone who knows that it is highly likely that their entire life will go on *like this*, moment by moment and year by year, till the end. And that, after their death, the life of their own children will also be, moment by moment, and year by year, *like this*" (2016, 8). In a stable climate of repression, whose end is not in sight, refusing all compromises requires an improbable, doubly heroic attitude of courage and endurance.[21] Developing duplicitous dispositions thus often emerges as the combined result of fear and a longing for normality.

The vulnerabilities inherent in the relationships attached to certain positionalities also influence where individuals end up on the spectrum. For example, class and economic precarity, but also gender via the institution of the family, create specific sets of vulnerabilities, that attach to the poor and to women in ways that often discourage them from joining resistance struggles and push them into forms of economic and political complicity. Having to provide for dependents under the conditions of scarcity and insecurity that characterized the German occupation of France made it natural for caregivers and providers to collaborate economically and politically. Testimonies by parents in all three case studies show how they sought to impede their children's political activism out of fear and love, effectively contributing to the systems' stability. Moreover, violent regimes open up important opportunities for social mobility and political empowerment, previously unavailable to many social categories. The upward economic mobility made possible by colluding with the authoritarian regime in Romania led many from economically disadvantaged classes to join the ranks of the party, including its repressive institutions. In France, the war opened the door for women to enter the public space, an entry previously denied: the possibility of having a career thus led some women to apply for jobs with Vichy's institutions—though their participation was always framed by the roles prescribed by their gender. Similarly, the material benefits of heading the Bantustan administrative institutions in South Africa led many impoverished Black people to recognize the homelands system, thus de facto reinforcing its racially segregationist agenda.

Some bystanders slide toward the other end of the spectrum, resistance. Resistance ranges from armed struggle and sabotage to protest, clandestine publishing, and refusals to collaborate, pay taxes, and obey laws. It can be motivated by various hopes, whose sources are multiple and whose objects translate political, ethical, or personal commitments. Members of the ANC fought for racial emancipation against the background of the Cold War, sometimes in ideological disagreement with other resistance organizations, such as Black Consciousness (BC) and the Communist Party of South Africa. The French *maquis* pursued national sovereignty, Communist ideals, and a certain idea of French masculinity that needed redeeming after the humiliatingly rapid defeat of 1939. All these organizations' structures and practices reflected the classed and gendered structures typical of the general population. Intellectual dissidents worldwide invoke principles of ethical integrity: staying true to oneself is part of a hegemonic idea of intellectuals' higher morals—an idea only few live up to. Avoiding the ethical harm to one's identity that complicity would involve has led some intellectuals to withdraw from politics and into the life of contemplation—a practice invoked defensively (yet never uncontroversially) as a form of resistance.[22] Moreover, many resisters are opportunists, driven by self-interest. For example, many French men joined the resistance late in the war, when they sensed the possibility of a German defeat and sought to dodge their regimentation as laborers in Germany—in the infamous *Service de Travail Obligatoire* (STO). The early anti-Communist armed resistance in Romania was mainly composed of propertied peasants who opposed the nationalization of their land and livestock (Dobrincu 2006, 2007a; Avram n.d.). This brings us to a conclusion difficult to square with national mythmaking: not all the alternative sources of meaning that resisters mobilize and not all motivations are immediately or overtly oriented by a noble commitment to the common good or lofty ideas of freedom.

Thus, just like different forms of complicity, different forms of resistance correspond to different positionalities within a community's lifeworld, influenced by habituses situated at the intersection of gender, class, ideology, profession, and religion, as well as traditions and memories of prior struggles. The decision to act is never absolutely free or spontaneous, but always necessarily influenced by political commitments and economic interests, professional roles, gendered relationships and hopes. The markers of one's identity and one's material conditions will determine *if, when,* and *how often* resisters act or remain passive and, as we shall see, how they are remembered post factum.

It is therefore unproductive to elide—in both political and academic discourses about complicity and resistance—the intersubjective dimension of hoping, imagining, and acting. A responsive social world is a precondition for hope, and "shared hopes become collective when individuals see themselves as hoping and so acting in concert for ends that they communally endorse" (McGeer 2004, 125). This is valid for both complicity and resistance. As the case studies show, perpetrators and collaborators offer each other the necessary support, mobilizing to act more efficiently in pursuit of their aims. On the other hand, while no two repressive regimes are alike, social trust is generally eroded. Fear of violent reprisals for dissent, anxieties about the ever-present possibility of betrayal (Mrovlje 2020), and wide-ranging hardships usually have an atomizing effect.[23] The social scaffolding that hopes for a different future need to flourish is often eroded. Opportunities for solidarity—which depend on cultivating hope in others' capacity to act in concert—are diminished, and with them the possibility of effective resistance. To give a few examples, without the Allies' aid and the moral and concrete support of local populations, the French maquis fighters' impact would have been even more doubtable. Without friends' and families' support, many Romanian dissidents would not have found the strength to sustain their opposition.[24] Without the ideological and material support that the USSR and its political satellites, but also local communities, provided, the ANC could not have imposed itself as the main opposition force in South Africa.

Such scaffolding support is not always available. Consequently, resistance is often feeble and wavering. The morally purist visions of resisters that dominate national myths—the "controlling image" (Hill Collins

2009) of lonely, absolute, unwavering courage—obscure the ambivalence, hesitations, compromises, silences, betrayals, violent abuses, and bitterness political resisters often feel toward the very communities they fight for, but whose members fail to show solidarity with their struggle. The hopelessness and despair resisters experience when the future seems foreclosed and their frustration and anger at their struggle's heavy personal costs rarely figure in heroic hagiographies. In contrast, this book hopes to foreground the many ways in which resisters depart from the dominant script, departures that, instead of subverting their standing, could render them more plausible and thus perhaps more inspiring.

This chapter's brief account of the positionality and relationality of memory, hope, and action paves the way for a more sophisticated understanding of the spectrum of involvement. All accomplices, bystanders, enablers, beneficiaries, and resisters take their bearing from the horizon of meaning and materiality within which they live and the relationships through which they are simultaneously constituted, both constrained and enabled. It is now time to turn to the second set of questions at the center of this project: how can we pierce through dominant ways of remembering, imagining, and hoping to undo the arbitrary excisions from the community's mnemonic horizon? What kind of media can illuminate the cartography of involvement sketched above, and by virtue of what features? In dialogue with social epistemologists, care ethicists, sociologists, and philosophers of art, chapter 2 suggest that certain artworks can interrupt the automatism of problematic modes of remembering, prosthetically enable us to travel in the past, and seduce us away from reductive visions of it. By virtue of their hedonic elements and mediated nature, certain artworks can effectively sabotage our cognitive, emotional, and sensorial investments in the double erasure at the core of this book. It is to this task that I now turn.

2   The Aesthetics of Care

PROBLEMATIZING REDUCTIVE PRACTICES and institutions of remembering poses enormous challenges, given communities' symbolic, emotional, and material investments in them. When individuals' schemes of perception, expectations, and aspirations are deeply emotionally anchored, when the scope of their political imagination is shaped by dominant narratives of who they are as a community, these erasures are often difficult to politically thematize and undo. The public camouflaging of violent and exclusionary forms of sociality allows them to remain recalcitrant, as sequelae on the body politic and sources of ongoing marginalizations in the present.

This chapter seeks to propose a potential strategy—one among others—for how these erasures, as well as the habits and relationships they nurture, can be challenged cognitively, emotionally, and sensorially: via artworks that could seductively sabotage reductive historical scripts and prosthetically enable spectators to see the world in its complexity, from different points of view. Such works, I argue, can trigger productive forms of mnemonic hesitation, which could open up a space for remembering and imagining differently.

Inspired by reflection on the role of art in the wake of the Shoah[1] and in response to other forms of historical oppression and forgetting (Lowenstein 2005; Hadj-Moussa and Nijhawan 2014; Guynn 2016; Winters 2016;

Asavei 2017) a rich literature tries to recuperate its political potential in relation to a past of violence. According to this literature, art is thought to achieve several crucial objectives. It can open political space for conflict transformation, kick-start justice processes, and create shared historical meanings in divided societies (Rush and Simić 2014); build solidarity between the wider public and the victims (Bilbija et al. 2005; Bennett 2005); facilitate historical learning (Hemer 2012); promote healing for the victims (Simić and Daly 2011); give voice to the suffering (Lorde 1993; Bisschoff and Peer 2013); constitute justice in itself (Dube 2011); offer a complex picture of victimization (Reinhardt et al. 2007; Mihai 2018); distort simplistic stories of linear historical causality (Zolkos 2008); and overcome ethno-national frames of commemoration (Asavei 2019).

Rejecting both romanticized views of art's revolutionary potential and elitist celebrations of avant-garde works' formal qualities, this book proposes that, by virtue of some specific characteristics, certain artworks might open the space of meaning to more complex accounts of historical agency, both complicit and resistant. I argue that certain—not all—works can trigger moments of mnemonic hesitation that generate an opportunity for publics to prosthetically experience the past in a way that seductively sabotages their received ideas, embedded as they are in their emotional and sensorial apparatus. Artworks that problematize the double erasure at the center of this book can provide a more nuanced and temporally sensitive picture of the spectrum of involvement, of its inhabitants' subjectivities and their position-takings. Moreover, in centering resisters' ambiguity, cowardice, and violence, they might also expand audiences' political imaginary. Last but not least, the chapter makes the case that, beyond their effect on immediate readers and viewers, as interventions in the hermeneutical space of the community, such artworks can be read as performing a labor of aesthetic care for the health of that very space. Leaning on feminist theorizing in care ethics, I argue that artists who, through their work, chip at dominant mystifications by uncovering their blind spots provide a crucial labor of mnemonic care for the political communities they address.

This is a modest proposal that could be added to broader institutional efforts aimed at tackling the social, economic, and cultural factors at play in ecological violence and its reproduction over time. Yet, contra what skeptics might argue, this is not merely wishful thinking: historically, artworks have made visible resilient exclusionary doxas and their sedimentation in national narratives and habituses. By simultaneously engaging the intellect, emotions, and the body, they have subverted individuals' investment in their own ignorance about the elisions at the center of their community's *grand récits*. Through the encounter with certain films, novels, or plays, communities have been seduced to become acute perceivers of others' experiences of violence and marginalization and reckon with their own participation in their reproduction over time. Let us now turn to the mechanisms through which such processes might take place.

THE GOOD OF HESITATION

How can we simultaneously and effectively engage individuals' faculties, emotions, and bodies in ways that steer them away from politically self-serving, reductive practices of remembrance? How can we transform the mnemonic habitus? This chapter proposes that certain artworks create a valuable tension between national reductive doxas—emotionally anchored and embodied ideas that reproduce violent habituses, relationships, and attitudes—on the one hand, and more discriminate visions of what happened, on the other. The power to trigger hesitation and thus render visible ideational, moral, and experiential limitations makes suck artworks valuable tools in problematizing and dislocating reified visions of history, in general, and the double erasure I outlined in the chapter 1, in particular.

Before delving into the argument, two caveats are necessary. First, this book does not naively assume that artistic encounters have a guaranteed effect or that they will be sufficient, on their own, to tackle these erasures. Given the picture of subjectification provided earlier, the thorny problem of pluralizing the space of meaning and socializing solidary citizens has no easy fixes. The canonization of resonating aesthetic works might help them reverberate socially—a possibility worth contemplating without falling prey to the temptation of self-delusion about its efficacy.

Second, again critically building on Pierre Bourdieu's work, this book subscribes to an institutionalist view of the artworld as a social field governed by rules, principles, and hierarchies of value and power. In unpacking the characteristics through which some artworks become valuable instruments against epistemic erasures, I assume they are all located within—yet simultaneously push at—the conventional boundaries that structure this field and regulate access to it. The aim is to highlight how, under certain circumstances, these conventions have been mobilized, channeled, stretched, or reinvented productively to articulate heretic visions that destabilize hegemonic memory regimes.

In considering art's epistemic functions, philosophers have argued that it can provide us with an awareness of, a perspective on, or insight into various dimensions of our world (C. Wilson 1983; John 1998; 2005; Young 2001). In political theory, following Hannah Arendt's argument that storytelling discloses important aspects of reality, researchers have claimed that both historical and fictional accounts can "stimulate and enrich political thought, as well as destabilize reductive, obfuscating narratives" (Stone-Mediatore 2003), help us comprehend unprecedented historical events (Disch 1996; Lara 2007; Bleiker 2009; Schiff 2014; Thaler 2014; Mrovlje 2019), illuminate the meaning of historical contingencies (E. Hutchison 2010), denounce historical injustices (Mihai 2014), and serve as means of self-presentation for subjects involved in struggles for social inclusion (Lara 1998). While political theorists agree that certain narratives can trigger individual and collective processes of reckoning with the limits of self-knowledge and knowledge about the political world, we need to consider the obstacles that can undermine the critical-political effect of encounters with artworks.

In what follows, I discuss the *features* and *processes* through which certain (not all) artworks can feed some (not all) individuals' and collectives' transformation. The argument is that certain works suspend the automatism of remembrance by inserting a moment of hesitation, disorienting ideational, moral, and experiential (emotional-sensorial) dispositions. In doing so, they simultaneously puzzle us intellectually, awaken our moral capacities, intensify our feelings, and surprise us sensorially. That is to say, they stimulate processes of what Medina (2013b) calls "epistemic friction" between, on the one hand, concepts, beliefs, attitudes, feelings, and experiences of an object and, on the other hand, alternative depictions of this object in art. Thus, they can undermine the "need not to know" (Medina 2013b, 215), rearranging desires and subverting the habituated "monoculture" of most minds.[2]

Alia Al-Saji's work (2014) is a great starting point for highlighting the difficulty of triggering epistemic friction. Her reflections on affective hesitation as a precondition for self- and collective transformation inform our discussion of artworks' effectiveness in their friction-inducing function at the level of the habitus. Her views of how we conceive of the world according to the common sense of our community in ways that remain beneath the radar of consciousness have strong affinities with the social-ontological sketch introduced in chapter 1. Building on Frantz Fanon's work, Al-Saji focuses on the stability of racializing vision. However, her problematization of the structural embeddedness of perception and of its recalcitrance and rigidity is relevant beyond the problem that triggers her reflection.

Al-Saji (2014, 138) writes, "Through sedimentation and habituation, the constitutive operations of vision remain tacit or unconscious; its intentionality works in us without our reflective awareness." The effect of these processes is the closing down of vision—the disabling of "its capacity to be affected, to be touched, by that which lies beyond or beneath its objectifying schemas" (2014, 140)—or what Al-Saji, following Fanon (2008, 92), calls "affective ankylosis." The medical metaphor points to how the hegemonic common sense structures the present and the future of the community whose schemes of perception and meaning-making it dominates: "the past is here congealed as schema and is, as such, overdetermined and fixed in its sense; this is the past as . . . myth, stereotype, distorted and isolated remnant" (2014, 141).

The ways in which individuals relate to each other are therefore permeated by the weight of this ankylotic past, as encapsulated in their practical sense, in ways that make alternative views of reality unthinkable. What is needed, Al-Saji argues, are moments of affective hesitation that open up the space and the time for a reorientation of what Keightley and Pickering (2012) named the "mnemonic imagination." This concept captures the routine interplay between these two faculties: our memories are organized into coherent narratives via the imagination, while the imagination builds on sources provided by memory. The imagination is also at work in bringing our memories into relation with the experiences of others who are differently positioned, actively building on past experiences and using them as raw material for dealing with new, unprecedented experiences.

This process is both about the intellectual contemplation of images and representations and about relying on and rehearsing embodied explorations of the world (Medina 2013a, 331).

I suggest that in hesitating, the routine relationship between memory and the imagination is broken. Hesitation invites the reconfiguration of our memories but also calls on our imagination to respond to a stimulus in the world that cannot be easily subsumed to our interpretive schemas: "unassimilable events pose an impediment for the perceiving self; they are experienced as 'adversity', as tension and, we may say, discomfort" (Al-Saji 2014, 158). Provided we do not reject them, tension and discomfort enable us to perceive the limits of our knowledge: "Hesitation is a deceleration that opens up the affective infrastructure of perception, in order both to make it responsive to what it has been unable to see and to make aware its contextual and constructed features" (2014, 147). The past is thus unlocked through a reorganization of memory, which means that both the present and the future are simultaneously rendered uncertain. Once the automatism of the mnemonic habitus and imagination is suspended, alternative ways of relating to others become possible. However, hesitation is only the beginning as it "happens within a context wherein it interposes an opening; this opening must yet be taken up for new possibility to be created" (2014, 149). The reconfiguration of individuals' vision and relationalities that hesitation makes possible requires opportunities for habitual encounters with different views of reality and ample opportunities for confronting the unassimilable. It is only thus that our "perceptual and affective map" could be redrawn (2014, 161).

Al-Saji's account of hesitation is particularly fruitful for thinking through what is at stake in trying to destabilize convenient mystifying doxas, and the forms of subjectivity and sociality they underpin. However, her prioritizing of hesitation at the affective level needs to be supplemented with an attention to the effect of the unassimilable on other dimensions of the individual's habitus—which is not reducible to affect—and also on the common sense, that is, on the doxa.[3] Hesitation brings one's embodied memories and one's imagination in a potentially productive tension—which may or may not fruitfully subvert the individual's schemas of perception, depending *both* on the nature of the stimulus *and* on the subject's welcoming or rejecting the discomfort associated with hesitation. In what follows, I argue that certain artworks can play a transformative role to the extent that they trigger affective but also cognitive, emotional, and moral hesitations. It is worth noting that certain identities are likely to be more propitious to hesitation than others, depending on the configuration of their habitus via socialization and the context in which hesitation is experienced. I will next delve into a discussion of the mechanisms by virtue of which artworks can minimize the risk of conservative entrenchment and productively support different ways of reconfiguring the doxastic past in relation to the present and the future. In the last section of this chapter, I will scale the discussion up to the level of the community, to think through the artistic practice of triggering shared hesitations as the expression of a labor of aesthetic care for memory.

ART'S KNOWLEDGE: SEDUCTIVE SABOTAGE
AND PROSTHETIC TRAVELING

Following in Al-Saji's footsteps but also departing from her exclusive focus on affect, this chapter recognizes the weight of the past as ankylosis, as embodied, institutionalized, and naturalized remainder—as habitus— and foregrounds its closing off the space for solidarity between individuals. It argues that, for hesitation to lead to a transformation of the individual's practical sense, it needs to enable processes of epistemic friction not just in the affective—or not primarily in the affective—register but also cognitively, ideationally, and morally. I argue that effective friction is powered by artworks' capacity to *pleasurably sabotage* the limitations inherent in our habits of perceiving, remembering, and imagining and to *prosthetically*[4] *expand* the pool of hermeneutical resources on which our engagement with the world relies. I suggest below that several features make artistic encounters particularly suited for provoking friction without risking reactionary reinvestment.

First, the plots in literary and cinematographic works are located within specific lifeworlds. Unlike national myths, they concretize, particularize, and exemplify broader processes and experiences shared by groups of people. Particularization facilitates rich and detailed accounts of the multiple and invisible ways in which individuals enter and move within the spectrum of involvement: their relationships, the axes of their identity, the vulnerabilities inherent in their positionalities, the scope of their imagination, and the strength of their hopes, which influence the level of their political efficacy. Thus, as Alison Landsberg (2004) argued, artworks can provide the spectator with a "prosthetic memory": through encounters with fiction, she argued, we acquire knowledge about experiences we never had. As our case studies show, certain artworks do supply the prosthetic knowledge necessary to tackle violent aftermaths and their mnemonic occlusion.

A brief problematization of the adjective *prosthetic* is necessary, however. This book's argument is not fully aligned with Landsberg's: *prosthetic* is used here in two senses. First, while artworks track experiences in the social world, these experiences are—and perpetually remain—alien to us: we never fully master or own them. We need to let go of the chimera that we could fully know and inhabit the position of another.[5] Secondly, these experiences are mediated through fiction. Therefore, they will inevitably be experienced as awkward, enabling our traveling beyond our narrow position, while sitting uncomfortably within our worldview. Prostheses can facilitate thought, emotions, and sensorial awareness in that they push us to go beyond our immediate habits of remembering, perceiving, thinking, feeling, and imagining—initially causing our habitus to falter in relation to the unassimilable events, identities, and social vistas they make available to us. As we shall see, heretic representations of complicity and resistance can sit uneasily with received ideas about what happened and with shared understandings regarding who the main actors of history are: victims, perpetrators and heroes.

Experiences that readers and viewers might only have an abstract idea of are thus made vividly present in a way that invites the reorganization of memory. Through hesitation, a gap opens between the viewer's horizon and that introduced in the artwork. In "this liminal, but creative space, the mnemonic imagination is at work" (Keightley and Pickering 2012, 189). I argue that productive "epistemic friction" (Medina 2013b)—can emerge in this opening, provided viewers and readers hesitate. Friction is successful when the imagination stretches to prosthetically include previously disconsonant instances—of victimhood, complicity, or resistance—within our repertoire of hermeneutical resources, which we actualize practically at various points in time. To the extent that the encounter with particularity through fiction props the mnemonic imagination in its active engagement with the unassimilable during moments of hesitation, changes in the individual's habitus might eventually obtain at the ideational, moral, emotional, and sensorial levels.

However, success is never guaranteed: individuals might reject the prosthesis—their memories, habits of thought, and affective investments weighing them down into despondency or even resentment. Given that the imagination does not start ab ovo, how adventurous or reticent we are to take the opportunities opened up by hesitation and to accept the prosthetic relationship to the artwork varies across individuals and groups.[6] Publics will move on a continuum ranging from refusal to deep transformation. Representations of complicity and resistance that provoke hesitation—that is, destabilize one's beliefs, emotions, and expectations in relation to the past (and implicitly to who "we" are as a community)—can unsettle and produce confusion, which can often lead to rejection. This is why, for the prosthetic experience to successfully put a break on the automatism of perception and memory, the encounter with a fictional lifeworld must be *seductive*. In what follows I try to flesh out the idea of *seductive sabotage* as a way of capturing artworks' unpredictable capacity to subvert doxastic investments.

Artworks' power to disrupt individuals' embodied habits of remembering, perceiving, and feeling relies on two main features: their hedonic and their mediated nature. I propose that the combination of hedonic and epistemic processes—of pleasure and knowledge—can lure spectators and readers to travel outside their comfort zone, welcome epistemic friction, and accept the prosthetic addition of other experiences within their hermeneutical pool of resources. Reflecting on the humanities, Spivak (2013, 9) uses the metaphor of "contamination," which is just as effective at articulating the idea that artworks insinuate themselves into the reader's memory, via the imagination, as "poison" or "medicine" (2013, 152), without us being fully aware of how exactly they get us to modify our memories, beliefs, and emotions.[7] The metaphor of "seduction" refers to the very fact that pleasure is involved in the encounter with art. Pleasure is understood here to incorporate discomfort and pain—this book subscribes to a "rich theory of art," according to which individuals purposefully seek and enjoy even painful art because they appreciate "experiences that are cognitively, sensorially, and affectively engaging: that is, rich experiences" (Smuts 2014, 132).

The traveling that artworks embark us upon is "safe" because the encounter is mediated. The spectator knows the representation "is not exactly about me"—but about types, some of which are mere possibilities—and can therefore feel freer, allowing themselves to learn, be captivated, and vicariously experience affectively and sensorially through the artwork, beyond their parochial positionality. To the extent that this mediated encounter disrupts the past as framework and to the extent that it enables a prosthetic learning from different pictures of reality, it contributes to the erosion of reductive mythologizing.

The discussion has so far remained at the level of process and mechanism. But what about the content of these seductive, prosthetic artworks? It is impossible to build, in abstracto, a catalogue of the kinds of narrative and form that are likely to serve our purposes. The next few chapters analyze a series of radically different artworks that all feature prosthetic visions of the past and all have—I argue—the potential to seductively sabotage audience's ankylosed habits of remembering. To the extent that we can generalize at all, novels and films that invite hesitation tend to trigger ideational, moral, emotional, and sensorial friction between the public's mnemonic habitus, on the one hand, and sacrilegious visions of the past, on the other. While I cannot hope to provide any comprehensive parameters here, here are some suggestions, tailored to this book's specific objectives.

First, ideationally, the artworks of interest to this project challenge our understanding of both complicity and resistance, both as concepts and historical realities. One way they can do this is by contesting the usual deployment of these heavily laden concepts to describe specific individuals and groups—that is, by disturbing entrenched hierarchies of valor and disgrace. Another is by not exclusively representing complicity and resistance in individualizing and psychologizing ways, as isolated, decontextualized acts in the case of the former, or as instances of sovereign heroism, in the case of the latter. To the extent that individualizing and psychologizing accounts dominate public debates, to the extent that we cannot see the social forest for the individual trees, our political use of the mnemonic imagination remains limited. Artworks that reveal the structural foundations of both complicity and resistance, their relationality, and the vulnerabilities that underpin both, as well as the temporal dynamism of the spectrum of involvement, are instrumental to dislodging the reductive social ontology of national mythologies. Bringing social and political forces back into the picture should not, however, lead us to an abdication of responsibility. Artistic engagements with complicity that balance the focus on individual responsibility with a concern for the social preconditions of individuals' patterns of behavior are more likely to trigger productive hesitations in relation to the limits of the official story.

Second, still ideationally, works that highlight the insulation of the national doxa and its categories from alternative communities of meaning, their narrative frameworks, and political categories are extremely valuable. To recall Winters (2016), it is important to remember what others cannot forget. Inserting accounts of "unlikely" resisters—that is, misrecognized resisters—or of resisters who waiver and hesitate, who are sometimes resentful and complicitly silent, who engage in abusive violence, and who betray or become double agents is also crucial for pluralizing the space of memory. So are artworks that foreground characters who fit neither the traitor nor the hero profile and who expose the very artificiality, reductionism, and implausibility of dominant ideas of historical agency.

Third, morally, friction then emerges between automatic habits of ascribing praise or guilt and more ambiguous, complex, and therefore more plausible renditions of the circumstances facing political actors. The reconfiguration of the public's sense of justice is thus encouraged by bringing to the fore cases that cannot be neatly subsumed under clear moral schemas. Films and novels that highlight the temporality, structural nature, uneven intensity, and psychological effects of violence can make it difficult for audiences to comfortably fall back on easy, moralizing, and individualizing judgments. Thematizing the burdens of resisting, the violence and the compromises involved, as well as the relationalities and vulnerabilities that make some more likely to get involved in ethically problematic practices and institutions than others, is another way of stimulating moral friction.

Emotionally and sensorially, depictions of the effect of systemic violence on victims but also scapegoats can lead us to question our capacity for empathy and sense of what it means to feel at home in the world. In this sense, artistic engagements with the violent abuses motivated by self-righteous indignation against real or imagined collaborators and traitors could cast doubt on the rigid moral grids through which we read reality. Artworks that highlight these effects over time, cross-generationally, can sabotage the limits of our compassion and ideas of deservingness, as well as nurture a solidary attunement to fellow human beings. Provided the spectator immerses themselves experimentally in alternative scenarios, scenarios that are uncomfortable but attractive and tolerable because of the pleasurable elements in art and its mediated nature, the opportunities created within the space of hesitation are not wasted.

This abstract sketch will be fleshed out—and vindicated—in the chapters that follow. I will investigate films and novels that, I suggest, have the capacity to trigger perceptual, mnemonic, and affective hesitation, to seduce readers and spectators to travel in the world of imagined others, becoming their apprentices.[8] Notwithstanding the phenomenological and sociological differences between film-watching and book-reading, I am interested here in how both films and books can similarly engage readers and spectators cognitively, emotionally, and sensorially in ways that can interrupt their habitus and enable them to prosthetically access alternative visions of the past. I cannot judge here whether book-reading or film-watching is more effective politically although, immersed as we are in the visual era, it is tempting to jump to conclusions. National cultures of art consumption will make a difference as well. Given the classed nature of the habitus, certain artforms will be more available and more favored by some groups and not by others. However, provided they reverberate in the public sphere or get canonized in national curricula, books and films alike can serve the objectives I outlined at the beginning of the book. To the extent that they shed light on the complexity and relationality of both resistance and complicity in a way that makes apparent the limits of moralistic, individualistic myths about the past, they have the potential to reveal—if not even undo—the double erasure at the core of this book.

Before I move on to the discussion of the case studies, the last section of this chapter suggests that artistic work aiming to pluralize a community's space of meaning can be best understood as the aesthetic form of a labor of mnemonic care for the health of that very space. Caring for its openness will often require rejecting certain occluding master narratives and assuming the risks that such moves necessarily involve, given their naturalization as part of the national doxa. It is to care ethicists and the resources they provide for advancing this argument that I now turn.

ARTISTIC PRACTICE AS MNEMONIC LABOR: INTRODUCING THE CARING REFUSENIK

The main argument advanced in this section is that caring for a plural space of memory requires the inclusion of accounts about the structural underpinnings of violence and the ambiguity of resistance within the public conversation. In refusing obscuring projects—that conceal violence-genic forms of social relationality and foreground implausible models of resistance—this labor of mnemonic care can nurture a more balanced space of intelligibility, preventing its monopolization by any "final" and reductive affirmation of the "truth" about heroes, victims, and perpetrators. In other words, we need hermeneutical care to impede new forms of dogmatic univocality from becoming politically hegemonic.

In their often-cited definition, Tronto and Fisher (1990, 40) claim care is "a species activity that includes everything that we do to maintain, continue and repair our 'world' so that we can live in it as well as possible. That world includes our bodies, our selves, and our environment, all of which we seek to interweave in a complex, life-sustaining web." Drawing the connection between care and democracy, elsewhere Tronto (2013, xiv) writes that "democracy itself, as a form of governing in which citizens participate, requires care." Tronto's making of democracy itself the object of care paves the way for my attempt to stretch care beyond the private and social-policy areas that deal directly with caring (for example, welfare, health, or education) and propose a new, more general, more abstract but still relational object of care: the hermeneutical space of a community— its doxa, its common sense, which includes political memory—and the relations that it constitutes. While some might disagree, worrying perhaps about the dilution of the concept of care, I argue that tending to a community's space of meaning, its silences and absences, laboring to pluralize it and criticize self-serving institutions of remembering, constitutes a form of valuable epistemological care. In what follows I delineate this chapter's second theoretical argument. However, the reader will have to wait for the empirical analysis for concrete illustrations, which will hopefully dispel doubts about the philosophical connection I am trying to make between artistic production, care, and the health of the doxastic space.

There are several aspects of (certain strands in) care ethics[9] that make this philosophical perspective a useful terrain for understanding what is at stake in the double erasure that concerns us. First, care ethics presupposes a relational ontology: it opposes Kantian accounts of atomistic individuals, conceiving of humans as always embedded in concrete, complex relations of mutual dependency and attachment (Gilligan 1982; Tronto 1995, 2013; Urban Walker 2007; Bowden 1997; Held 2007; Sevenhuijsen 2003; Stensöta 2015; Dingler 2015; Koggel and Orme 2013; Engster and Hamington 2015). These relations constitute us as individuals, and, therefore, human agency and responsibility can only be understood by taking relationality seriously, in its political, economic, and hermeneutical dimensions. Dependency and vulnerability are not aspects of human existence to be overcome but an inextricable part of that very existence (Robinson 2011; Dingler 2015). This perspective mirrors this book's commitments and its conviction that complicity with and resistance to violence can only be understood relationally. Moreover, hermeneutical relations—within collective meaning-making processes, including meaning-making about the past, its violence, complicities, and resistances—are an important part of the social webs we always find ourselves in. Moreover, we are dependent on others to have our voices heard, and, reversely, we are vulnerable to practices of hermeneutical exclusion. The hermeneutical space between us can collapse when the imposition—the trumpeting—of a certain vision silences competing accounts. Caring for that space in its plurality, nurturing the conditions that enable it to thrive, is, I will argue, an important political practice.

Second and relatedly, building and maintaining relationships is the goal of care. Taking the relationality of human experience seriously means that living well requires us to care—broadly speaking to nurture, sustain, and protect (Robinson 1998; Tronto 1996; Ruddick 1995)—these relationships. Caring is thus nor merely a disposition but a practice and, as Tronto (2013, 48–49) clearly argued, the motivation need not precede the practice: we begin to care in the act of caring. Given that care must adjust and respond to the needs of the object of care, communication is central to caring. Yet breakdowns in communication can always occur, since caring is not assumed to be a tension-free activity (Bowden 1997, 173). Tensions and conflict are not the only aspects of caring that need acknowledging if we are to avoid a romantic vision thereof: not all relationships are worth nurturing and protecting; on the contrary, some need discouraging and transforming. As Fiona Robinson (1998, 30) writes, "An ethics of care must, in the context of social and practical relations, seek to uncover the relationships which exist among and within groups while, at the same time, maintaining a critical stance towards those relations . . . This, in turn, involves a thorough understanding of how relations are constructed and how difference is perceived and maintained through institutions and structures in societies."

Caring therefore must confront the conditions and complex relationships that create the suffering it addresses, whatever its nature might be. In other words, it requires that we excavate the source of exclusions in oppressive sociopolitical ecologies. Indeed, a deep knowledge of how these structures have historically burdened and silenced certain individuals and groups within our communities is a precondition for nurturing different, more solidary relations: "When an ethics of care is combined with a critical examination of how structural features of institutional relations enable or deform the abilities of all concerned to hear and to be heard, an ethics of care can combat exclusion and oppression" (Robinson 1998, 46–47).

Refocusing on our main objective in this book, caring for political memory aims to make sure that problematic hermeneutical and political occlusions do not inform collective meaning-making intergenerationally, especially given the risk of resilient violent sequelae—that is, of widespread susceptibility to mystification and absolutist impositions. Caring for the plurivocality of the hermeneutical space requires a sustained fight *against* the stamping out of heretic accounts of the past—accounts of the past that, if preserved, might keep us vigilant—and *for* inclusive relationships. While activists, historians, and social scientists have often provided mnemonic care via their political and scientific work, I focus here on aesthetic care for its capacity to seductively sabotage intransigent, absolutist trumpeting via the inclusion of mnemonic prostheses—that is, of dissenting cognitive, emotional, and sensorial knowledges.

Third, caring is conceptualized as a practice that presupposes several virtues.[10] It demands a sustained effort to become aware of and pay attention to the object of care, assume responsibility, meet caring needs, and be responsive to communication about those needs (Tronto 1996). Caring is concrete, culturally specific, and historically variable (1996, 149). Good care involves an ongoing commitment to sustaining the *labor* of care and a set of characteristics: thoughtfulness, patience, deliberativeness, good judgment, self-knowledge, and knowledge of the situation one cares for (Ruddick 1995). The availability of adequate resources for caring—material and intellectual—is also essential. These prerequisites emerge in existing practices of care, such as mothering, nursing, and friendship, but also in political practices of hospitability: in welcoming refugees and showing solidarity with marginalized groups publicly.[11]

This book focuses on caring that targets the sustained preservation and nurturing of "the social ties that bind groups together, . . . the bonds on which political and social institutions can be built" (Held 2007, 31). In the wake of violence, these bonds need special attention so that the erasures in the community's doxa don't reproduce exclusionary understandings of the community across generations. Care for inclusive political relationships obliges us to ask "a qualitative question: *what* world do we want to build as responsible subjects?" (Pulcini 2013, 13). I suggest that, in undermining triumphant, self-congratulatory *grands récits*, certain artworks contribute to building a world where we care *about* how our past influences our relationships in the present and *for* more complex and discriminate practices of memory-making. In seducing the public away from their socialized misremembering, they prosthetically enable them to see, think, and feel otherwise.

In light of these features of caring, I propose to conceptualize artists' refusal of the double erasure at the center of this project as the expression of a commitment to a balanced hermeneutical space of memory. As I show in the second half of the book, the erasure of certain inconvenient, shameful, or not-so-glorious episodes from political memory, in the name of intransigent, selective views of "the past" has been successfully countered via practices of aesthetic care. Redress cannot, however, emerge from episodic attempts: it requires a dedicated effort to thwart the reproduction of intolerant dogmatism and nurture the flourishing of multiperspectival visions of the past.

Caring is neither straightforward, nor risk-free. Crucially, it involves vigilance over the ever-present twin dangers of contamination and rejection. On the one hand, contamination defuses the power of caring to transform its object: caring requires a form of commitment that, while emotionally anchored, remains lucid and avoids falling into both uncritical sentimentality and intransigent invocations of an alternative, exclusionary "truth."[12] On the other hand, rejection ranges from dismissal to stigmatization, marginalization, and ostracism. Caring can also involve frustration, conflict, and getting hurt (Conradi 2015). The memory actors who insist on problematizing national master narratives are shunned—the label "Nestbeschmutzer" (nest fouler) is often applied to them—and, as we shall see, various strategies are deployed to delegitimize their claims. In trying to silence them, the spaces where productive friction between different perspectives can yield alternative meanings are closed off.

To the deprecating metaphor of "Nestbeschmutzer" I oppose that of the "caring refusenik"—dissenting memory agents who reject reductive national narratives and who nurture (rather than treasonously befouling) a plural space of memory-making. The caring refusenik challenges the political and practical continuities left untouched by the official sanctioning of neutralizing projects of "moving forward." Avoiding both lamentation and morally inflexible invocations of alternative complete "truths"—that risk replacing one form of loud absolutism with another—they cultivate a self-reflective, humble clarity of vision. Most importantly, they remain wary of any totalizing vision of the past that renders invisible the uncomfortable in-between and the impure aspects of resistance.

Before concluding this section, it should be noted that the refusenik's caring work will not be a painless affair—and it will be all the more valuable for the discomfort it causes. Comfort is complacent and it cannot be the goal of care, not without qualification. Caring is motivated by a deep commitment to inclusiveness and equality, often by love, but this does not exclude tension. The French, Romanian, and South African refuseniks featured in this book have opened prematurely closed books, excavated the structural underpinning of violence, and iconoclastically depicted heroes and resisters—all with the aesthetic tools at their disposal.

Moreover, they have illuminated the artificiality of memory-making and its vulnerability to mystification. In response, official memory's gate-keepers have often attacked their caring work as a treacherous maneuver to taint the "Nation," the "People," the "Resistance." However, despite such hostile rejection, their labor of hermeneutical care has effectively and irreversibly dented mnemonic doxas. Before moving on to a detailed discussion of the three case studies that vindicate my abstract theoretical proposals, however, it is time for a reality check.

REALITY CHECK

At this stage, several legitimate questions could be raised about my theoretical project. Let me address them in turn.

First, one might worry the proposal advanced in this chapter is naive as art has historically played ideological, propagandistic roles. To respond, I have no trust in art's transformational power per se. Its seductive power can be—and historically has been—harnessed to confirm oppressive social relations. Not all artworks enrich and perplex us productively along the dimensions outlined above; not all narratives are revelatory. On the contrary, many cultivate insensitivity, bad faith, and thought-lessness (Schiff 2014). The failure to provide epistemic insight cannot be explained—despite what many philosophers of art argue—by exclusive reference to the aesthetic qualities of a work of art. As a field of the social world, art is not immune to power relations: there is no point in investing in the chimera of artistic independence.[13] The artistic imagination is not always necessarily emancipatory; its value depends on its content and use. Romantic beliefs in the heroic, autonomous artist should give way to the realization that independence is a matter of degree: some artists do a better job than others at ensuring sufficient critical distance to provoke epistemic friction and at caring for inclusive hermeneutical relationships. What we are interested in recuperating here are particular artworks by caring refuseniks who, one way or another, insightfully problematized the double erasure.

Second, whose art is likely to cause friction and provoke hesitation? Should we focus on artworks by victims and survivors only? I propose that aesthetically caring works will find their authors both within and without the community of victims and survivors. Moreover, plenty of works by victims, survivors, and resisters can reproduce problematic visions of the past. I am interested here in artists who tackle ankylotic mystifications, their anchoring in social imaginaries and affective registers, who denounce their effects and the interests underpinning their hegemony while proposing alternative, more inclusive visions of the past and its protagonists.[14] As we will see in the chapters that follow, certain films and novels can and have opened up the possibility of political transformation, all the while acknowledging that our grasp of the past can never amount to full mastery. On the contrary, it is perpetually precarious and incomplete, a continuous experimental process of apprenticeship and world-traveling, helped by artistic props.

Third, are works that depict the misery and nefarious effects of widespread complicity and the weaknesses of heroes best for sabotaging the double erasure? Engagements with the relationality and vulnerabilities inherent in systemic violence and their murderous effects, as well as depictions of less-than-heroic forms of resistance and their complex ambivalence can activate the mnemonic imagination productively. I analyze filmic and literary representations of political accommodation and of the multiple reasons—not all equally condemnable—why individuals become complicit with violence, from within positionalities that are marked by a variety of vulnerabilities. I also included artworks that highlight how enduring violent orders constrict individuals' horizons of hope and political imagination, as well as works about improbable resisters and resisters who act sometimes courageously, sometimes cowardly. Last but not least, works about communities' yearning for exceptional heroes and for clear demarcation lines between the past and the future, with all the costs that accrue from such aspirations, are also given space in the chapters that follow.

Fourth, it must be reiterated that the double erasure is not merely a hermeneutical problem: as I have been suggesting throughout, hermeneutical exclusions from memory-making processes are inextricably connected to historically resilient patterns of exclusion—political, economic, cultural. Histories of marginalization inform *both* systemic violence against certain groups *and* the erasure of collective responsibility for their victimization from national political memory. Mythmaking is never divorced from the materiality of past and present violence. To put it straightforwardly, how societies remember the past is not unconnected from how they organize their institutions and how they distribute their wealth.

Lastly, how can we ensure that encounters with challenging artworks will not lead to negative reactions that block the possibility of hesitation? The answer is simple: we cannot. There will always be spectators and readers who remain indifferent or resistant to artistic seduction, and there will be others who—perhaps because of a socialized capacity to appreciate artworks or because of specific features of their identity—will be more welcoming to its pull. Hesitation can be invited, encouraged, but not regimented. The beliefs, values, interests, and emotional dispositions entrenched in the habitus are the most important obstacle. The lack of exposure to art or an inadequate aesthetic socialization—often related to class and other markers of social distinction—constitutes another important impediment: "The 'eye' is a product of history reproduced by education" (Bourdieu 2010, xxvi). National cultures of art consumption will also influence caring refuseniks' success. While receptiveness inescapably relies on a measure of effort and openness by the audience, democratic societies have at their disposal institutional mechanisms to cultivate it: sponsoring citizens' more equal access to art, socializing their habits of appreciating it, and ensuring that the art they are exposed to is plurivocal. Guaranteeing a more equal access to funding and dissemination channels for all artists and expanding canons to include marginalized authors constitute two more strategies for rectifying skewed perceptions of the social world in its historicity. In sum, undoing the double erasure can only result from a concerted institutional effort.

The chapters that follow aim to render concrete the theoretical proposal advanced so far through an analysis of three case studies: France during the German occupation, Romania during the Communist dictatorship, and South-Africa under apartheid. I turn to these messy histories in an attempt to map their spectrum of involvement and identify illuminating examples of committed caring refuseniks, but also in search of insights that might render this book's theoretical proposals more sophisticated, more plausible, and more productive.

3   France's "Dark Years"

COMPLICITIES AND RESISTANCES DURING THE OCCUPATION

France was partially and then fully occupied by Germany between 1940 and 1944. This chapter kicks off by analyzing several forms of complicity and resistance, focusing on the multiple, overlapping structures that influenced people's complex positions in relation to the occupier, positions that were neither static, nor reducible to one single identity vector. Complex ideological legacies and commitments that preceded the war, gender, class, religion, the opacity of the future, and severe economic hardships, as well as ambivalent views regarding the occupier—all contributed to where individuals ended up on the spectrum of involvement. As will become evident, individualizing, time-slice approaches to parsing out historical responsibility—whether to blame or praise—fail when faced with such complexity. Moreover, the map of the in-between introduced below will cast a dark shadow over the mystifications that dominated French political memory for decades after the war.

Temporally, French people's horizons of expectation was marked by these several vectors, which affected the scope of their imagination and the courage of their hopes, as well as the relationships they entertained and the practices they participated in. While collaboration and resistance were both, to a great extent, correlated with the degree of uncertainty regarding the result of the war, the painful memory of World War I—which killed almost 1.5 million Frenchmen—made pacifism widespread before 1939 (Rousso 1992). Pacifism paradoxically motivated various collaborators, who saw the occupation as marking the beginning of an enduring peace between France and Germany (Joly 2011, 14). *La drôle de guerre*—the short, quiet period between September 1939 and May 1940—blunted the spirits and made the shock of the defeat extremely acute. Following the capitulation, everyday pressures and relief that "the war was over" made most people acquiescent supporters of the collaborationist government in Vichy, incapable of imagining a way out (Diamond 1999, 72). Many saw its leader, Pétain, as the hero of Verdun, the savior who could provide some sense of normalcy and secure the return of war prisoners (Paxton 2001; Wieviorka 2010). Signs of resentment against the Germans were documented already in 1940, though distinctions between Nazism and Germany, good and bad Germans, and a sense of admiration based in old stereotypes about German culture were common (Burrin 1996, 195). But, as Jackson (2003, 240) writes, "until at least the end of 1942, the resistance was too small to be a presence in the experience, event consciousness, of most people: choices did not seem to exist in 1940." The year 1942 brought a major shift in French people's horizon of hope and their attitude toward the occupier: the occupation of France's entire territory, the great roundups of Jews, and the plausible hope that Germany could be defeated shifted public perceptions. Consequently, and gradually, resistant activities intensified from then on.

Structurally, individuals' locations on the spectrum of involvement was influenced by their habitus (gender, class, religion) and the social, economic and cultural capital they accrued against the background of historical, doxastic anti-Semitism, the painful memory of World War I, and the split ideological horizon that predated and was exacerbated by the war. The laws and policies institutionalized by Vichy and the occupier constituted the institutional infrastructure *within* and *against which* complicity and resistance shaped up as practices. These temporally dynamic structures incited, elicited, inspired, or facilitated various forms of both collaboration and resistance that cannot be reduced to the discrete, intentional, fully reflexive acts that the individualizing imaginaries discussed in chapter 1 presuppose.

Following the armistice, Marshal Pétain launched the doctrine of "state collaboration" with Germany, kick-starting the "National Revolution" in the free zone: a Fascist cultural revolution replacing "Liberty, Equality, Fraternity" with "Work, Family, Motherland." "Motherland" excluded "groups that, by virtue of their race or convictions, could not or would not subscribe to the primacy of the French nation: foreigners, Jews, masons, Communists, internationalists of all origins and loyalties" (R. Gillouin cited in Rousso 1992). Political repression was legally authorized. Anti-Semitic laws were passed, mostly but not exclusively instigated by the Germans (Joly 2012, 2015; Joly and Passera 2016), unequivocally tapping into a doxastic horizon of French anti-Semitism. The subordination of the judiciary to political control happened gradually, via new legislation and the purging of some of the magistrates. Virginie Sansico traces this development in three steps: first, political repression via ordinary courts was institutionalized already in 1940; second, in response to heightened Communist resistance after Germany's invasion of the USSR, extraordinary courts were set in place in 1942; lastly, in 1944, the establishment of martial courts, usually run by the Milice—the regime's political super-police—were meant to deal with the growing risk of a civil war and increased international pressures (2002). Apoliticism and a mechanical understanding of the role of magistrates—a certain professional habitus—made most judges acquiescent vis-à-vis the regime, paradoxically enough at a time when the latter was eroding the very principles of the rule of law. The same apolitical attitude characterized many of the leaders of professional associations, universities, and local administrations, who diligently implemented the laws despite not being virulent anti-Semites (Jackson 2003). Out of Pétainist convictions, or sheer thoughtless pragmatism, universities applied anti-Jewish laws (Burrin 1996). The infrastructure of the ecology of violence was thus laid out. In what follows, I mark several key positions on the dynamic space of implication this ecology enabled.

The gravest form of complicity, collaborationism, was rare. In French, *collabo*, or "collaborationist"—as opposed to *collaborateur*—is the term reserved for the "ultra"-ideologically motivated collaborator (Joly 2011, 6). Few collabos supported the institutionalization of anti-Semitism without any scruples. A mix of ambitious megalomaniacs, irresponsible gangsters, and useful idiots (2011), the collabos tapped into pacifism, fascism, and Catholicism (Jackson 2003) and tried to benefit politically, symbolically, and economically from the occupation. Notwithstanding their heterogeneity, the collabos presented themselves as the only true "patriots," who took the initiative and sanctioned anti-Semitic laws in 1940–41, when the Nazis had not yet formulated the Final Solution (Rousso 1992, 86–92). The passing and enforcement of anti-Semitic measures was meant as proof of Vichy's capacity to govern. Organizations such as Jacques Doriot's Le parti populaire français, Marcel Déat's Rassemblement National Populaire and Eugène Deloncle's Mouvement social révolutionnaire were potent vehicles for anti-Semitic, anti-Communist, and anti-Masonic propaganda, articulating a new contribution to a long French tradition of extreme-right politics and militarism. Their newspapers—*Le Francisme*, *Le cri du peuple*, and *Au pilori*—had rubrics dedicated to the denunciation of Jewish illegal behavior. In terms of public support, at their peak, these organizations gathered an estimated maximum of 220,000—mostly urban, low middle-class people (Jackson 2003, 195).

When it comes to the Church's position, the regime's Catholic conservatism translated into a glorification of motherhood, which led to a natalist policy between 1940 and 1944 (Jennings 2002). Women who did not conform to the conservative image of passive domesticity celebrated by the regime were viciously attacked (Hawthorne and Golsan 1997). As Pollard shows, although the gender-conservative doxa predated the war, Vichy's aggressive heteronormative familialism led to a heavy editing of sexuality norms along gender lines: education was accordingly reformed, ensuring the production of devoted mothers and virile fighters (Pollard 1998). Abortion became a capital offense in 1942, analogous to treason. With Pétain in power, the Catholic Church was emboldened, especially since its main ideological opponents—Communists and masons—were targeted by both the government and the occupier. However, few prelates openly endorsed the regime, the Church preferring to silently benefit (Burrin 1996).

Right-wing intellectuals were not immune to the lure of power: many collaborated out of conviction, promoting racist propaganda (Joly 2011). Figures as different as Louis-Ferdinand Céline, Robert Brasillach, Pierre Drieu La Rochelle, and Xavier de Magallon lent their talents to the anti-Semitic cause, legitimizing it. Le Groupe Collaboration assembled ideologically motivated writers, scientists, clerics, and artists—who were also pursuing personal fame. Under the aegis of the Institute for the Study of Jewish Questions, they organized the anti-Semitic exhibition "The Jew and France": two hundred thousand ticket-paying French citizens, including pupils, visited it in 1941 (Rousso 1992, 98).

Beyond outright intellectual collaboration lies the issue of censorship and self-censorship. Already in 1940, most editors committed to censoring publications contrary to German interest—a deal meant to allow them to publish during the occupation. A list of banned authors—Jewish or suspected of belonging to the resistance—was imposed on all publishers (Assouline 1985). German pro-Nazi authors were translated and works by authors favorable to collaboration were assiduously printed (Burrin 1996). As in the other countries discussed in this book, a great debate ensued over whether continuing to write and publish despite these measures constituted a form of complicity with the regime, even though the author's motives did not always align with the censor's.[1] Some artists and intellectuals went into exile; others withdrew into the life of the mind; others, still, joined the resistance. Many wrote to regain a sense of normality or out of a desire to keep the French intellectual life going, self-censoring and eliminating whole chapters to enable publication—Camus's excluding his analysis of Kafka from *The Myth of Sisyphus* a clear case in point. It is worth noting that more than four hundred plays, including by consecrated playwrights such as Sartre, Camus, Anouilh, Cocteau, and Giraudoux, were performed during the occupation. Coded writing flourished—though not as much as it was later claimed—especially in poetry, a genre that lent itself more easily to ambiguity (Jackson 2003). Clandestinely, however, the famous press Éditions de Minuit was created, opening a space for resistance publishing.

Moving along in the spectrum, we find another form of complicity: applying for a job with the repressive state apparatus, an important target of postwar purges. In 1943–44 there were two thousand German gestapistes in France and thirty thousand French agents working for the Germans (Nettelbeck 1985, 83). The *milice* was founded as a political police in 1943. In its ranks we could find fanatic Catholics and anti-Communists, representatives of the landed gentry, ex-convicts, and outlaws, but also many driven by classed, economic need and especially by the desire to escape the Service de Travail Obligatoire (STO)—the forced recruitment of French laborers sent to German factories (Grégoire 2007). Moreover, gender played a great role in joining such institutions: cultural and political historians argue that France suffered a crisis of virility because of the tension between the masculinist and militarist national doxa and the stunning defeat of 1940 (Kelly 1995; Capdevila 2002, 2001a). In public discourse and imagery, including artistic production, various ideological discourses converged on the centrality of virility in visions of honor, patriotism, and action after 1940. Vichy advanced two such visions of virility: the father-worker who spearheaded the Catholic national revolution and the anti-Bolshevist legionnaires, Fascist knights promising to restore masculine strength to a country feminized by democracy. Studies argue that young Frenchmen bearing the generational shame of defeat were attracted to collaborationism to recapture a sense of self-worth, which the Fascist virile mythology and its institutions—the milice, the LVF—provided all-too-easily (Capdevila 2001b).

Another institution in the repressive machine was the General Commissariat for Jewish Questions, which "administered" the Jewish population and the spoliation of their property. "Economic aryanisation" required an army of clerks (Bruttmann 2013). Two categories of employees emerge from the archives. First, those recommended by personal contacts in Vichy's bureaucratic apparatus. Political connections and professional networks of trust—one's social capital—framed clerks' image of professional success and the means for achieving it: working as a public servant was a legitimate and worthy aspiration within France's centralized and bureaucratized state imaginary. The second category is the "bureaucratic proletariat," stuck on temporary, underpaid jobs: secretaries, accountants, and the office personnel of businesses and publications discontinued after 1940. Many applied to the commissariat—seen as an "ordinary" institution—to secure a stable job (Joly 2016). Thus, a different positionality, marked by stark economic vulnerability, pushed older, unemployed, and underqualified men and women—some of them war refugees or repatriated POWs—to apply for jobs that paid salaries above average (2016, 170). The number of fervent anti-Semites among the applicants was rather low, an estimated 10 percent.[2]

After 1942, the increasing hope in an Allied victory, budgetary cuts, and a dramatic decrease in unemployment led to a recruitment crisis for the repressive institutions. Assassinations of milice members by resistance fighters did not help. By 1944, the milice could no longer be scrupulous (Joly 2016, 172). The Commissariat started contracting "unqualified" personnel, some with criminal records, young men seduced by the sense of power they got from bearing weapons (Grégoire 2007)—a clear reflection of the dominant gender order and the habitus it underpinned. This dynamic picture renders obvious the temporal and structural underpinnings of the collaborator's position, who sat at the intersection of several economic and political vectors of identity and whose horizon of hope constricted or expanded according to the evolution of the war.

Perhaps in spite of the regime's conservatism, women did gain certain freedoms during the occupation. The economic pressures of the time weighed disproportionately on them as main carers, pushing them to enter the public realm, sometimes in complicitous, other times in resistant ways (Hawthorne and Golsan 1997). Women, too, joined anti-Semitic organizations and Vichy's repressive institutions—including the milice, where they accounted for 15 percent of the cadres (Burrin 1996)—for political, religious, economic, and personal reasons, a historical fact that sat uneasily with the gendered image of women as nurturing beings (Schwartz 1995). Imagined political futures animated some miliciennes: visions of a "new French order, national and socialist" with the milice as "the only guarantor of the French order, the only hope for a brighter future" (Simonin 2010, 19). When it comes to socioeconomic status, statistics show the milicienne as a young, single, economically vulnerable woman with limited education—a secretary, dactylographer, or telephone operator.[3] The socio-professional status determined the economic options for these women, whose precarious situation was often manipulated. For example, Déat's RNP recruited many women by promising to help bring back family members who were POWs.

In general, however, women's political hopes and imagination were filtered through the matrix of gender, but also that of Catholicism. Paradoxically enough, post–World War I pacifism motivated some to join repressive institutions. Religiously inflexed duties of charity—often combined with *maréchalisme* (an attachment to Pétain's virile, heroic past and fatherly image)—also played a role. Building on an existing tradition of "social citizenship" that went back at least to World War I, Catholic women did social work for the wounded and the displaced, thus simultaneously adhering to their Catholic faith and serving Pétain (Fageot 2008): they became "universal mothers" (Simonin 2010, 22). Gendered notions of work and citizenship thus informed their positioning on the complicity spectrum as their collaboration perversely empowered them, fueling a hope for public engagement, at a time when they could not vote.

These examples highlight gender, class, and religion as important structures of the war experiences and the role of habitus in shaping the aspirations and relations one could cultivate. Pointing to the ecological nature of violence is not meant to exculpate. Many were favorable to Vichy's agenda, socialized within an anti-Semitic national doxa with deep roots in French history. This is nowhere more evident than in the practice of *délation*, another insidious and dangerous form of collaboration bolstered by Vichy's racist legislation. Individuals belonging to certain socioeconomic and cultural strata participated in uncoordinated yet widespread denunciations of Jews, Communists, and freemasons to the French police, the Gestapo, or the General Commissariat for Jewish Questions. Some délateurs addressed several institutions at the same time, keen to maximize the chances of "success" (Joly 2017). The anti-Semitic press had dedicated rubrics for délations—*Au pilori* being perhaps the most infamous. The Institute for the Study of Jewish Questions served as intermediary between those who provided information and the other repressive institutions. Thousands of such letters were submitted in writing and orally, contributing to the generalized harassment of Jewish people, Communists, and other "undesirables."

To emphasize the need to expand the temporal horizon of analysis when investigating systemic violence, it should be noted that the practice of délation had a long history in France, going back to the nineteenth century: Édouard Drumont's newspaper *La libre parole*, launched in 1892, contained "revelations" about Jewish interference in French affairs—a clear precursor to the practices of the 1940s (Joly 2007). Disclosing this lineage simultaneously highlights the role of institutional and political memory in shaping patterns of behavior—the ankylotic past as schema of perception and interaction—and the limits of the individualistic, act-based paradigm in tackling systemic patterns of behavior. Outraged or meek, délateurs were mostly men, contrary to the gendered association of women and betrayal and perfidy (Joly 2017, 37). Most délations— oral or written, signed or anonymous—invoked the common good and noble ideas of justice but were often motivated by personal reasons: an unneighborly conflict, jealousy, greed,[4] bitterness and frustration linked to deprivation, professional rivalries, an excessive and misguided respect for the law, or duress (Joly 2013), always tainted by anti-Semitism, visceral or circumstantial, militant and cultivated or rough, and always normalized by ecological institutionalization and the general political atmosphere (Joly 2007).

Temporally speaking, the numbers of denunciations spiked around the main roundups, when Jews went into clandestinity and délateurs were emboldened by the abusive and spectacular actions taken by the authorities. Moreover, the general situation on the front affected the number of letters that led to inquiries, and so did the profile of the person in charge at the General Commissariat for Jewish Questions and its police branch, the Department for Investigation and Control: anti-Semitic careerists as much as extreme-right activists pursued the délations methodically (Joly 2017). Scaffolded by the official policy, which rendered hate legitimate and nurtured the hope for a "Jewish people- and communist-free France," some used this well-tested, old instrument to settle personal and professional scores, but also to feed their political aspirations, often with bravado or self-righteous outrage. The world was responsive to the délateur's hopes: Jewish people were regularly arrested and deported, thus encouraging repetition. Vichy's laws and institutions and parts of the press thus created a propitious environment for the systemic elimination of the unassimilable other, against the background of a hostile common sense.

More diffuse, nonofficial acts of collaboration took place in the occupied zone. Servility was normal, and the occupation was initially seen, by many, to be less terrible than expected and preferable to open hostilities. People on the political right saw the defeat as "providential"—an opportunity to form an enduring alliance with Germany against the Soviet threat—while others argued for a more realistic form of collaboration, hoping for a "bloodless peace," but also for Germany's defeat in the long run (Burrin 1996, 183–84). The rich could live in relative comfort

(Nettelbeck 1985). Direct terror affected few categories, principally Jews and Communists. However, economic shortages related to the war and the general exploitation of the French labor force gradually led to widescale impoverishment and increasing resentment toward the occupier—which did not, however, automatically translate into strong public support for the resistance (Burrin 1996).

Germans became the biggest consumers of French goods (Sebba 2016), including French culture. While a sense of general pragmatism dominated the market, some businesses focused on survival while others tried to make the best of the lucrative opportunities opened by the occupation, thus effectively supporting the German war effort. Businesses' positions differed depending on their branch of industry and the pressures that Germany could exert but, in general, "it was impossible for most employers or workers to avoid some degree of implication in the German war economy unless they wished to go out of business or find themselves unemployed" (Jackson 2003, 299): where commercial and national interest were not aligned, the former trumped the latter. Few industrialists saw the German–French "cooperation" as essential to peace and a new Europe. More generally, a flourishing black market in French goods, including delicatessen, artworks, and antiques enabled various speculators, racketeers, and middlemen who often took advantage of "economic Aryanisation" to get obscenely rich (Burrin 1996). However, after the watershed year of 1942, businessmen and industrialists became more reserved when it came to economic collaboration (Burrin 1996).

Culture thrived under the occupation, providing much-needed distraction and relief. On the one hand, the French took German language classes and bought tickets to concerts and public lectures by German musicians, scientists, and philosophers—all part of the German cultural offensive. Researchers and artists forged relationships with German companies and institutions and went on work visits to Germany and Austria— out of political conviction, professional ambition, or a combination of both (Burrin 1996). On the other hand, French entertainers such as Edith Piaf and Charles Trenet, aware of the need to keep French culture and patriotism alive, faced the moral dilemma of singing for German audiences, French workers, or French POWs in Germany (Nettelbeck 1985, 83). The term "larval collaboration" covers this flourishing cultural life: cinemas, theaters, and libraries were always full (Rousso 1992). Cinema audiences soared, and many productions promoted Vichy's conservative values. No single explanation suffices: cultural life could have simultaneously been a coping, escapist mechanism, a sign of political blindness, or a means to support national intellectual traditions. Many, therefore, adjusted to the situation, for psychological and economic rather than ideological reasons, and mostly for want of a better alternative: the Germans appeared to be there to stay, making the horizon of hope and the scope of French political imagination contract.

As mentioned already, the experience of the occupation was highly gendered and classed. French farmers in certain areas of the countryside could pass the entire war without experiencing food shortages or ever encountering the occupier: hierarchies of class privilege were partly destabilized during the war (Fogg 2009). Refugees and Jewish and Roma people had great difficulties getting food and supplies. While men were deported, trapped as POWs, or working in Germany, women's experience was filtered through class and religion. I have already discussed women who joined the repressive institutions. Poor urban women bore the brunt of food shortages in cities, solely responsible for the physical survival of their families.[5] German employers of domestic servants, cooks, secretaries, drivers, and mechanics paid better salaries, an important incentive in times of hardship. Volunteers for the STO also existed, attracted by the higher pay, especially given high unemployment in the first part of the war (Burrin 1996; Diamond 1999).

Particularly in cities, bonds of solidarity formed in response to shared hardship: women's organizations emerged, scaffolding hopes and encouraging cooperation. Supported by the Communists, women protested against the meager food ratios (Schwartz 1999) and published newspapers to put pressure on the authorities (Veillon 2003, 96). The much-discussed "sexual collaboration"—less widespread than assumed (Simonin 2010)—was also often motivated by imperious economic needs, but also by love (Weitz 1995).

As already mentioned, 1942 was a breaking point for French perceptions of political time and hopes: it marked an important shift in public opinion with regard to the occupation and Vichy. Germans' exploitation of the French economy led to painful scarcities, which mobilized the population against the regime, the occupier, and black-market profiteers (Diamond 1999, 75). The STO fueled a dramatic change in public opinion that made it difficult for repressive institutions to recruit French personnel (Simonin 2010). It has been argued that the increase in the number of resisters after 1942 can be at least partially explained by the lack of options for French men, facing forced departures to German factories (Nettelbeck 1985). In November, the Allied "Operation Torch" began in North Africa, nurturing hopes in the possibility of liberation, as well as simultaneously worrying collaborationists who proceeded to rethink their political alliances.[6] Parisians reportedly exhausted the stocks of USSR maps, feverishly following the successes of the Red Army. This coincided with Germans occupying the whole French territory, revealing Vichy's shambolic pretense of sovereignty (Drake 2015). From this point on, the structural and temporal coordinates changed and, while collaboration practices continued till the end of the war, motivations and strategies adjusted to the plausibility of liberation.

Like complicity, resistance was an internally heterogeneous phenomenon, including military and civilian resistance and resistance from within occupied France and from abroad. Counting only a few thousand in late 1940, by 1944 the organized resistance comprised anything between three hundred thousand and five hundred thousand people (Marcot 2006). This increase in number matches the timeline introduced in the discussion of complicity above: the effects of the STO, the gradual disenchantment with Pétain's regime, growing shortages, and Allied bombings turned public opinion toward resistance. Armed struggle, the printing and distribution of illegal publications, political strikes, sabotage, and transporting weapons were all forms of organized resistance by people who consciously engaged in a sustained, risky fight. Beyond organized resistance, public acts of support increased as the war progressed. Resisters shared the broad cause of fighting the occupier but were moved by a variety of political, economic, and personal commitments.

Organized resisters' motivations were in stark tension with the Gaullist mythology of the noble and unified resistance, a mythology that—as we shall see—the state cultivated for many years after the war, not uncontroversially (Wieviorka 2016). Class, ideology, age, religion, and gender shaped the contours of the armed resistance. Within the French territory, the working class and the bourgeois were overrepresented in organized, sustained struggles, while farmers provided mostly local, punctual support: the resistance was generally an urban phenomenon, with Paris, Lyon, and Marseille as its key centers. Class and gender hierarchies were reflected in the ranks of the organized resistance. Ideologically, alternative communities of judgment fed the struggle: Communists and nationalists were much more in favor of—and much better prepared for—the underground fight, in contrast to the Socialists, who traditionally preferred institutional reform. Italians, Spanish Republicans, and Polish agents working for Great Britain operated on French territory. Catholics were divided: some supported the conservative values of Vichy, others tapped into a tradition of contempt toward temporal powers to engage in resistance. Catholics who sheltered Jewish fugitives were sometimes driven by humanitarianism, other times by a desire to convert them. Communist and Zionist Jews were quicker to engage in resistance than were the majority of assimilated Jewish people. The young were overrepresented in the armed resistance because of their rejection of the STO, an incapacity to identify with the octogenarian Pétain, and their age-specific attitude to risk (2016).

As in the case of complicity, professional and political experiences pushed women—in particular, those who had already studied to become professionals or had been affiliated with the Communist youth organizations (such as Jeunes Filles de France) before the war—into the resistance (Schwartz 1995). Joining the resistance opened the public to those normally confined to the private: they traveled, moved to the city, and escaped the moral constraints imposed by their families (Weitz 1995). Women acted as explosives experts, evasion specialists, and exceptionally as leaders of cells, networks, and organizations (Gorrara 1998). However, societal gender roles dictated their position in the struggle: they were overrepresented as secretaries, liaison agents, and social workers and only exceptionally did they occupy leadership positions (C. Andrieu 2000; Gilzmer, Levisse-Touzé, and Martens 2003). Imbricated in family relations with organized male resisters, women contributed by housing, feeding, and caring for resisters, escapees, and allied aviators (Veillon 2003). Most women resisters contributed by forging documents, copying and distributing propaganda materials, transporting arms, and transmitting messages, instrumentalizing gendered stereotypes to their advantage (Veillon 2003). Their relative social invisibility was deployed to great effect in clandestine operations. The general socioeconomic and professional structure of the women population was reflected in the resistance: housewives, workers, and clerks, motivated by various ideologies and relations to male resisters, dominated, with few rural women farmers represented. When caught and imprisoned, women resisters did not benefit from any indulgence (Jaladieu 2003). Those few who did become leaders faced the skepticism of male resisters and were often labeled "honorary men." Given that women themselves had internalized their secondary status in society—a status confirmed even by the Communists, who addressed them as mothers and wives, beings of sacrifice relegated to supportive roles in their propaganda publications (Adler 1995)—they effaced themselves after the war, a fact that partially explains why they officially appear to have accounted for only 11 percent to 12 percent of the organized resistance (C. Andrieu 2000): the gendered doxa and habitus shaped women's experience of the resistance and subsequently erased them from national registers of valor.

Beyond women's activities in the organized resistance, nonarmed resistance work included hiding potential victims, demonstrating, striking, and industrial sabotage. Contributing to clandestine publications was especially important at the initial stages of organizing the resistance, when the propaganda function was key (Jackson 2003). While illegal food production and transactions, as well as counterfeiting rationing documents and theft, have been proposed as authentic forms of political resistance, they should more plausibly be read as expressions of a need to survive under the harsh war conditions and as symptomatic of the normalization of illegality: only 25 percent of the population had sufficient food after the armistice (Cépède 1961).

Alongside the resistance's sexism and misrecognition of women's roles, the anti-Semitism and initial Pétainism of some resister groups, as well as the internal power struggles between them during and after the war, posed challenges to the legends that leaders tried to mythologize (Wieviorka 2016). A particularly disruptive force was that of the violent abuses committed by resisters after the liberation, as well as the self-aggrandizing, self-righteous politics that developed both on the Gaullist and the Communist sides. The less savory elements of the liberation were elided from the master narrative entrenched after 1945, only to be problematized—especially by artists—later. Before discussing the countervisions proposed by caring refuseniks, I now turn to outlining the French official story.

THE OFFICIAL STORY

Beyond the main figures of the Vichy regime, the challenge of deciding who was a victim and who was a collaborator raised extreme difficulties for the post-liberation governments, especially given the moralist indignation many indulged in. To give just one example, the mixed reasons for which French people ended up working in German factories—some volunteered for economic reasons, others went against their will—made it very difficult for the political elite to subsume these workers under either the category of victims (and thus entitled to compensation) or collaborators (liable for punishment). Eventually, an indulgent policy was adopted, enabling their reintegration in their home communities (Wieviorka 2010).

In terms of broader punitive measures, legal purges led to 1,500 executions; 13,339 forced-labor sentences; 2,044 criminal sentences; and 22,883 general prison terms. Administrative internment—outside the court system—was deployed extensively to avoid wild purges, which nonetheless took place along ideological and gendered lines: twenty thousand women were victims of abusive public shaming rituals, which reaffirmed the patriarchal view of patriotic loyalty (Brossat 1993; Weitz 1995; Virgili 2002). Professional lustration in the judiciary and the police focused on the top ranks, while the purging of the army had to be reversed because of anticolonial challenges beginning in 1948 (Wieviorka 2010). To temper the judiciary's frequent and moralistic excess of zeal after the liberation and to promote national unity, de Gaulle used his amnesty power widely and discretely (Gacon 2002). He was also hoping to pacify the Right and avoid upsetting the Communists: the number of imprisoned collaborators therefore dropped from forty thousand in 1945 to just nineteen in 1958 (Rousso 1987, 70).

Scholars of French political memory tend to distinguish between three phases, beginning with the Gaullist vision (Flower 2014). Since there was no unifying experience of the war, there was no shared memory either. The task facing the state in the wake of the liberation was highly complex: "bury the dead, celebrate the heroes, punish the traitors and push them into the flood of opprobrium—or of forgetting—compensate the victims and recognize their status" (Wieviorka 2010, 18). Given the uncertainty and contestability of all the categories listed above, as well as the political need to provide the country with a fabricated, reassuring narrative that could underpin processes of recovery, de Gaulle adopted a strategic politics of memory, heavily contested by various groups and especially by the Communists. This narrative reduced the war to a military encounter and did not thematize the extermination of the Jewish people, downplayed Communists' and the Allies' roles in the liberation, distanced the French nation from the Vichy regime, and projected the image of a unified resistance (Wieviorka 2010). Military leaders were sacralized, while civilian fighters were considered secondary. No distinction was made between Jewish and work deportations. The official account thus denied the specificity of the genocide, obscured France's enthusiastic participation in it, and the broad popular support for Vichy. Moreover, largely forgotten were the wild executions of collaborators at the hour of the liberation, the embarrassment caused to Communists by the Ribbentrop-Molotov pact, and the large fortunes made via spoliation (Flower 2014).

Politically and aesthetically, de Gaulle embraced the language of virility, associating defeat and collaboration with femininity and cowardice, and resistance with masculine honor (Capdevila 2001b). A discursive and visual equivalence between active resistance and manliness was established, an image that outlived the war and shaped the hegemonic memory thereof (Mosse 1990). During the liberation, theatrical displays of masculinity were common: resisters brandished their weapons; buried the dead with military honors; and arrested, judged, and executed supposed and real collaborators. The trial of Robert Brasillach—an anti-Semitic collaborationist intellectual—is infamous for the prosecution's allusions to his homosexuality and supposed enjoyment of German domination, as well as equating treason with "sleeping with Germany" (Kaplan 2000). In many ways, after 1945, the French masculine order reasserted itself with a vengeance.

The gendered reclaiming of the national space was most visible during the purges, which appear to validate the "masculinity crisis" thesis (Capdevila 1998): thousands of women accused of "horizontal" or "sentimental" collaboration were publicly humiliated in an effort to reaffirm masculine authority over their bodies (Virgili 2002; Wieviorka 2010). Mobilizing intense negative emotions during and after the war, the issue of "sentimental" or "horizontal" collaboration became the object of both legal and wild purges. In his detailed study, Virgili highlighted the role of nationalist patriarchal investments underpinning the widespread public degradation of women suspected of such forms of collaboration, often at the hands of last-minute heroes (2002). The purges were undertaken as a satisfactory analgesic for the defeated and their collective humiliation after the *drôle de guerre*: "The sexuality of the sentimental collaborator represented a corrigible transgressive femininity that could only be amended through a public purification ritual operating in three distinct phases: objectification, de-sexualization and marginalization" (Prundeanu 2017, 200).

Deploring the loss of military virtue by a "womanly" France who had been easily overpowered and had submissively "slept with the enemy," the Gaullist and Communist resistance discourses and aesthetics consequently framed national reconstruction as a project of restoring national dignity via a return to virile values. While only 10 percent of men nineteen to forty years old participated in the French Forces of the Interior (FFI) (the armed volunteers who fought alongside Allied forces), it was the male armed combatant who overdetermined the symbolic imagery of France's reconstruction. As Capdevila (1998, 616–17) showed, the collective memory orchestrated after the war was a masculine memory that valorized salvific violence: the war was a men-only business, and reconstruction required masculine knowledges. "Compensatory hyper-masculinity" triumphed, politically and mnemonically.

The first phase of memory was marked by an intense and rich artistic production about the war. Films such as *La bataille du rail* by René Clément (1946)—the result of a political compromise between de Gaulle and the Communists and the winner of the Palme d'Or award at Cannes— presented the image of the unified struggle; *Paris, brûle-t-il?* (1966), also by Clément, fitted the same bill. *La Grande Vadrouille* (1966) by Gérard Oury—an extraordinary box-office success—highlighted civil society's support for the Allies, portraying the occupiers as ridiculous buffoons. The Jewish victims, the other resistance groups, and the popularity of Pétainism were obscured in favor of the "lofty figure of the soldier in the army of shadows" (Wieviorka 2016, 461). These moralizing stories separated the French population into two camps: a majority committed to universal ideals and a few traitors driven by self-interest (Hamel 2005).

Patriarchal norms and bourgeois ideas about women's sexuality were central to some artists' engagements with "sexual collaboration." Many of the occupation novels adopted a sexist, ultramoralistic, and sociologically reductive view of the relationships between French women and German soldiers. In Bory's *Mon village à l'heure allemande* (Prix Goncourt 1945), most women had little else on their minds except romantic relations with the occupier. One of the key resistance works also turned into a film, Vercors's *Le silence de la mer* (1942), already identified feminine sexual virtue with patriotic sentiment.[7] Among the early works, it was perhaps only Jean-Louis Curtis's *Les forêts de la nuit* (1947) that thematized the abusive shearing of women and FFI's hypocrisy.

However, alternative narratives about the war and the occupation were formulated from the beginning by Communists, artists harboring right-wing ideological commitments, combatants, and deportees' associations (Atack and Lloyd 2012). The artistic field was thus divided between, on the one hand, accounts that moralized a voluntaristic idea of individual choice—by both celebrated heroes and reviled traitors—and, on the other hand, accounts that foreground the overdetermining role of chance in exculpatory and implausible ways.[8] Jean-Louis Bory's *Mon village* (1945), Romain Gary's *Éducation européenne* (1945), and Roger Vailland's *Drôle de jeu* (1945) offered unflattering perspectives on the war. Curtis's *Les forêts de la nuit* and Jean Dutourd's *Au bon beurre* (1954) disturbed moralistic visions of valor and victimization by foregrounding collaborators, black marketers, and opportunists. On the political right, Marcel Aymé's *Le chemin des écoliers* (1946) and *Uranus* (1954), while revealing French *attentisme*, profiteering, and accommodationism also questioned the noble ideals of the resistance and condemned the abuses of the purges. Roger Nimier's *Les épées* (1948) and *Le Hussard bleu* (1950) as well as Jacques Laurent's *Le petit canard* (1954) sought to challenge the mythologies of the resistance by introducing main characters who appeared to be immoral or morally relativistic; who saw themselves as belonging to a cultural and intellectual elite; and who, the authors suggested (unpersuasively), ended up on the wrong side of history by sheer chance. Despite this diversity, before de Gaulle's death and the coming of age of a new generation in the 1970s, the state's orchestration of national commemorations, its control over school curricula, its generous use of amnesty, and its compensatory and honorary policies kept the self-serving hegemonic view quite safely in place (Nettelbeck 1985; Wieviorka 2010).

The 1970s marked the change of a generation—a generation that erupted in 1968—and the end of the Gaullist, Manichean vision's domination (Nettelbeck 1985; Flower 2014). In the second phase, neither Pompidou nor Giscard d'Estaing continued the veneration of the resistance in the cultish form it developed under de Gaulle (Wieviorka 2010). Memory became more fragmented, and it is perhaps in France that we most vividly witness the crucial epistemic and political role of aesthetic mnemonic care. Several films and novels contributed to destabilizing the silences and blind spots of the official story. Marcel Ophüls's documentary, *Le chagrin et la pitié* (1969) revealed the multiple positions occupied by various French citizens on the spectrum of involvement and thus dislocated the vision of a united, resisting France. Because of political pressure by the government, the film was not bought by the national television.[9] Patrick Modiano's trilogy of novels, *La Place de L'Étoile* (1968), *La ronde de nuit* (1969), and *Les boulevards de ceinture* (1972), as well as his script for *Lacombe, Lucien*—Louis Malle's 1974 film—problematized French anti-Semitism and opened up a vista on the multiple faces and motivations in the murky in-between, not uncontroversially (Foucault, Bonitzer, and Toubiana 2000; Morris 1992; Atack 2016). Historians also brought their contribution: Robert Paxton's *La France de Vichy* (1973) showed that state collaboration was a deliberate policy, which enjoyed sufficient internal autonomy to initiate anti-Semitic legislation on its own.[10] In parallel, Serge and Beate Klarsfeld's pursuit of Nazis foregrounded the Jewish nature of the genocide (Wieviorka 2010, 197). While not without moralistic or reductionist entrepreneurs, the memory of the war was eroded by a variety of refuseniks who insisted on excavating the unassimilable.

The third phase, beginning with Mitterrand's presidency, added further ambiguity, to a large extent because of the president's own involvement with Vichy.[11] It was during his presidency, however, that the study of the occupation and the Shoah were included in school curricula and that some of the most important trials took place: Klaus Barbie, Paul Touvier, and Maurice Papon were all sentenced during this period.[12] While trials functioned within an individualistic framework of responsibility, they did contribute to increasing public awareness about French participation in crimes against humanity. The picture of the heroic resistance was further challenged not only by artists but also by historians who found misrecognized resisters in the archives—such as women, Jewish people, and colonial troops[13]—and who questioned why so many French citizens, on the left and on the right, had embraced *attentisme* (Wieviorka 2010, 229–30). Films such as Jean-Marie Poiré's *Papy fait de la résistance* (1982) and Claude Berri's *Uranus* (1990) contributed to the demystification of the exalted vision of underground heroism (Wieviorka 2016, 464). It is films such as these that displaced the public's "confused image of the resistance fighter that combines the secret agent, the sheriff or the outlaw as played by an actor in a western, and the fearless knights beyond reproach, who, submachine gun in hand, blow up an incalculable number of factories and trains" (Azéma 1979, 169).

However, it was not until Chirac's mandate that the status of Vichy was addressed directly: in 1995 the president recognized Vichy's being an integral part of France—a view in tension with de Gaulle's refusal to acknowledge its legality. Chirac foregrounded the Shoah and offered reparations to various groups of victims (Wieviorka 2010).

While Sarkozy reaffirmed the specificity of the Jewish genocide, he returned to the Gaullist cult of the resistance—though by then many artists, biographers, and historians had permanently taken it off the pedestal (Flower 2014). Sarkozy's presidency was also marked by a very intense—and not always critical—artistic interest in the occupation, with many novels, films, and exhibitions trying to educate new generations about the war (Flower 2014). In the 2010s, we witness a return of the Gaullist myths—especially in relation to the 2014 commemorations of D-Day ministered by François Hollande and the multiple revisionist publications by historians and public intellectuals (Golsan 2017). Highly successful—yet controversial—novels such as Irène Némirovsky's *Suite française* (2004), Jonathan Littell's *Les Bienveillantes* (2006), Laurent Binet's *HHhH* (2010), and Yannick Haenel's *Jan Karski* (2009), as well as films such as Rachid Bouchareb's *Indigènes* (2006), Roselyne Bosch's *La rafle* (2010), and the television series *Un village français* (2009–17), kept alive the theme of the war, sometimes true to the historical ambivalences, other times falling prey to propagandist temptations.

HERETIC VISIONS OF THE OCCUPATION

Having sketched the phases of French political memory, I turn to several positions on the spectrum of involvement as captured by artists' imagination. I read them through the prosthetic and seductive lens of literary and cinematographic work, seeking to highlight their potential to trigger friction between internalized, reductive doxas and more lucid and discriminating visions of the past, thus highlighting their contribution to the decolonization and reconfiguration of the memoryscape.

I begin with an examination of a gestapiste and a legionnaire and discuss a novel and a film that were received as assaults on the pieties of postwar memory-making. Jacques Laurent's *Le petit canard* (1954) and Louis Malle's *Lacombe, Lucien* (1974) are firmly situated in patriarchal territory. They are analyzed for revealing the complex positionalities from within which people glide within the spectrum of involvement and for thematizing the liberation purges. The chapter then tackles treason. Patrick Modiano's *La ronde de nuit* (2015b) and Brigitte Friang's *Comme un verger avant l'hiver* (1978) offer lucid and pluriperspectival treatments of organized resistance and collaboration, thus making an important dent in the national hierarchy of honor and abjection. Last but not least, I look into artworks that thematize "unpatriotic" forms of sexual desire and give voice to previously silenced historical actors: women resisters and *les tondues*—the women publicly shorn during the liberation. Marguerite Duras's *La douleur* (2011)—in particular, the section titled *Ter le milicien*—and *Hiroshima, mon amour* (1959), a film directed by Alain Resnais on a script by Duras are examined for their foregrounding the gendered unassimilable and the threat it posed to resistance hagiographies.

GESTAPISTES ET LEGIONNAIRES: COMPLICITY WITHIN THE PATRIARCHAL HORIZON

Lacombe, Lucien: Police Allemande!

The much-studied *Lacombe, Lucien* (1974, directed by Louis Malle, script by Patrick Modiano) faced distribution problems and instigated a public scandal (Milne 1974; Walsh 1974; Sineux 1974; Keyser 1975; Foucault, Bonitzer, and Toubiana 2000; Cieutat 2005; Sarnecki 2006; Singerman 2007). Because of its timing, its historical veracity was thought to outweigh its artistic qualities: the French hoped for an accurate snapshot of the war and representative characters (Golsan 2000). Its realistic style fed this expectation: the film meticulously reconstructed the homes, cars, clothing, music, and mannerisms of the period. Yet spectators were disappointed by its refusal to provide an unambiguous moral account of the war. Therefore, in light of the political, symbolic, and affective investment in the Gaullian myth of united resistance and its controlling images of virile, armed heroes and cowardly, effeminate traitors, the film polarized the French public. While some saw it as a masterpiece, critics from opposing ideological camps expressed virulent outrage, targeting both the film and the director.

In this section, I discuss *Lacombe, Lucien* along several dimensions of caring refusal. First, the war is narrated from a collaborator's perspective, not the resisters'—as the norm dictated. In making Lucien his main character, Malle rejects the dominant melodramatic script. Second, the film thematizes the complex positionalities from within which people glide into and move within the spectrum of complicity. In particular, I focus on how it tackles the classed and gendered nature of Lucien's hopes and deeds. Malle chooses a poor farmer's young son as his protagonist and follows him during the last months of World War II, on his quest for social recognition and prosperity, which he eventually obtains by joining the Gestapo. While the film has often been subsumed to the *mode rétro*[14]— broadly understood as a genre deploying nostalgic aesthetics by artists aiming to justify their own or their families' problematic positioning during the occupation—I suggest that the ambiguity of Lucien's opaque character, capable of both cruelty and love, of pettiness and courage, as well as his apparently inescapable position in a web of competitive masculine relations, render implausible both hypermoralistic, psychologizing readings of the film and ideologically overdetermined rejections thereof. Lucien is neither an unambiguous villain nor a weak coward, as per the national mythology. In introducing a hypermasculine traitor, the film troubles gendered imaginaries that associated valor and patriotism with virility and shame and perfidy with femininity. Lastly, I suggest that

Modiano's diverse cast of gestapistes and collaborators—moved both by political and economic imperatives—and his foregrounding of the institutional face of complicity sabotages the reductive narratives peddled by both the Left and the Right after the liberation.

The film starts by showing Lucien working as a cleaner in a nursing home—a menial job he detests. The setup is an idyllic French countryside: long shots follow Lucien cycling amid rolling green hills on the soundtrack of Django Reinhardt's music, a staple of French culture at the time. Like Duras's stories analyzed below, the film is firmly located in French moral territory: Germans make only episodic, marginal appearances. Lucien's father is a POW, while his mother is involved with her employer, Mr. Laborit, who makes Lucien feel unwelcome on his farm. To change his life, Lucien approaches a known resister, the village teacher, asking to join the struggle. Lucien's hopes are quelled when the teacher firmly rejects him, patronizing him as ignorant and too young, derisively informing him that resisting was unlike poaching, Lucien's favorite pastime. This first rejection by a father figure—a painful denial of entry into the realm of manly valor—embitters him deeply.

Lucien has no choice but return to the nursing home job, yet, because of a flat tire, he fails to arrive before the curfew. In the streets, he encounters contrabandists, but also French gestapistes and their entourage, heading for a party in the Gestapo headquarters. The latter catch him spying on their party and arrest him; on realizing he could be a source, they get him drunk and easily extract information from him. Inebriated and resentful at the teacher's earlier dismissal, Lucien eventually betrays him to the gestapistes, a gesture he appears to regret when, hungover, he faces the arrested man in the morning and realizes the gravity of his deed. The teacher calls Lucien a "bastard," a second admonition that, against the background of his general frustration with his socially subordinate position, contributes to Lucien's feeling flattered by the Gestapo's job offer, which comes a few minutes later.

In the Gestapo, he joins a diverse cast of characters that troubles the official doxa of French people's united resistance. In the group, few are ideologically committed; many are opportunists, who work closely with black marketers to make the best of the end of the war. Most disrespect Pétain, calling him names and practicing their shooting on his portrait. Part of their everyday job is to sort out the many délation letters the Gestapo received from French people, which they do, scoffing at informers' petty motivations. Malle's insertion of office-set, secretarial scenes depicting this routine, bureaucratized process as part of a violent ecology contribute to his refusal of national doxastic pieties. While some gestapistes are rabid anti-Semites, many appear simply bent on getting rich—stealing from those they arrest is the norm. This picture of the diversity of positionalities within the group troubles Manichaeistic and reductive views of agency, relativizing the role of ideology and confirming historians' emphasis on the role of economic gain. More importantly, it hollows the comforting picture that de Gaulle hegemonized after the war by casting a critical light on the interstitial practices of complicity that could not be assimilated to his "official story": délation, black marketeering, and implementing the occupier's policies willingly and self-interestedly.

The material benefits that Lucien derives from the job boost his self-esteem. He is moved by a simple, class-inflected manliness: economic prosperity and control over a woman—both instrumental for gaining other men's respect—are his key objectives.[15] He rejoices in his social climb and thrives on the power he has over villagers as gestapiste, especially over older men, including Mr. Horn, the Jewish tailor who makes his first suit.

Mr. Horn is in hiding with his mother, Bella, and daughter, France, a pianist whose studies were stalled by Vichy's anti-Semitic laws. The family is bourgeois and assimilated. It is in the encounter with the Horns that class divisions and Lucien's desire to affirm himself as a mature, manly provider become even clearer. His classed and gendered habitus—his attitudes and ideas but also his bodily hexis—clashes with their bourgeois tastes and manners: he has no idea of fashion, is clumsy and out of place, and doesn't know how to court France. He tries to impress her by lying that he was a student before the war and by using his badge to get her ahead in the queue for food, unsuccessfully. He brings the Horns various confiscated luxury goods in awkward and unwanted gestures of "generosity" meant to endear him to them. He later threatens Horn with giving him in to the police just to get his permission to take France to a party. Once there, Lucien gets violently jealous when another gestapiste gropes France on the dance floor. The film also suggests that on one occasion Lucien raped France. In everything he does, Lucien is driven by regressive gender norms and a desire to be recognized and respected, and any slight opposition angers him.

Mr. Horn and his mother, Bella, adopt a very reserved attitude toward Lucien and his acolytes. Bella never speaks to them and moves about the house in her routines as if they did not exist, refusing to acknowledge their reality. France is romantically intrigued by Lucien but, sensing his roughness, maintains an ambivalent attitude throughout. Toward the end, she even contemplates murdering him. Because of the centrality of armed struggle within the national mnemonic imagination, the family's reticence and refusals did not register with the film's critics.

Lucien's ambiguity as a character emerges via the juxtaposition of instances of petty cruelty and acts of kindness and justice. He uses his authority to chase away Horn's landlord, who extorts an exorbitant rent from his Jewish tenants. When France is attacked by an anti-Semitic maid, he defends and comforts her tenderly. In an open confrontation with the resistance—which, contrary to critics, does make an appearance in the film—Lucien is distracted and prefers to shoot rabbits, failing to fight alongside his Gestapo mates. Mr. Horn, whom Lucien harasses in his own home, confesses that he cannot bring himself to detest the young man. Lucien loves his mother and regularly sends her money. Though he humiliates Gestapo's victims, Lucien kills a German soldier and rescues France and her grandmother from deportation—though it is not clear whether out of concern for the women or sheer resentment toward the soldier who had chastened him minutes earlier. On the run, he provides for France and her frail grandmother. Therefore, the last scene, which introduces the news of Lucien's execution in text overlaying a medium shot of him resting in the grass, leaves the spectator uneasy.

Malle claimed that Lucien could have easily ended up as a resister, under different circumstances. This statement outraged many former resisters, who thought Malle was devaluing their political commitment— also an exaggeration given how many young men became last-minute resisters as the war was ending, to avoid the STO or reap the benefits of victory. A non sequitur, I argue, plagues the director's position, one that the film does not actually vindicate. There is an unwarranted argumentative leap from stating: "everyone reacted according to the circumstances" to "Lucien could just as well have been a resister." I argue that Lucien's

class and his location within a competitive horizon of masculinity and
the relationships it opened influenced where he ended up on the spectrum
of involvement. His main reason—like the reasons of other gestapistes in
the film—is negative: he has a strong desire to escape his humble social
condition. His trajectory in the last few months of the war is situated
relationally, based on how the people around him support or obfuscate
his hopes. His longing for social validation and social proximity to the
members of the maquis make him approach the resistance first. Rejected
and humiliated by his elders—a rejection that could be attributed to
a problematic, haughty self-righteousness by the leader who gatekeeps
resistance's ranks as a "men only" business—Lucien eventually joins an
institution that promises to give him that much-needed sense of self-worth
and access to the material resources he longed for. Being patronized by
older men unfailingly pushes him to oppose them, whoever they might be.
He denounces the teacher for his rejection. He harasses Horn incessantly
and becomes France's lover against Horn's will. When a victim of the
Gestapo reprimands Lucien for betraying his country, Lucien reasserts his
authority by sticking tape over the man's mouth. Upon being admonished
by a German soldier, Lucien kills him.

Malle purposefully makes Lucien's thoughts and desires unavailable to
viewers, explicitly rejecting a pedagogical approach to political memory[16]:
with few exceptions, close shots of Lucien's young face give no clues as
to his inner life, and the spectator is forced to judge on the basis of a few
dialogues and his actions alone. I suggest this is a valuable formal choice
that prevented psychologizing, individualizing readings, allowing for
class-inflected competitive masculinity to emerge as key to comprehend-
ing Lucien's actions. His overcompensatory virile brutality is predictable
in the context in which he strives to affirm himself. His behavior is far
from the mythologies of passivity, effeminacy, and homosexuality that
framed the dominant understandings of collaboration after the war. Malle
shoots the amateur actor he cast as Lucien in flattering medium shots,
brandishing machine guns, clad in leather jackets or open-neck white
shirts, sleeves rolled up, Basque beret perched on the head, or in full
shots while in action, running or aiming his gun, producing an aesthetics
that blasphemously evokes that of the maquis and Communist fighters.
In choosing as protagonist a hypermasculine collaborator, the film thus

invites epistemic friction between the convenient mnemonic common sense and an alternative vision of the occupation, populated by virile traitors and a heterogenous fauna of war profiteers and délateurs.

While Lucien remains Malle's character (Nettelbeck and Hueston 1986), Modiano's indisputable contribution is the human debris associated with the *police allemande*. The figures that gravitate around Lucien make up a heterogeneous group of *déclassés*, professional failures, speculators, black marketers, ex-convicts, farmers, men, and women who try to make the best of the situation, fully aware of the risks. Malle was criticized for presenting a bleak image of France, one that foregrounded collaboration to the detriment of the resistance (Foucault, Bonitzer, and Toubiana 2000). This very reaction vindicates the value of the film's refusal of soothing mnemonic doxas and its injecting of a healthy dose of lucidity in ideologically saturated debates about the glorious past of the "Nation." In pluralizing the cast of history's protagonists, foregrounding ambiguous characters, and decoupling patriotism from masculinity, the film successfully short-circuits national mnemonic reflexes and can therefore be read as an example of mnemonic care.

Fathers and Sons: *Le petit canard*

A prolific writer and journalist, Jacques Laurent belonged to the Hussards, a literary movement on the political right that forcefully opposed the engaged-intellectual model promoted by Jean-Paul Sartre. Published in 1954, *Le petit canard*[17] takes us back to 1939. The choice of a legionnaire for a protagonist and the centering of his father's pain at his impending execution after the liberation plunged the novel in the great debates on the political role of literature after the war. The book contributes two insights to this project. First, it prosthetically takes us into the world of Antoine, an insecure, sexually inexperienced teenager, raised in a Catholic, bourgeois, highly conservative family. Like Lucien, Antoine is deeply embedded in relationships of competitive masculinity and his aspirations are shaped by the regulating ideal of sovereign heroism. We follow him during the early stages of the war as he experiences some of the most formative events of his life. The novel sheds light on the complex ways in which both Antoine's social positionality within a masculinist, militarist doxa and his individual choices—as filtered through his class and religion—come together to determine his trajectory, in ways that show the limits of individualizing and temporally static accounts of complicity. Second, readers also enter Antoine's father's world during the days preceding his son's trial and execution for treason. I suggest that the novel enlarges our horizon of moral relevance, making available neglected hermeneutical vistas on the war and its aftermath, thus potentially provoking epistemic friction between mnemonically ignored perspectives and socialized memory. In problematizing the costs of postwar purges and their liberal deployment of capital punishment, Laurent goes much further than Malle in questioning any strong certainty or enthusiasm about their moral rightness and political value. *Le petit canard* thus strongly refuses the moral self-righteousness that became dominant after the war.

In the first part of the novel, we follow an insecure eighteen-year-old Antoine on his quest to become a "real" man. The story is told in the third person by an unknown narrator who privileges the boy's point of view. In a rather traditional, highly accessible narrative style, Laurent contours the main characters and evokes the life of a bourgeois, Catholic family with its rhythms and routines, which are suddenly disturbed by the war. Antoine's father is a World War I veteran mobilized in Alsace. The boy is very excited and longs to join the army. For him, this is not at all a matter of patriotism but one of masculine affirmation: he dreams of getting a wound that would permanently scar his face and make him look older and less innocent—that is, like a "patented man, and a prestigious man" (1975, 27). Socialized in a conservative patriarchal horizon, he sees the war as essential to his individualization and liberation from his father's shadow and fantasizes about his hypothetical scar being remarked upon by girls—at the swimming pool or in intimate settings. He imagines them asking him about it and his nonchalantly responding: "Ah! This little nothing! I got it in '39, out of sheer distraction. A perforating bullet" (1975, 28).

To persuade his devout mother to allow him to enlist, Antoine makes deliberate efforts to fail in school. His reading is almost exclusively about wars and heroes. The regulatory norm of sovereign heroism is shown here in its overbearing shaping of teenagers' imagination and aspirations. Antoine is torn by an existential dilemma: can he participate heroically in war while also being in love with his school mate, Sophie? His worries are soon dissipated when Sophie, less shy than he is, kisses him, thus confirming their chaste teenage love.

Antoine's social circle is enlarged when Sonia, a Polish woman; Vladi, a Polish officer and Sonia's lover; and Paule, a teacher, enter his life. They meet to discuss literature, listen to music, flirt, and pass the time. Antoine becomes slowly annoyed and resentful toward Sophie, especially after she rejects his clumsy sexual advances. He is jealous of two men: of Vladi, whose war stories enthrall Sonia, and of a new history teacher, a veteran who gives her private lessons. Both men are older and more experienced, and both have known war. Antoine grows particularly disdainful of Vladi, toward whom he nourishes racist and classist views.

The second part of the novel recounts Antoine's escape, in Sophie's mother's car, as the German invasion begins. At some point, the two teenagers find themselves alone, having to find their way together. This challenge brings them closer together, enjoying an unexpected autonomy. Their romantic adventure is cut short by Antoine's irredeemable jealousy when he learns that Sophie has already had affairs with both Vladi and the history teacher. The idea that she had a flourishing sexual life, that she chose her partners and hadn't been seduced or fooled by Vladi is unacceptable to Antoine, whose ideas of women's sexuality are deeply conservative. The gender doxa regulates not only his ideas of his own worth but also those of the women around him. As Bourdieu insightfully remarked, "Exaltation of masculine values has as its dark negative side in the fears and anxiety aroused by femininity" (2001, 51), connoted simultaneously as weak and "devilishly cunning." The second part of the novel ends with Antoine angrily leaving Sophie, heading to join the defeated French soldiers, a move he sees as his integration into a masculine world of valor: to Sophie's lax morality he counterpoises their (supposed) moral purity and courage. The novel's first two parts thus give us a prosthetic glimpse of the misogynistic world that later made possible both the post-liberation scapegoating of (mostly imagined) women collaborators and the consecration of overcompensatory masculinity.

The last part skips to June 1945 and stretches over two days. The narrator is Antoine's father, who has to face his son's death sentence for treason—Antoine had joined the LVF. The story is told in the first person, and the tone is sometimes confessional, sometimes nostalgic. The father is torn between desperation and hope in the possibility of a pardon. Crucially for this book's argument, in foregrounding the father's suffering and giving him an authorial voice, Laurent undermines any self-righteous, intransigent belief in the moral certainties of the liberation purges.

The father does not excuse his son's choices. Laurent shows him recording with great emotional and sensorial acuity people's attitudes and feeding off memories of Antoine's childhood, recalling in flashback the good times they spent together. His pain is tangible in his recounting of endearing stories but also in his reliving mentally Antoine's arrest and trial. We understand that, during his interrogation, Antoine had displayed incriminatory, treasonous positions, including a hate of the Polish people and a refusal to recant. Details about Antoine's life after 1939 emerge in snippets from the father's meandering thoughts: we learn that at some point he started displaying an incomprehensible aversion to Poland and the Polish people and that he cynically thought Americans politically smarter than the Nazis, since, unlike the latter, they did not announce their war crimes in advance. The reasons that the father and the defense lawyer think Antoine joined the LVF are slowly revealed: they know he was bent on fighting the war. On whose side, they wondered? That was a secondary question, as far as they could tell. They conclude it must have been LVF's offices' proximity to their house—as per Laurent's desire to emphasize the role of chance.

The father's portrait emerges from his memories. A former architect, he loves his son above everyone else, in standard patriarchal manner. He confesses his own—politically superficial—preferences in 1942: he would have loved to move to Algiers, for the "easy life" of the colony and the warm weather. He seems baffled by Antoine's decision to go to the freezing East front dressed in the "ugly" German uniform. The father seems to suspect that Antoine wanted to affirm himself as a man in his own right but does not fully grasp the weight of this psychological truth. His militarism and masculine pride makes the idea of asking the jury for clemency on behalf of his son look like an unfathomable humiliation. To stay sane, he is writing a book on Roman history, whose proofs arrive for correction on the very day of the execution. The novel ends with the father's own marveling at how he continues to live despite his son's death—that he can eat and laugh, in spite of it all.

While Laurent makes the two main male characters completely transparent by meticulously recording their inner thoughts, emotions, and sensorial reactions to the materiality surrounding them, the structure of the novel—the temporal break in the narrative between parts II and III—inserts a degree of uncertainty. *Le petit canard* invites the reader to put together a coherent narrative about Antoine's war experience, his motivations, and his complicities. In the interview that prefaces the 1973 edition of the novel, Laurent refuses to consider the novel political. He consistently repeats that Antoine joined the LVF because of a certain mood (*humeur*), and not out of patriotic or political honor (*honneur*). He emphasizes, again and again, the role of chance in his ending up in the Legion and then executed after the war. Laurent's—exaggerated and implausible—denial of the novel's political nature has to be read against the background of his rejection of the engaged literature promoted at the time by the existentialists, particularly by Sartre.[18] However, I argue that the novel gives us plenty of resources to read it otherwise, *with* but also *contra* Laurent: the complex ways in which age, class, gender, and religion come together to move Antoine to join an extreme Right—as opposed to a resistant—group are evident in the text.

Antoine is a politically immature man. He sees the war as the only possible certifier of manliness and adulthood, an idea inculcated into schoolchildren by teachers, the books they read, and the division of labor in the family. Antoine's view of the world is informed by his extensive reading—a reflection of his family's class, politics, and religion: Corneille's *Le Cid*, Montherlant's misogynistic writings, and histories of various wars and revolutions dominate his reading list. These books constitute his main source of information about the world (including about manliness, feminine virtues, sexuality, and politics) and, alongside his mother's fervent Catholicism, the only source of values. Laurent seduces us into Antoine's psychic life and helps us see how his identity develops as a response to his milieu and its multiple determinations. It therefore comes as no surprise when Antoine behaves as if his virility could only be confirmed in competitive relationships with other, more experienced older men—his father, the history teacher, Vladi—and in the exclusive possession of a pure and sexually unexperienced woman, which he believes Sophie to be.[19] Antoine is guided by a very conservative, sexist, and naive vision of intimate and romantic relationships, and his insertion within a Catholic, bourgeois, and patriarchal horizon determines how he sees himself as well as what he aspires to be and to have.

The third part of the novel suggests a simple reconstruction: deeply disappointed by Sophie's deliberate choice of other men over him and her refusal to be shamed by his invectives, Antoine decides to join the LVF, in the hope of affirming his moral superiority over the depraved lovers. However, given the picture already portrayed of Antoine's social, economic, and cultural background, this suggestion is too quick, on the novel's own terms. Antoine's parents' Anglophobia and Catholicism, his immersion in a patriarchal order where he is yet to be consecrated, his internalization of impossible standards of heroism in their militarist guise (as embodied by his father and romantic rivals, but also canonized in the books he reads), his racism and possessive understanding of relations to women—all come together in constellations of ideas, relationships, and processes of subject formation that make Antoine's choice for the political Right quite predictable. Laurent's effort to challenge the moralistic can-onization of the heroic figure of the Communist resister by foregrounding the role of chance in collaboration is bound to fail because the trajectory of his protagonist is anything but arbitrary. The story we get in the first two parts—that of Antoine's socialization—makes his choice of the LVF eminently logical and sociologically foreseeable: the structural and relational underpinnings of his actions are laid bare in front of our eyes.

The book also successfully challenges the moral—and often hypocritical—intransigence animating the post-liberation purges and executions. Antoine's father's pain is deeply moving as Laurent provides us with a powerful emotional and sensorial prosthesis into his collapsing world: we feel with him the weight of his neighbors' half-compassionate gaze, the psychological burden of waiting for his son's execution within the oppressive walls of his home, his unappeased anguish, and the partial efficiency of his coping mechanisms. Laurent records the father's slow movements about his room in short, descriptive sentences that conjure an overwhelming atmosphere of psychological tension. The father an-chors himself in the unbearable present by paying minute attention to objects—a table, a wine glass, the light switch. The few chapters dedicated to the father's recollections of Antoine's childhood show how memories provide a support mechanism for the agonizing parent: he recalls snippets of conversations, shared laughter, the feel of Antoine's small hand in his. In giving the traitor's father a voice and centering his horrific torment, Laurent thus invites a moment of hesitation in the automatism of socialized memory and aims to interrupt quick and moralistic judgments about treason and what traitors deserve. As we shall also see in the discussion of Marguerite Duras's story *Ter le milicien*, facing the immediacy of retributive death in all its enormity and horror, through the eyes of the condemned and their close ones, can suspend mnemonic reflexes, artistically pierce the armature of sanctimonious master narratives of blame and just deserts, and invite readers to readjust their moral, emotional, and political compass.

TRAITORS, IMPOSTORS, AND DOUBLE AGENTS
La ronde de nuit: The Ever-Swinging Pendulum of Identification

Patrick Modiano's *La ronde de nuit* (1969) belongs to his iconoclastic "Occupation Trilogy," one of the most celebrated outputs of his vast literary production on the period, on which the Nobel jury commented in justifying their decision in 2014.[20] A writer obsessed with memory, identity, and their inescapable elusiveness and uncertainty (Nettelbeck and Hueston 1986; Morris 1996; Roux 1999; Flower 2007; Butaud 2008; Cooke 2005), Modiano's novels are often akin to detective stories with inconclusive ends. Frequently, the object of the unsuccessful investigation is the identity of the detective himself, modeled on Modiano and his own identity struggle: born at the end of the war, the novelist autofictionalizes his search for his absent father, a Jewish-Italian black marketer connected to French collaborationist circles, who barely escaped deportation.[21] As we will see, *La ronde de nuit* also dramatizes identity, and it does so in a way that provides a sophisticated engagement with the double erasure at the center of this project.

While the novel has often been read as asking readers to inhabit the world of the occupation and make moral judgments, I suggest that the book transports the reader sensorially, emotionally, and morally into the tense atmosphere of occupied Paris to reveal the implausibility of standard accounts of both heroism and collaborationism. First, Modiano decenters the Germans and foregrounds French people's compromises, silences, and internecine ideological confrontations: by portraying a bestiary that includes war profiteers, collaborators, and a double agent tormented by guilt and loneliness, Modiano decouples readers' socialized memory from the exercise of the imagination, enabling them to rethink the category of "traitor" and its capaciousness. Second, the book's tackling of obdurate models of resistance, their moralism and assumed purity—all in tension with political and military imperatives of efficacy—highlights the intangibility, implausibility, and alienating effect of heroic models on ordinary individuals and thematizes their constricting role in relation to a community's register of resistant action and critique.

The novel seduces the reader into the ambiance of Paris in the summer of 1942. Modiano reconstructs the sounds, the smells, the furnishings, and the urban map of a double underground: of collaboration and of resistance. Precise geographical references, characters modeled on known historical figures, sartorial details, snippets of popular songs in French and German, and inventories of objects and consumer goods typical of the time—cigarettes, drinks, foods—are introduced to firmly situate the plot in an authentic historical horizon. The elegiac, elliptic writing is strongly evocative of the chaos, confusion, and lawlessness that dominated that otherwise beautiful, warm, and dusty summer: Paris was left to the "rats that take over the city after the plague has wiped out the populace" (2015a, 128). Against this background, the first-person narrator is a double agent who works under the code name "Swing Troubadour" for a band of extortionists, black marketers, torturers, and killers subordinated to the French police and, simultaneously, as "Princesse de Lamballe" for a resistance cell made of former military officers.

Modiano formally splits the double agent's experiential world into three. First, there are his criminal activities alongside the crooks who compose the Cimarosa Square band—modeled on two real bands active during the occupation, the Lafont and Berger bands (Nettelbeck and Hueston 1986, 27). The leader is a man nicknamed the Khedive, after the cigarettes he smokes. The Khedive comes from a disadvantaged social background: orphaned as a child, he had no education and passed his youth going through various reformatories and prisons. He recognizes the many opportunities the war created for people like him. He hopes and longs for upward social mobility and for gaining respectability—his biggest dream is to one day become the Préfet de Police. The Khedive is surrounded by ex-convicts, actresses, addicts, nightclub owners, impoverished aristocrats, procurers, speculators, and black marketers. They "work" as informants, torture and assassinate suspected resisters, and get rich from trafficking in goods they pillage from deserted houses under the indulgent eye of the French police. The band recalls the group of gestapistes in *Lacombe, Lucien,* gathering a similarly diverse fauna: Modiano fictionally recuperates historical figures, infamous for their crimes and racism, with deep roots in French history (Golsan 1998; Roux 1999). By digging deep into archives to highlight these continuities, Modiano historically embeds the ecology of violence in the *longue durée,* making it difficult for memory entrepreneurs to ascribe all responsibility to the occupier and a few traitors and to persuasively argue for "clean slates."

The Swing Troubadour finds a home and a father figure in the band. He is trusted as an efficient informer and infiltrator, but he also loots emptied houses, whose owners fled or were deported. This well-remunerated "employment" allows him to provide generously for his mother and derive an incredible sense of power: "The city was mine" (Modiano 2015a, 138). However, the Troubadour is aware of his lack of will to extricate himself form the corrupt group who scaffold his hopes. At no point does he believe that he will get away with his crimes, yet he also knows that his actions were partly made possible by the generalized collapse of morality and law. As Roux observes, Modiano's goal was to reconstitute "a general atmosphere of institutionalized corruption and degeneration, which allows the reader to grasp the essence of abjection" (Roux 1999, 65): complicity is relational and underpinned by a series of practices, institutions, and forms of sociability—many of which had roots before the war.

Because he appears to have an "innocent" look, the Troubadour is considered particularly good for infiltrating resistance cells, which is what the Khedive asks him to do. Therefore, second, he joins a resistance cell, under the code name "Princesse de Lamballe"—gendered female. The decadent, film-noir atmosphere in the Cimarosa Square villa is counterpoised to the austere life of the somber, self-denying, idealistic resisters. The cell is led by the Lieutenant. The Princesse both admires and resents the Lieutenant for his moral sanctimoniousness and intimidating integrity. The Lieutenant's fatherly attitude moves him. However, he is soon disappointed to learn that resisters also deal in deceit: the Lieutenant asks the Princesse to penetrate the band in Cimarosa square and execute its leaders. And thus a disillusioned Princesse begins his career as a double agent.

The third world is an imaginary one: escapism is the Troubadour's only relief. He has two fictitious friends, an old blind man, Coco Lacour, and a fragile elderly lady, Esmeralda, in whose well-being he is heavily emotionally invested—they are a "palliative" (Morris 1996, 24) for his loneliness and constant sense of impending doom. The Troubadour's reveries about caring for them help him deal with his hopelessness and feelings of guilt. Projecting himself imaginatively as their protector provides a measure of relief: caring for the weak, be they real or imagined, offers some meaning and comfort. The introduction of this tripartite world-structure is Modiano's key formal trick for troubling black-and-white judgments about his protagonist's character and actions: like Lucien Lacombe, he cannot be completely written off morally. As I argue below, within this pluriverse, the reader is faced with a character whose conflicting allegiances shed light on reductive views of historical agency and models of identification.

The Troubadour/Princesse moves between these three worlds, changing personae as he does so. Modiano contours his profile by taking the reader on a journey in his rich psychological life: the protagonist is often hyperreflective and Modiano makes us witness to the working of his mnemonic imagination: memories in flashback are juxtaposed to imagined scenarios—some comforting in their escapism, others foreboding. In reckoning with his having become a double agent, the protagonist invokes his childhood and his psychological dispositions: "Not enough fibre to be a hero. Too dispassionate and distracted to be a real villain. On the other hand, I was malleable, I had a fondness for action and I was plainly good-natured" (2015a, 139).

The Troubadour/Princesse's oscillations sabotage easy subsumption to pregiven moralized categories. Son of a famous fraudster from the 1930s, he grows up fatherless. His being attracted to the Khedive and the Lieutenant, both of whom address him with "mon petit," is thus no surprise: like Lucien, he is in search of a surrogate father. His loneliness makes him emotionally dependent on these two men and gets him entangled in webs of relationships that structure his actions. However, he remains at a certain distance from both: unlike the Khedive, he is tormented by his conscience and expects to be punished for his deeds; unlike the Lieutenant, he is not ready to die for his beliefs. A most ordinary man, neither a monster nor a saint, he is easily seduced by money, which—like Lucien—he uses to be a good son to his mother, something that assuages his bad conscience. The double agent's greatest dream—almost touching in its ordinariness and lack of ambition—is to become a bartender somewhere outside Paris. And still, while often akratic, he is not indifferent to the moral consequences of his choices: he even imagines his own trial and how journalists might report his crimes.[22]

Most importantly, the Troubadour sees both the crooks and the resisters as "lunatics" and feels he cannot identify with either of these opposing camps. Both "wear him down" (2015a, 207). He feels like a weathervane, cowardly and weak, like somebody who can fit neither the hero nor the villain profile, living in permanent fear of both worlds. While his actions bring him much closer to the crooks, the Troubadour experiences deep remorse and guilt. Thus, I argue, Modiano gestures to the implausibility of the prototypes of both heroism and villainy, invites us to approach them with circumspection and to imagine that being complicit does not necessarily extinguish one's moral sense. By introducing such a vacillating, morally complex character, the book subtly undermines ossified ideological visions and their reductive categories of worthiness and wickedness. The troubadour's multiple, contradictory drives, his conscience and his fears, make him plausible as a susceptible individual, inextricably caught in a tiresome in-between.

On the one hand, while the Troubadour is touched by the Lieutenant's kindness and by his followers' vulnerabilities, fears, and hopes, he does not share their idealism and political commitment. Their invocations of the "Revolution," "moral awakenings," and "a just world", as well as their veneration of Robespierre and Breton alienate him. He thinks to himself, in a somewhat self-exculpatory manner: "They were lucky, these boys, to be able to daydream . . . I was the one sent out to battle in the real world, and I was flailing against the current" (2015a, 189). To their imperious need to bear witness and break the silence about suffering, he opposes brutal realism: "Silence is easily earnt: a couple of kicks in the teeth will do the trick" (2015a, 189). When they ask him to infiltrate the

Cimarosa band, he feels used and is deeply disappointed by their resorting to subterfuge and assassinations.

On the other hand, his pangs of conscience and his deep need to care for the weak distance him from the Khedive and his acolytes. He is uneasy at his mates' torturing and killing of resisters. Despite his inertial disposition, his moral sense is alive. He confesses that his heart skips every time the word "informer" is enunciated. He lies to the Khedive as to who the leader of the resister cell is, claiming all orders come from a man named Princesse de Lamballe, his own code name. He stalls the attack on the resistance cell, trying to convince the Khedive that their power was negligible and identifying the Princesse de Lamballe as the only worthy target. Moments before the resisters' arrest, he feels queasy and doubts whether he would be able to live with himself. The only thing that makes this feeling tolerable is the resisters' disdain at realizing who betrayed them, a disdain that feeds his resentment: "Ten, perhaps twenty other faces filled with contempt. Since they're determined to go out with a flourish, let them die!" (2015a, 148). The heroes' intangibility—their "triumphant scorn" (2015a, 157) alienates him. He knows, however, that the time of punishment will eventually come, and he accepts this unreservedly.[23]

The Troubadour/Princesse's final grand gesture, of trying—unsuccessfully—to kill the Khedive confirms the texts' ideological uselessness: subsuming it to the category of "novels of the anxious conscience," Hamel (2005) persuasively argues that Modiano refuses to instruct and cannot be easily co-opted by either the Right or the Left. The novel's ambivalent protagonist, trapped between two contradictory options, deeply invested in his identity as a provider, acts against the background of the breakdown of principles and laws, generalized theft and profiteering—that is, from within a complex ecology of violence in which Modiano marginalizes the Germans. The novel implicates the French and offers an acute panorama of a "world obscured by textbooks, forgotten or repressed by those who had experienced it, simply unknown to the young generation," which he "brings to the surface of collective consciousness with a shocking force that pulverises the received ideas of the official history" (Nettelbeck and Hueston 1986, 27).

The effort to muddy the memorial waters does not limit itself to the collaborators: the portraits of the resisters—intransigently moralistic, unwavering, haughty, and thus distant and intimidating, but also weak as a military and political force and comfortable with treachery—destabilizes the master narrative institutionalized after the war. In inserting ambiguity in the hermeneutical space of the late 1960s and early 1970s, Modiano interpellates readers to travel prosthetically into the worlds that the Troubadour/Princesse uncomfortably inhabited, in the psyche of an ordinary man, who is neither politically committed, nor amoral, a man of modest ambition, whose trajectory cannot be easily judged, a man who, most importantly for this book, cannot find himself in any of the categories that the postwar mythology offers as matrices of identification. In doing so, Modiano gets at the core of the double erasure that motivates this project, highlighting the poverty of hegemonic tropes of remembering in relation to the complexities of lived experience under the occupation.

The Honor Trap: *Come un verger avant l'hiver*

Come un verger avant l'hiver by Brigitte Friang was published in 1978, joining an already rich corpus of works problematizing the hegemonic vision of the war.[24] Like her woman protagonist, Friang was active as a resister during the war. She was arrested, tortured, and interned in Ravensbrück but survived a grueling death march to Dachau and returned to Paris in 1945. Later, she became a successful war correspondent.

The novel analyzed in this section heretically foregrounds a woman resister and her perspective, illuminating her multifaceted positionality, the webs of relationships that inform her decisions, and the moral impurity of her motivations. In shedding light on the complexity, ambivalence, and murkiness of this mnemonically marginalized perspective, Friang avoids reproducing the blind spots of the masculinist, absolutist model. Perhaps most importantly, the novel tackles head-on Gaullist resisters' own complicitous support for a skewed, self-serving, and dangerous mythology of the past, one that helped convert their moral capital into political capital after the war and that precluded an honest discussion about their own complicities, cowardice, and violence, as well as the recognition of other groups of resisters, in particular the Communists. Friang thus uses treason within the resistance as a starting point for thematizing the different, mutually reinforcing, institutionalized silences that keep the regulative ideal of heroism in place. In this sense, she illuminates the risks of subsequent colonizations of the space of meaning by various forms of dogmatic univocality.

The novel follows a logic of discovery, jumping back and forth in time over a period of twenty years. Consisting of a collage of conversations, letters, long passages of self-introspection, and confessions, it offers a plural perspective on a group of resisters who had been close childhood friends, despite important class and gender differences. We gradually meet Jeanne-Claude and her brother Philippe, belonging to an impoverished aristocratic family with Pétainist sympathies. Gérard, Alain, and Sophie are the children of the rich businessman Gilbert Bonhomme. Alain, Gilbert's favorite son and Jeanne Claude's teenage love interest, is killed alongside Philippe in action in 1942. Gilbert joins the resistance in London, while Jeanne-Claude and Sophie work for a local cell. Jeanne-Claude eventually recruits Gérard who, as an adult, retained much of his childhood awkwardness, which had made him the resentful object of his friends' jokes and his father's disdain.

A novel of introspection, the structure reflects the plurivocality of memory and its vulnerability to self-serving mystifications, individual and collective. The reader is confronted with a medley of fragmented stories, each with their own narrator, inviting them to inhabit the world of several key characters brought together on the evening of February 20, 1944, when the resistance cell to which they all belonged was decimated by the Gestapo. Friang thus formally challenges the reader to embark on a detective quest and make sense of this fictional archive of multiple, competing accounts, in a way that vindicates this project's theoretical proposals: the resisters' habitus and the complex web of relationalities that anchor them socially determine how they experience this fateful night and its aftermath, but also how they remember it. The author draws her characters with a fine brush, offering us rich psychological portraits; however, a structural filter is permanently superimposed on these portraits, particularly in relation to the role that gender, class, and religion played in agents' positioning—both resistant and complicit—during both the war and the race for honors that followed.

What happened that evening? We are initially led to believe that Gérard betrayed the resisters under horrific torture. As a result, Jeanne-Claude and Sophie were sent to Buchenwald, where Sophie eventually died. Various other cell members were killed or committed suicide. Before being sent to a concentration camp himself, a disconsolate Gérard confessed his betrayal to Jeanne-Claude, whom he met by chance in one of Gestapo's cells.

Gérard's character emerges from his own reflections and his friends' memories in flashback. Living in the shadow of his brother's heroic life and death, his shame at having caved in and shown himself to be a lesser man is deep. Once his much-envied brother dies, however, Gérard decides to marry Jeanne-Claude, who survived Buchenwald and returned to France, welcomed as a certified resister with full public honors. Marrying her was, to his mind, his best revenge on Alain, a compensatory move to restore his manly self-esteem. Gérard tells himself that it is "better to be a traitor and alive rather than a dead hero" (1978, 60) and sees the marriage as best suited for his gaining control over the woman who knew his most shameful secret. Moreover, her aristocratic title brought his bourgeois family some much-desired social prestige.

Surprisingly enough, she accepts his proposal, mediated by Gilbert, also keen to add her resistant credentials to his family. Jeanne-Claude's ambivalent motivations are presented in the first person, in conversations and letters sent to another woman survivor, Marie-Laure—the frank exchanges between the two friends inserting important, usually marginalized voices in discussions about the memory of the war: those of women resisters. Jeanne-Claude is highly reflective and motivated by a mixture of personal and overtly political reasons, which reflect her complex positionality as a woman for whom the war created a first opportunity to escape her gender and oppressive family. Peace, which brought men back in control of the public sphere, brutally pushed her again into a secondary role in the private sphere, a reality she never ceases to lament: she experiences the reaffirmation of patriarchal power as an affront and a closing down of her horizon of hope.

Her decision to marry her traitor is informed by her Catholic sense of guilt, a gendered idea of herself, and a strong political commitment to the Gaullist resistance and its reputation within postwar political struggles. Initially, Jeanne-Claude is compassionate toward Gérard and doubts whether she herself could have kept silent under torture. As his recruiter, she feels responsible for him and his betrayal. In marrying him, she wants to "compensate" his family for the pain she thinks she caused them—Sophie's death, Gérard's torture and deportation—through her political work. A devout Catholic, Jeanne-Claude also feels a deep compassion for the burden of guilt Gérard carries, that of having betrayed his friends. The union is meant to prove her forgiveness to him, and she decides to dedicate herself as a wife to helping him reconcile with his own weakness.

However, Friang also reveals Jeanne-Claude's less virtuous reasons, enabling us to imperfectly inhabit her difficult social position. Because of her gender and class, she has no professional skills, so she chooses marriage as a financial safety net—something she experiences as a painful compromise imposed on women by gender structures. In a way, to her mind, keeping Gérard's secret gave her some power over him, something that balanced the field of their marriage, by default skewed toward the man. This also allowed her to confront her own conservative parents, who looked down on the bourgeoisie while envying their money. Moreover, while she does not love him, upon being reinserted in an indifferent French society, she feels more comfortable with her own traitor—himself a former camp inmate—than with anyone else.

Politically, Jeanne-Claude is deeply invested in cultivating the glorious image of the Gaullist resistance and refuses to give any satisfaction to collaborationists and Communists, who would have gloated at learning about their betrayals. She is also loath to give any form of excuse to the millions of *attentistes*. Her silence over her husband's treason is encouraged by local and national resistance leaders, concerned about potential reputational damages and bent on consolidating their political capital. Things get complicated by Gilbert's becoming an MP, whose influence is key to resistance's institutionalizing itself as a redoubtable political force after the war, against the Communists' competing claims. Very fond of Gilbert since childhood, Jeanne-Claude does not want to endanger all the benefits he conferred on former Gaullist resisters by virtue of his parliamentary seat.

Gérard capitalizes on her silence and, insinuating horrific suffering while in the camp, works assiduously to obtain public recognition for his "heroism," medals, and institutional positions of power. Jeanne-Claude becomes gradually disenchanted with her husband's relentless efforts to accumulate public honors. Her disappointment and alienation are compounded by the slow understanding of the political processes via which de Gaulle sacralized forty million French people as resisters simply because "we cannot shoot all of them" (1978, 93). She wearily notes how "each small groups of ambiguous friends who had heroically listened to the BBC and marked on a map the advance of the allied armies called itself a 'network.' And to get some relief and save appearances, resister cards were distributed to everyone who bothered to ask" (1978, 196).

However, she also casts a ruthless, sarcastic eye on resisters' dishonest, self-righteous moralism after the war, her own included: "We perceived ourselves to be an elite. From the heights of our small, mutual admiration committee, we contemplated the mass of the weak, slaves to cowardice, to their own wallets and to ignorant tranquility. We were medieval knights who had sacrificed themselves to protect the mass of terrorized uglies. How delightful." (1978, 103).

Her husband's hunger for social prestige and the resistance chiefs' readiness to provide the relevant medals eventually push Jeanne-Claude into a deep depression and alcoholism. Gérard prudently shares his spoils with other "heroes" who fabricate flattering biographies, thereby buying their silence: he surrounds himself with people in his debt, who would be negatively affected by his potential downfall. He cynically accumulates influence and esteem, sponsored by an organization too invested in its own mythology to risk a scandal. As Gérard bluntly observes, "Ah, resistance, how many crimes were forgotten in your name" (1978, 46).

The reader gradually realizes Gérard had never been tortured and that the names of the resisters were found on a paper he carelessly carried on him when he was arrested. Introspectively, he confesses to himself that betraying his friends gave him a certain sense of satisfaction, avenging his resentment for having always been thought to be a failed man. His feeling of grievance is real: Jeanne-Claude confesses she only ever felt repugnance or tender pity toward him. Thus, betrayal made him feel in control for the first time in his life—a moment when his complexes of inferiority were suspended. He feels proud of having escaped torture and looks down on the deported, the tortured, and the killed. Simultaneously, he cannot help but see his wife's strength and integrity as a perpetual reminder of his own insufficiencies. He therefore encourages her drinking and consumption of antidepressants, hoping for her early demise.

Jeanne-Claude reaches the edge of despair after she decides to divorce him. Her Catholic parents oppose her plans, while former resisters put immense pressure on her to stay silent and married. She is perpetually reminded of her gender and of her duty "to accept reality," especially when it comes to an eminently masculine domain, war, and the hierarchies of honor it produces. She is particularly aggrieved by how her own complicitous silence enabled Gérard's lies but also, much worse, the bigger lies that got institutionalized around them. Alone and fearing for her children's well-being, she keeps the secret till she dies by an overdose that Gérard facilitates—a death foretold by the novel's epigraph, which Friang borrows from Balzac: "We don't hate ourselves for compromised interests, for an injury, not even for a slap in the face; everything is repairable. But being found a coward? . . . the conflict that emerges between the criminal and the witness to the crime only ends with the death of one or the other." Once free of all witnesses to his shame, Gérard is finally reassured, realizing that "at the highest levels of the Republic, everyone is interested in silence" (1978, 338).

Via its formal multiperspectivism, the book helps us enter the complex world of gendered and classed resistance, its betrayals and mystifications. Friang's epistolary style seduces readers into occupying her characters' positions, revealing their ever-changing, complex, and contradictory desires, hopes, fears, and intentions, which are recorded painstakingly, often in confessional mode, with a view to troubling assumptions about resistance, its gender, its drivers, and especially its purity. As a young woman stifled by Catholic conservatism, Jeanne-Claude is mainly motivated by a desire to act as a subject. She remains, however, at least partially trapped in a Christian outlook, which shapes her key decisions: she derives great satisfaction from protecting Gérard, a decision that, however, also confirms her moral superiority over him. While slowly growing aware of the pernicious effects of her silence in conjunction with broader, institutionalized silences, she remains loyal, out of hopelessness but also because she wants to preserve Gaullist resisters' political gains against the Communists, their redoubtable competitors in the race for national honor. However, throughout, her position is shaped by her gender and the supporting role the societal doxa assigns to her.

By the end of the book, Gérard's character becomes implausible as he veers toward radical cynicism. Nonetheless, the story of his lifelong insecurities, his physical ineptitude, his difficult relationships with his father and his friends, and his ongoing awkwardness and deep envy of his brother—all account for the sense of power he experienced in the act of betrayal, as well as for his feverishly planned overcompensatory projects after the war. Just like Antoine and Lucien, he is embedded in a patriarchal order that finds him wanting. Acquiring public honor and dominating the worthier resister his wife is—accumulating moral and political capital—become vehicles for asserting his virility.

Friang thus caringly refuses the complicitous, institutionalized silences that kept a certain vision of history in place—a vision that enabled many to fabricate profitable biographies and dodge a meaningful conversation about historical responsibility. Resisters' self-righteous moralism after the war is not spared, and neither are their dubious political maneuvers, their arrogant self-perception, and their exclusions and univocal trumpeting of a self-serving vision of the past. The public projection of a pure, martyrial image and the sustained machinations necessary to keep that image in place for political gain are vividly illuminated: the book effectively sabotages any naive sentimentality about national inventories of valor and exposes the irresistible lure of the honor trap.

"SENTIMENTAL" COLLABORATORS: BETRAYING THE FATHERLAND

"Ter le milicien": Rewriting the Script of Infamy

Based on her own war experience, Marguerite Duras's explicitly autobiographical *La douleur*[25] was published in 1982 and includes several stories, among which is "Ter le milicien," which I will discuss in detail below. A towering figure of twentieth-century French culture, Duras's range is exceptional: novelist, playwright, screenwriter, essayist, and experimental filmmaker, she left an indelible mark on public debates about the war, colonialism, writing, gender, sexuality, and alienation. In *La douleur*, Duras's memories are filtered through her imagination to construct a multifaceted portrait of herself during the occupation, presented not only as anxiously waiting for her deported husband but also as a resister capable of cruel and unnecessary violence. The stories take the readers on a realistic tour of Paris during the occupation and the liberation, recording in minute detail the complex atmosphere of fear, hope and violence. While Modiano's tone is elegiac, Duras's is abrupt and involved, confessional yet pressing, reflectively and lucidly recording in the present tense emotional reactions, tics, and colloquial dialogues, as well as postures, clothing details, and gestures. Against an urban background meticulously reconstructed via precise geographical references, her urgent writing ushers the reader into a time of suspense, when the typical protagonists of official history disappoint, confuse, or outrage by their departures from the required script.

The short story "Ter le milicien"[26] centers on a woman resister—Thérèse—and her desire for a milicien arrested during the liberation days. "Horizontal" or "sentimental" collaboration was a legal offence established after the war, and it typically featured a French woman and a German soldier. Duras sabotages this scenario by casting as key characters a Communist woman who is a resister—thus dislodging masculinist visions of salvific heroism—and a French *milicien,* that is, a young man enlisted in one of the most reviled institutions of French complicity, *la milice.* Gendering the resister as a woman and the collaborator as a French man sabotages the compensatory hypermasculinism of the resistance projected by both Communists and Gaullists, during and after the war. Thus, Duras provocatively takes the occupier out of the moral calculus: the story is firmly rooted in French moral soil. Like Friang, she recuperates women's historical agency, while simultaneously avoiding the honor trap: the naturalistic, brutal depiction of Thérèse and her actions in no way reproduces the propagandistic, heroizing, and martyrizing tropes of the dominant hagiographic literature. On the contrary, it pitilessly displays the resister's unquenched thirst for revenge, her relentless violence, and her blasphemous sexual desires: no convincing lines of moral demarcation can be found in the book.

The protagonist's portrait is drawn across several stories. In the same volume, in "Albert des Capitales,"[27] also set during the purges and during the long period of waiting for her deported husband, Thérèse is featured in the role of the resister-torturer, who unleashes her ferocious hatred against a French man suspected of having been an informer for the German police. Duras casts a cold, analytic eye on her own rage and vindictive excesses via a third-person narrative that does not omit any of the gruesome details. Her senseless, indomitable, and extreme violence is clinically recorded: the smell of sweat and blood, the texture of bruised flesh, the sound of despairing cries. This violence provides Thérèse with psychic relief, yet, in all its enormity, it alienates her fellow resisters, whom she disgusts, and points to the outrage and uselessness of having secured a confession through torture at the end of the war. In not portraying Thérèse in glowing colors, in tackling her pointless excess head on, Duras sheds light on the unassimilable aspects of resistance—its gratuitous violence—while avoiding the kind of revisionism that replaces one form of reductive trumpeting with another.[28]

In "Ter, le milicien" Thérèse takes over the dominant sexual gaze, a gaze that travels across tabooed ideological—but not national—boundaries. The object of her desire is a milicien —who strongly recalls Lucien Lacombe. Duras introduces his hypersexualized portrait as drawn through Thérèse's eyes. In the short explanatory text that sets up this story and "Albert des Capitales," Duras writes bluntly that "Thérèse is me. She who tortures the informer is me. Also, the woman who wants to make love to Ter the militiaman is me" (2011, 116). This confessional text—meant to enhance the authenticity of the story—is doubly sacrilegious since, at that moment in the novel's timeline, her husband was in a concentration camp. While living through *la douleur* —that is, the extraordinary pain of missing her husband and not knowing whether she would ever see him again (recorded in the first part of the book)—she is still capable of sexual desire, and toward, of all people, a traitor of the nation, a militiaman. She does not act on her irreverent desire, yet that is beside the point. Her yearning across the trenches sits in tension with the alignment between feminine sexual virtue and patriotism that, as historians and cultural theorists have shown, both the Gaullist and the Communist narratives prescribed. The distance between Vercors's virtuous, chaste, and self-controlled young woman—a metaphor for an idealized vision of France—who stoically resists the charms of the invader in *Le silence de la mer*, and Duras's Thérèse could not be any greater.

The book's dissidence cannot, however, be reduced to the choice and features of its main characters. Duras also invites us into the space where adversaries encounter each other and into contemplating the possibility of human compassion across ideological divides. The resisters who arrest Ter are torn between a deep, seething hatred and a hunger for revenge, on the one hand, and pity for the immature and attractive young man that sits before them, on the other. The Communists are touched by Ter's naivety, thoughtlessness, and evident fear of dying in a way that casts doubt on the implacable, moral sanctimony of the liberation purges. As we shall see, to a certain degree, Duras joins Malle and Laurent: in invoking the horror of capital punishment, they seek to insert a moment of hesitation in the automatism of moralistic mnemonic impulses.

The story follows Thérèse and D., two Communist resisters, driving Ter through Paris in the immediate wake of the liberation. They move from one building to another, in an effort to distribute the men and women they arrested to different locations in the city. An unexpected event influences the relationship between the three for the rest of the story: upon arriving at their first stop, they realize somebody had just been executed by a group of Spanish Republicans—the three see the blood and the dead body. The enormity of witnessing death and Ter's horrified reaction to it—recorded in great detail by Thérèse—brings them close together: "Ter is leaning against the fireplace. He is real, Ter. Ter the militiaman. Ter is pale . . . he has become green, his lips are chalky and he is grey under his eyes" (2011, 149).

Expecting to be executed—something he fully accepts, without looking for excuses—Ter wants to write a note to his family and asks D. for permission. D. reassures him: they won't execute him. Hinting that this was the group's first execution and that the resisters were themselves nervous, Thérèse records a form of sympathy developing in the Communists, who perceive his wild fear, as they simultaneously become aware of their exclusive power to dissipate it. For different reasons, both D. and Thérèse are hypnotized by Ter, they cannot help staring at him while he is smoking with trembling hands. His puerile reasons for joining the milice—Thérèse compares him to a plant and a child—makes D. grow well-disposed toward him. His simplemindedness and sincerity during the interrogation make D. feel almost paternal toward Ter. Ter responds to the changes in D.'s attitude, he wants to be liked by D., he trusts D., even when he calls him an abject human being who deserves to die.

As for Thérèse, he is gallant toward her. His physical portrait is drawn through Thérèse's objectifying gaze: "Ter is 23. He is a handsome man. He doesn't have a jacket and one can see the muscles on his arms, long, young. He has a thin waist, fastened with a leather belt" (2011, 152). She notices his beard, clothes, and shoes and remembers that he had looked at her insistently a few days back. She observes that he has "the mouth of a roisterer and kisser" (2011, 155) and suspects he must miss women. While attracted to him, Thérèse nonetheless remembers: "But Ter has a dirty past. There's no avoiding it. An enormous past has grown onto Ter's young life, because of which he will surely die" (2011, 152).

Despite this certainty, the two Communists continue to talk to him, baffled by his ignorance and recklessness: "He has no thoughts in his head, only appetites, he has a body made for pleasure, for excess, for fighting, and for women" (2011, 152). He entered the milice because he wanted a gun, which he considered "chic." At the end of the war, he insinuated himself into an FFI group but was quickly caught. Asked why he did it, he responded that he wanted to fight: not because he hated the Germans, simply for the sake of fighting. For the sake of getting a car and wearing a gun, he became complicit. Driving around with Thérèse and D., he is happy to witness the liberation festivities, without understanding that the public celebration marks the end of his world—and probably of his own life. Once back at the resistance headquarters, he mindlessly plays cards and eats as if he had no reason to worry. The only thing he seems to understand is that he would have pushed things too far if he had actually worn the FFI armband to mask his crimes—even for him, this would have implied crossing an ethical line. The story ends without revealing Ter's fate. Thérèse suspects that, if he survived, he must have ended on that side of society where "money is easy, ideas short and the mystique of the leader replaces ideology and justifies murder" (2011, 160).

The story's style ushers readers into a day of great uncertainty, fear, and violence alongside a heterogenous group of resisters. While her work has been associated with the Nouveau Roman, most commentators agree that it is less self-consciously driven by form. Short and sharp sentences suggest the heightened levels of political and psychological tension characteristic of the liberation. The characterization of Ter is built via a series of such blunt sentences with his name always as the subject—an allusion to his being the focus of the resister's perceptual and sexual attention. This style also captures the emotional rush of thoughts through Thérèse's and D.'s heads—two resisters who, despite their apparent calm, are thrown off by the execution witnessed at the beginning of the story.

The urgent writing—minimal and close to spoken language (Bordeleau 1985)—rhythmically suggests the feverish search for collaborators and resisters' hurried conversations, oscillating between righteous indignation, fear, and mundane concerns, such as procuring food and cigarettes. The reader is thus immersed in an atmosphere of amplified anticipation, typical of the power vacuum characterizing the liberation.

Ter's story opens up several uncomfortable conversations. First, his immaturity and thoughtlessness were already problematized by Malle: Ter and Lucien share a desire for money, power, and women as both men are part of patriarchal, competitive masculinity. Like Lucien, Ter is not clearly politically engaged. Like Modiano's Swing Troubadour, however, he has an active sense of justice: he deferentially accepts D's moral judgment of his crimes and his probable execution. Second, Duras troubles hegemonic accounts of the resistance on several levels. She highlights resisters' ambivalence toward capital punishment: Ter's terror at the prospect of being executed elicits the Communists' compassion; they cannot see him only with hate, especially since they appear to be themselves novices in the practice of killing their opponents. Moreover, in centering a woman resister's experience, the book adds yet another layer of complexity: Duras genders the Communist resistance—like Friang gendered the Gaullist. Moreover, via Thérèse's merciless and senseless torturing of a suspected informer, Duras triggers friction between her depiction of resisters' violent abuses and the regulative ideal of noble heroism. Last but not least, in fully and candidly confessing her sexual attraction to Ter, Thérèse/Duras opens up one of the toughest taboos in French political memory and highlights the hypocrisy of the wild purges of women. The author thus destabilizes the moralistic nationalism and sexist certainties of the liberation, casting a critical light on the self-serving scapegoating of women and the patriarchal doxa that reaffirmed itself after the war.

Unsilencing la tondue: Hiroshima, mon amour

Alain Resnais's career as a director spanned over six decades. His first feature film, *Hiroshima, mon amour* (1959), based on a script by Marguerite Duras, is included here for its highlighting the construction and enforcement of an abusive, sexist, and hypermoralistic conception of complicity in the context of a conservative, nationalist, and patriarchal order. Resnais and Duras's refusal is complex. First, it subverts the annals of the war by foregrounding a *tondue*, a woman whose voice had been conveniently silenced in the fury of public "patriotic" shaming that marked the liberation. Formally alternating between an "objective," institutional view of the past and a personal, subjective voice of experience, it reveals the vulnerability of the former to the latter. Second, it convincingly thematizes the imperfection of the prosthetic experience enabled by all attempts to remember the past—be they official or unofficial, conservative or subversive—in a way that buttresses the arguments I advanced in chapter 2.

The film was well received by critics and was nominated for several awards—although its unconventional dealing with the highly sensitive topic of the nuclear bomb disadvantaged it in the festival circuit (Thomson 2014). It centers on the short affair between a French actress who finds herself shooting a film "about peace" in Hiroshima in 1957 and a Japanese architect. Both characters remain unnamed throughout the film. Both are happily married. They live the affair with incandescent passion and find it difficult to separate. Little happens in the film, and it is the dialogues between the two that, laden with metaphorical content, take center stage. The lovers' conversation uncovers, first, the structural underpinnings and arbitrariness of instituting and punishing a specific form of complicity, "horizontal" or "sentimental" collaboration. Slowly revealing that the actress is a former *tondue*, who had had a romantic relationship with a German soldier in Névers and who had been bitterly punished for it, the film questions the criminalization of women's desire and the abuses of the liberation.[29] The story of her suffering, marginalization, and humiliation is told in the first person via flashbacks that bear a high emotional, perceptual, and sensorial charge, in a way that tests ankylosed ideas about the gender of patriotism.

Second, the scenes recording the lovers' differentiated memories of the atomic bomb underscore the artificiality and inescapable incompleteness of all political memory—as well as the risk of forgetting. Their recollections are narrated against the background of documentary footage taken in the immediate aftermath of the bomb, but also photography and images from the history museum—a designated space of authorized national memory—and footage from the film the actress stars in. The scenes on the film set, showing the crew doing makeup and managing the crowd of extras, as well as the images shot inside the museum, powerfully serve as Resnais's shorthand for official memory. The same images of suffering and mutilation appear in different media and settings, highlighting the mediatedness of political memory-making, as well as the fact that, though film-watching or museum-visiting, we can only get what I called a prosthetic experience of the event, which falls short of full mastery. As ethical witness, the actress is committed to learning everything about the event: she recalls seeing reports of it on the news in France and visits the museum four times during her stay. She insists she "saw everything in Hiroshima," only to be contradicted, again and again, in a calm voice, by her lover: "You saw nothing in Hiroshima." The juxtaposition of images—documentary and reconstructive—with the lovers' dialogue in voice-over, leads the spectators to get "caught in the epistemological crisis, confronted repeatedly with the limits of vision and the impossibility of 'knowledge'" (Craig 2005). In this way, the film reflects on the limits of official and nonofficial efforts to narrativize the past, and especially on its own capacity to confront deeply held certainties. It therefore displays one of the key virtues of aesthetic mnemonic care: in performing a reflexive practice of self-vigilance and humility, it reminds us of the bounds of what can be achieved via the prosthetic and seductive power of artistic engagements.

In addition to the imperfection of memory, the always present possibility of forgetting—individually and collectively—is hinted at in the first part of the film. Shifting between the actress's worries about forgetting her lover and the possibility of forgetting the bomb, Resnais makes her honestly reflect on how illusory it is to believe that one can ever keep an "inconsolable memory." She believes that remaining unconsoled is central to respecting the "obvious necessity of memory." And yet forgetting is always a real risk but also, I suggest, a blessing: Resnais suggests this ambiguity by superimposing the actresses' warnings about the reproduction of violence with images of reconstructed Hiroshima and catastrophe tourism. Therefore, the subject in the actress's prophetic statement, "It will begin all over again"—can be read to refer both to recurring violence and the life that can restart in the shadow of forgetting.[30]

The Japanese lover serves as a stand-in for the German lover she had during the occupation and a prop in the actress's efforts to recover the traumatic story of their forbidden love, his death, and her punishment—shown in flashbacks and narrated in voice-overs—for the first time in fourteen years. According to the psychologizing reading that the film invites, the architect represents a cathartic or therapeutical opportunity for her repressed memories of another lover to be worked through and mourned (Buys 2009; Cazenave 2011; Grégoire 2018). The actress remembers being a young woman, deeply in love for the first time, hiding her affair from the vigilant eyes of the inhabitants of Névers, the city where she lived, on the river Loire. Her father, a pharmacist, is disgraced at the liberation by his daughter's relationship with the German soldier, who is killed. Her hair is shorn by young people "who thought it was a duty" to punish her. Duras speaks through the architect: "Are you ashamed for them, my love?"—the preposition "for" makes all the difference in terms of the judgment the spectator is invited to make: Duras suspends the frame for remembering "horizontal collaboration" through the mere substitution of one preposition for another.

Her parents lock her in the house and, when she begins to scream with grief, they put her in a cold, damp cellar, hidden away, while life goes on above her—she sees passersby through her cellar's window and hears the Marseillaise playing in the street, a symbol of rediscovered patriotism. *La tondue* is thus physically erased from reality, her voice inaudible. While the mother seems to show some affection for her daughter, her actions are aligned with the patriarchal order: it is the mother who, when the hair has grown back and the girl returns to being "reasonable"—obedient to the norms that regulated her gender—sends her into the night, riding her bicycle toward Paris, in an attempt to expunge the shame she brought upon both family and country.

As she traverses these experiences, the actress suffers immensely. Images of her father's strict face appear in flashback, a symbol of the nationalist patriarchal order that proscribed her desire. Alongside the paternal strict gaze, the close shots of the cellar's walls suggest the constraints the woman faces: Resnais locks the viewer in the cellar, whose walls are damp, cold, and rough. However, they are made of saltpeter: the actress scratches them with bloodied hands and ingests the salty dust—gestures of powerless resistance that nonetheless erode the boundaries imposed on her. A growing lucidity of judgment against these boundaries—both material and symbolic—emerges out of this experience of suffering. Fourteen years later, telling the story to another man she desires against the rules of her society, she articulates the hate she nurtured toward Névers: "Night after night, month after month, I set you on fire, as my body was ablaze with his memory."

The actress assumes firmly and honestly her sexuality: "I like boys," just as the architect "loves women," thus establishing an equivalent legitimacy of desire for both lovers. The actress sarcastically and unabashedly counterpoises her desires to the social norms that make of her a "shameful" girl, a "silly" girl, a *tondue*. The trauma is formative for who she is—and the Japanese lover understands this very clearly, "This is where I lost you, this is where you became you." However, the trauma and the suffering that followed coincided with her strongest experience of clarity: "In my dreams, morality and immorality mixed together to the point where they were indiscernible," she tells the architect. Earlier, she states, "I have doubtful morals, you know." When asked what that meant, she says she is doubtful of the morals of other people—another play on words that exemplifies the acuity of her vision and judgment after the *tonte*. This is why the film is important not merely for broaching the topic of the shearing ritual (Cazenave 2011) but also because it does so critically, revealing its abuses and the artificiality of the form of "complicity" it was supposed to punish, often by former bystanders and last-minute resisters.

For both lovers, the end of the war marked the deepest moment of despair: while everyone was celebrating, they were mourning. The experience of the bomb and the liberation's purges mark personal catastrophe for both protagonists. Inviting us to travel into their anguished world and see the effects of victory on scapegoats and losers, the film disrupts western triumphalist narratives of history: the atomic bomb and the public humiliation of French women tackled in the film unsettles the socialized dichotomic mnemonic habits and the clear distinctions they presuppose between victims and perpetrators, heroes and traitors.

To reinsert both *la tondue* and the vanquished back into history, the film prioritizes the experience of the senses—pleasure and pain—via the use of both long and close shots, different textures, and variations in lighting. Images of the lovers' entwined bodies are juxtaposed to images of bodies carbonized or mutilated by the bomb, of hair lost to radiation or shearing, horrifically scarred skin and severed limbs—as captured in documentary footage or in the museum's exhibits, but also in their reconstruction by makeup artists for the film the actress is shooting in Hiroshima. All evoke a complex tactile experience and invite a powerful sensorial response in the viewer. Long shots of scorched earth; piles of bricks, dead cows, and tuna fish; and ruined urban landscapes are coupled with the calm voice of the actress in a way that encourages ideational but especially emotional and sensorial friction between sanitized, Manichaeistic memory and the suffering this wounded materiality conjures. As Royer argues, "Our eyes become less a means to understand the meaning of the image and more like fingers feeling the grain of the skin, its temperature and humidity" (2019, 59). The same can be said of the scenes depicting the actress locked in her parents' cellar: its small window that allows little light to pierce its darkness and the close shots of the actress's bleeding hands scoring the rough walls and of her shorn skull help the viewer imaginatively inhabit a hostile world where the alignment between women's sexuality and patriotism is required and transgressions are fiercely punished.

Numerous contemporary critics condemned the actress's loose morals, while not subjecting the Japanese man's character to the same rigors, in a way that reflected the cultural and the legal norms about adultery in France at the time and vindicated the film's caring refusal of the masculinist narrative of the liberation. Many missed the critical force of its sophisticated reflection on what knowing and acting against one's community's norms involved and how complicities could be constituted out of historically resilient structures—patriarchy and nationalism—to serve the exculpatory needs of the present. The psychologizing reading, however, missed something even more valuable: the film's tackling the difficult matter of what one can know, understand, and feel about an experience one has not lived through—but to which one has access prosthetically. Its injection of a healthy dose of uncertainty invites circumspection and humility in thinking about how one can relate to the past, whoever its narrator might be and whatever authority they may enjoy.

CONCLUSIONS

In the first press release for the popular TV series *Un village Français*, the director, Frédéric Krivine, stated that "the majority of French people have certainly been more attentist and accommodating than was said in '45–'70, and much less pétainist and passive than was said after Ophüls and Paxton" (Bragança 2015b). This quote insightfully captures the political nature of French official memory and its malleability. It also foregrounds the difficulty of making clear-cut judgments and the precise parsing out of historical responsibility. However, what it leaves unanswered is the question about the connection between mnemonic distortions, on the one hand, and configurations of power and privilege in the present, on the other—a difficult question that some of the caring refuseniks included in this chapter tackled head on.

Thus, an important first specificity of works covered in relation to the French case is the way in which artists traced the link between mnemonic hierarchies of valor—especially in their gendered dimension—and the reproduction of hierarchical relations of citizenship in the wake of systemic violence. Friang, Duras, and Resnais perhaps most vividly reveal how gender informed the experience of the war and of the resistance but also how it structured the social construction of both treason and heroism within the space of public memory, with crucial consequences for women's sociopolitical status. Moreover, Duras and Malle effectively decoupled patriotism from masculinity and treason from femininity via characters that rewrote the standard scripts of both valor and abjection. A second and related specificity lies in artists' shedding light on resistance's own investment in the entrenchment of its power—not merely at the symbolic level but at the concrete, institutional level: far from being lofty, disinterested fighters, resisters belonged to different, conflicting ideological groups, with vested interests in using their moral capital politically. Their hold on political power required the institutionalization of certain practices of silencing, which would otherwise have endangered their hegemonic project. Lastly, some of the works in this chapter address directly the prosthetic—incomplete, fragmentary, and partial—nature of all attempts at narrating the past. Via different formal choices, Modiano, Friang, and Resnais take a position of exteriority on the very medium of their craft, thereby powerfully exemplifying one of the key principles of aesthetic mnemonic care: that of a hypervigilant practice of self-reflection.

French people's heterogeneous experience of the war and their multiply determined complicities and resistances, as well as the ways in which they have been remembered—celebrated or denounced—make the object of an extremely rich artistic production that, up to the present, does not seem to have exhausted its energies. Driven by specific questions, the selection included here cannot do it justice. Novels such as Anna Langfus's *Les bagages de sable*, Jean-François Deniau's *Un héros très discret* (and the film based on it by Jacques Audiard), Irène Némirovsky's *Suite Française*, Patrick Modiano's *La Place de l'Étoile,* Didier Daeninckx's *Itinéraire d'un salaud ordinaire,* or Pierre Assouline's *La cliente* would have been good alternative choices for achieving my critical and interpretive objectives. The same could be said about films such as *Indigènes* by Rachid Bouchareb, *Les guichets du Louvre* by Michel Mitrani, *Une affaire des femmes* by Claude Chabrol, or *Monsieur Klein* by Joseph Losey. All research choices yield some goods, but they also involve some costs—in this case, the possibility of pursuing different aspects of the historical experiences of both complicity and resistance and the ways in which they have been (mis) remembered politically. However, this chapter will have offered sufficient evidence of caring refuseniks' capacity to effectively interpellate a community's mnemonic imagination, inviting them to collectively assume responsibility for *what, whom,* and *how* they remember so that they can re-envisage *who* they can be, as heirs and survivors.

4   Romania's Horizons of Hope and Despair

THE RHINOCEROS: *LA LONGUE DURÉE*

Nineteen-eighty-nine marked the end of Nicolae Ceaușescu's dictatorship and faced Romanians with a complex past (Ciobanu 2015a): Romania's participation in the Shoah and the two stages of the Communist regime, which lasted from 1945 to 1989 and roughly corresponded to its two main leaders—Gheorghe Gheorghiu-Dej, until 1965, and Ceaușescu himself, from 1965 to 1989. The dictatorship was marked by several watershed years—1956, 1965, 1968, 1977, and 1987—that either expanded or constricted Romanians' horizons of hope, in ways that influenced how they positioned themselves on the spectrum of involvement. As in the French case, these positions emerged along intersecting axes of identity that include ideology, ethnicity, religion, class, profession, gender, and geographical location.

Ideologically, the nationalist version of communism that gripped Romania cannot be understood without a brief excursus in the interwar period.[1] The 1930s saw the rise of extreme-right political organizations that governed for a brief period in the 1940s, alongside a military dictator, Marshal Ion Antonescu, who eventually assumed power as sole Fascist leader. During their short administration, the extreme Right initiated a killing campaign against Jewish Romanians. Anti-Semitic legislation and pogroms characterized the violent ecology of the early 1940s, and so did the transformation of key intellectuals into rhinoceros: tapping into a long doxastic tradition of anti-Semitism, top luminaries contributed to the normalization of widespread violence.

Romania eventually joined the war on Germany's side in 1941, participating in the invasion of the USSR, avowedly in the hope of recuperating several territories lost in 1940 (Bessarabia, North Bukovina, and Herța). As Romanian troops entered these provinces, they engaged in mass killings, deportations, and internments, causing hundreds of thousands of deaths. It was only when the tide turned against Germany, in August 1944, that King Michael organized a coup against Antonescu and pulled out of the alliance with Germany, switching sides. The Red Army entered Romania a few days later. As we shall see, the ultranationalist colonization of the political space by the extreme Right reverberated in the decades that followed.

During the first stage of Romanian communism—the "unleashed Stalinism" of the 1947–64—the Communist Party consolidated its grip over the country, with the support of the USSR. The key social, political and economic transformations of this period were the turn to internationalism, the nationalization of private property, the forced collectivization of agriculture, the purging of institutions, the ideological targeting of several socio-professional categories, the elimination of political rivals, and the infiltration of the state by the party and its secret police (the Securitate).

A hypernationalism that uncannily evoked the rhinoceros of the 1930s and the 1940s and an increasing distance from the Kremlin are the staples of the second period, inaugurated in 1965. During the 1968 Prague Spring, Ceaușescu denounced the Soviet invasion, thus legitimizing his rule, currying the favor of western powers and the support of Romanian citizens, who interpreted his position-taking as a crucial moment of defiance against the USSR. A period of political relaxation in the 1960s was followed by the intensification of the personality cult, aggressive urbanization and industrialization, and oppressive pronatalist policies, as well as an economic crisis in the 1980s, which led to widespread impoverishment and despair. While temporally variable in intensity, the terror exercised by the Securitate, punitively or prophylactically, greatly affected the possibility of solidary resistance throughout.

Besides political prisoners, thousands of people of "unhealthy social origins" were sent to labor camps, while the propagandistic machine and its army of censors attacked intellectual plurality to consolidate the national-Communist project (Corobca 2016a). The number of people imprisoned, interned in labor camps, or deported on political grounds is estimated at 640,762 (Oprea 2008, 13), although, as historians rightly admit, a great deal of uncertainty remains (Boia 2016, 70). By 1989, an estimated 1,162,418 individuals were under surveillance by the Securitate (Stan 2013, 69). The party-state infiltrated workplaces, churches, homes, textbooks, minds, bodies, and intimate relations (Kligman 1998; Copilaș 2015; Corobca 2016a; Marcu 2016; Mareș and Vasilescu 2015; L. Vasile, Vasilescu, and Urs 2016). Via the hijacking of law, violence, fear, and suspicion but also through rewards, co-optation, and increased social mobility for disadvantaged social groups, the regime remained stable for more than forty years.

As in the French case, certain positions on the spectrum of involvement need highlighting. To reiterate, I do not purport to offer an exhaustive account here, only to zoom in on some of the most emblematic institutions and practices, to give a sense of the complexity of *the in-between* and its evolution over time in relation to a sophisticated institutional and legislative ecology of violence: the party-state system, its colonizing the public space of meaning, and its control over the collective horizon of hope. This analysis is meant to challenge a highly moralistic, apolitical, and sociologically naive denunciation of Communist leaders that individualized responsibility and demonized those who compromised and colluded, obscuring the systemic nature of violence and extensive participation in it. As we shall see, this narrative has its strong entrepreneurs: it underpins the virulent anti-communism that dominates the "official story" as formulated in the report of the Presidential Commission for the Analysis of the Communist Dictatorship published in 2006 and the discourse of many key NGOs and memory entrepreneurs focusing on commemorating the victims of communism and the canonization of saintly martyrs.

The party's elites were strongly ideologically motivated. In the initial stages, many in the top ranks were Soviet agents who helped build Romanian institutions on the USSR model—including the secret police.

Others enjoyed the symbolic capital of having been imprisoned after the banning of the Communist Party in 1924. The top leadership aimed to dismantle the old constitutional order and found another that would generate a new type of citizen. To do so, no effort was spared, no means excluded, not even the brutal purging of the leadership itself.

The second rank of apparatchiks enjoyed professional benefits and material goods not available to the wider population. They had above-average salaries, could travel abroad, live in nationalized buildings, and purchase western consumer goods. Gradually, their strong ideological commitment was replaced by patronage relationships, so much so that the party slowly became a "conglomerate of interests, a market for trafficking power and influence, according to the rules of demand and supply" (Oprea 2008, 16). Under circumstances of great penury during the 1980s economic crisis, the differences between this class and the many who faced strict rationing policies became glaring.

Regular cadres, activists, and bureaucrats were recruited according to very strict criteria, including social origin and level of ideological commitment: key axes of distinction structured the experience of the Communist regime. In the first decade, the propaganda apparatus targeted the socially disadvantaged: many of the new party members were workers or peasants suffering from severe economic deprivation. Joining the party ensured an important degree of upward social mobility, not negligible under the dire circumstances of post–World War II Eastern Europe.

No analysis of the Romanian spectrum of involvement is complete without a serious engagement with the infamous Securitate and its tentacular network of spies. Its privileged place in the repressive apparatus, its use of informers, and its prominent role in Romanians' perception of the party's power cannot be overestimated. The first two decades of the regime were marked by visible, brutal, intimidating violence by the Securitate. Illegal arrests, summary executions, systematic torture, large internal deportations, wide-scale imprisonment and internment in labor camps, expropriations, and expulsions from schools and universities were among its key strategies. The principal targets were members of the democratic parties, Fascists, priests (many of whom harbored Fascist sympathies[2]), intellectuals, artists, and rich peasants who resisted the national collectivization project, among others. While the most visible forms of brutality decreased after 1964, the control over the population, organized bureaucratically in classes and socio-professional categories, continued through the management of their hopes and fears. Romanians assumed the omnipresence of the Securitate and behaved as if the faceless institution was always watching. Even though not everyone had dealings with the service, fear had become part of individuals' habitus, embodied and firmly lodged within their psyches.

Established in 1948, the Securitate had three Soviet agents as its initial leaders (Oprea 2008). The Soviet control over the institution lasted until 1960 when, on a wave of nationalist aspirations, it was "romanianized." Its troops were used against the armed anti-Communist resistance, to "pacify" villagers who resisted collectivization, surveil dissidents, and run prisons and labor camps. In the mid-1950s, its personnel reached 165,000 (including artillery); by 1989 it had decreased to 25,000 (Oprea 2008, 64). The number of salaried cadres was around 25,468 in the mid-1950s, out of which 14,841 were officers, 4,451 were subofficers, and 6,112 were civilian employees. After several reshufflings, the number stabilized at 11,340—which remained more or less constant until 1989 (2008, 70). These figures do not include collaborators and informers.

The Securitate's demography reflected that of the country. In terms of gender, Stan remarks that, because of sexism—spying was considered too dangerous to be a feminine activity—the vast majority of employees and informers were men: of the 2,293 full-time officers identified by the Council for the Study of the Securitate File by 2013, only 1.04 percent were women, and of the 265 informers unveiled, only 5.66 percent were women (2014a, 86). Ninety percent of Securitate agents were party members (Stan 2013, 61). The recruitment of salaried staff was ultrarigorous: each file contained a written pledge of commitment and a personal biography. The archives show that many who applied and signed the pledge changed their minds once in post, often because of remorse (Albu 2008): they invoked illness, family matters, "adjustment" issues—more likely related to the inhumane "work" they were expected to perform (Oprea 2008, 75). Most of the employees were poorly educated and had no experience in policing, especially in the first decade. Salaries were, on average, ten times the average income—a compensation for the professional stress associated with the institution's activities. Moreover, bonuses were awarded proportionally to the number of "class enemies" arrested, which naturally led to abuses (2008, 77–78).

From its inception, the Securitate developed a network of informers and collaborators recruited to provide important information about
"class enemies"—that is, former politicians, bureaucrats, intellectuals, and
other politically "dubious" categories. A great leap in informers' numbers
happens in 1965—marking the switch form brutal, visible violence to the
subtler administration of fear. Délation thus became the main instrument
of terror and control. The estimated number of informers had reached
400,000 in 1989, out of which about 137,000 were active (2008, 81).

Informers had to sign a pledge of commitment as well, which could
be used as blackmail in case of "a change of heart." They fulfilled different roles and occupied precise hierarchical positions in the institution.
Some informers were recruited, others volunteered—which made them
less valuable. Certain groups of informers had been themselves targeted
as members of the Fascist movements or of banned democratic parties[3]:
by offering to inform, they hoped to "redeem" themselves and be treated
clemently by Communists, whose power seemed eternal. Others were
simply aiming for the "external markers of a respectable life: professional
prestige, a financially comfortable situation, the respect of their peers" (L.
Vasile, Vasilescu, and Urs 2016, 11). Given the stability of the geopolitical
constellation, individuals' horizon of expectations was severely constrained
and hope in meaningful political changes was almost inexistent. As Alina
Urs insightfully remarks: "When 'Mary' or 'Artur' signed their reports,
hardly could they imagine that the entire Communist era would become
a historical parenthesis and that their decisions would be put under the
microscope, in search for punctual or social explanations" (L. Vasile,
Vasilescu, and Urs 2016, 11). The best confirmation of the widely spread
belief that Ceaușescu's version of communism had become immutable
is that political change was broadly imagined to be inextricably—and
almost exclusively—related to the dictator's natural death.

Historians examining the Securitate archives record a variety of motivations and social positions. Some pledges are so fanatical that they leave
one wondering whether exalted political commitment or wild fear was at
play. As in the case of the French Milice, a deep sense of one's mission in
protecting the "people's revolutionary accomplishments" emerges from
some of the documents, whose authenticity cannot be verified. Beyond
their absurdity, informers' code names—"Brutus," "Zorro," "Ulysses,"

"the white condor"—testify to the sense of self-importance and empowerment they experienced. Many official reports by Securitate officers
highlight informers' problematic self-entitlement and arrogance: some
were dismissed because they boasted publicly about their "work." The
tone of the pledges changed in the 1960s and 1970s (Oprea 2008, 66–73),
reflecting the changes in the regime's repressive policy and in the geopolitical situation, as well as the bureaucratization of the institution—which
confirms our argument that any assessment of the *in-between* must be
structurally attuned and temporally dynamic.

When "patriotism" was not sufficiently motivating, recruiters used
other incentives: the promise of relocating from the countryside to the
city and career advancement are just two examples of their bargaining
chips (Stan 2013, 64). Money was also a non-negligible pull factor, and
so was access to other benefits, such as a passport, fast-track access to an
apartment, or western consumer goods. As in the French case, some hoped
to take revenge on former rivals, while others sought remuneration. When
money and other incentives failed, fear and blackmail were ordinary recruitment strategies, pushing many into despair and even suicide (Oprea
2008). Former political prisoners—often victims of torture and abusive
detention—were recruited while still in prison, their positional vulnerabilities limiting their choices.[4] Entrapment was yet another strategy (Albu
2008). Sometimes, members of the same family were simultaneously and
separately enlisted to spy on each other. By the end of 1989, an estimated
30 percent of informers were minors (Oprea 2008), who mostly provided
information on their families and colleagues (Albu 2008).

Not everyone gave in to pressure, however. Some stoically accepted
the repercussions of their refusal, which ranged from the loss of a job,
expulsion from an educational institution, harassment, and psychological
terror all the way to imprisonment. Archives also show how religious
beliefs and fear of public opprobrium led some to renege on their pledges
(Albu 2008). Some informers nobly hoped to protect their own friends
and family by passing on what they thought was useless information.
Numerous recruits gradually stopped providing information and showing
up for meetings, giving the institution no choice but to dismiss them.
Changing jobs or relocating to a different town released informers of the
pressure to report. Some felt deep regret—the files reveal a plethora of

excuses for failure to report (marital problems, poor health, professional issues) and testimonies of mental illness (depression, paranoia). Remorse led some to extol the moral and professional virtues of the target before including compromising intelligence in their reports (2008, 104). Shame led some de facto informers to provide information without signing a pledge, hoping to leave no trace. As expected, therefore, the murky *in-between* is not a purely demonic place.

Reflecting this book's argument about the temporally changing nature of involvement, informers changed their behavior in response to the consolidation of the regime and their own private circumstances. Thus, zealous informers slowly became useless, and resisters gave in to pressures to collaborate. Over a lifetime, one could turn from being a target to being an informer, and back again, sometimes simultaneously occupying the position of both victim and victimizer (Stan and Turcescu 2005; Urs 2015). Last but not least, informers were themselves under surveillance— through phone tapping, stakeouts, intercepted correspondence—to ensure their loyalty (Albu 2008). For all these reasons, the legalistic, individualizing, and criminalizing framework is unsuitable: moralizing, temporally static, and personalizing assessments must give way to a lucid, contextual, structural, and temporally sensitive analysis of this evolving institution.

Moving along the spectrum, the Militia—the regular police—had an important role in the ecology of repression. It controlled the population through the national ID system: all changes of domicile had to be reported officially. The Militia also kept a record of typing machines' profiles—lest they be used to disseminate antiregime propaganda. Though less feared than the Securitate—with which it closely collaborated—citizens knew the Militia to be a key part of the repressive apparatus. Therefore, the institution was a privileged object of fear and resentment, especially since its superior ranks also enjoyed important social and material privileges.

The Orthodox Church—the dominant church—suffered repressive measures, but it also closely collaborated with the regime to protect its assets and hegemony over the multiconfessional country (Stan and Turcescu 2005; 2017). By the 1980s, the Orthodox Church was subordinated to the party-state, its leaders were appointed by the regime, and its influence over the intellectual and public life of the country was strictly limited. Many top clerics had become collaborators and informers, while subsequent patriarchs—the national leaders of the church—played a game of accommodation to preserve the church's precarious position (Ciobanu 2017).

Intellectuals constitute a special category of academic inquiry when it comes to political responsibility since, as we also saw in the case of France, there is a general—yet unfounded—expectation that they be exemplars of lucidity and moral integrity. In the first stage of Communist consolidation, several categories were purged, and thousands of publications were banned (Mareş 2012). Academic freedom was suspended, and many university professors were fired or arrested, while Marxism-Leninism became compulsory in schools. The social sciences and the humanities were the worst affected by Stalinization. All presses, galleries, cinemas, and private art collections were nationalized (Preda 2017b). Translations of Soviet literature increased exponentially, while Socialist realism became the state-sponsored artistic style. The profession of writer was institutionalized—the state paid writers salaries and entrusted them with the task of "educating the people." Thus, a great degree of ideological control was accomplished.[5] Some artists willingly adhered to the new order; others hesitated for years before doing so. The general stabilization of the party-state and of the Iron Curtain closed the horizon of hope and diluted the energy to refuse, take risks, and resist. Through the institution of censorship and the political control of research and artistic creation, the intellectual life of the country became regimented.

A system of carrots and sticks regulated artistic production. In the literary world, the Writers' Union enforced the rules (Mareş 2012). Writers who adhered to the party's guiding principles were rewarded with translations of their work, trips abroad, awards, and prestigious lecture series—a combination of material and symbolic goods that encouraged alignment. In contrast, deviationism, "servile" cosmopolitanism, formalism, idealism, opportunism, decadence, objectivism, escapism, and pessimism were unacceptable. Public character assassinations became a common delegitimization practice, to which many succumbed (2012). Under such circumstances, some artists became sycophants, loyal cogs in the propaganda machine (Bosomitu, Burcea, and Diac 2012). Intellectuals were also recruited to spy on other intellectuals, and many did, for a variety of reasons. The more ambitious an intellectual was, the readier they were to compromise. Summarizing the results of his study of intellectual-informers in the Securitate archives, Andreescu (2013, 17) gives us this compassionate assessment:

> Individuals were sometimes courageous, even inflexible, sometimes fragile; some were rational, others confused, some fought, others gave in, overwhelmed by their own drama or saved by separating themselves from the drama of others; some found satisfaction in implicating colleagues, just for the sake of sharing the dock with someone. It mattered whether they were single or had a family, whether they were old or young—their whole life ahead of them. Their behavior depended on their education, social intelligence, on how much they understood of what was happening, on how much they had lost and what they could still hope for. The life of those surveiled by the Securitate, those questioned, asked to sign pledges, threatened, blackmailed into informing, enticed with various benefits, ultimately depended on the numerous crevices of their being.

Andreescu's conclusions highlight the multiple determinations of the intellectuals' positionality—age, socioeconomic status, cultural capital, the vulnerabilities involved in having dependents—which in turn affected the shape of their horizon of hope and actions. For artists and intellectuals, one of the most important constraints was a key clandestine institution: censorship (Corobca 2016a; 2016b).

From the very founding of the regime, numerous books and publications were banned—a move met with various levels of resistance by librarians and publishers (2015). Recruiting censors was a delicate task because they were charged with controlling the output of national and local newspapers, publishing houses, universities, radio and television shows, conferences, theaters, cinemas, and museums, among others (Németi 2016). From the archives, the censor emerges as a politically committed, middle-rank clerk, whose activity was minutely monitored, so much so that they were not thought to have much initiative, though they could, through excess of zeal, cause great harm (Corobca 2016b). Good practices of vigilance were rewarded materially—a strong incentive given the gradual economic immiseration of the population. In case mistakes were made and politically problematic materials saw the light of print, penalties were applied (2016b).

Censors were not alone in carrying on this work. Editors of publishing presses did the initial checking of manuscripts, working with authors to render manuscripts safe. Some sided with the authors and resorted to all sorts of maneuvers to help them pass the censor's vigilant eye. Self-censorship, however, was the most effective means of control. Self-censorship was intellectuals' means of coping with the order's apparent "eternity," a strategy that, however, inevitably shored up the regime. Most writers thus learned to adapt to the circumstances and write in a way that helped them get published.

Having sketched a rough map of complicity that uses ideology, class, profession, religion, and age as organizing criteria, I now turn to the heterogeneous resistances that punctuated the regime, where the same markers of distinction are at play. Despite swift generalizations about the population's passive victimization, the recent historical literature has excavated important modalities of resistance. In what follows, I review some of them, which include the well-known anti-Communist armed struggle that took place in the mountains until the 1960s, dissident intellectuals' efforts, the miners' strike in Valea Jiului, and the workers' strike in Brașov in 1987. I will review these in turn, contouring resisters' horizon of hope and the role their social positionality played in shaping their actions.

During the first period of party consolidation—until the mid-1960s—several small, uncoordinated, ideologically diverse, and geographically scattered groups of armed resisters withdrew into the Carpathian Mountains and fought, for radically different reasons, to prevent the country's integration into the Soviet bloc. These groups disproportionately captured the attention of historians and national mythmakers after 1989—themselves captive to masculinist visions of heroic armed struggle—but they did not constitute the only forms of resistance in this first period. Terrorist attacks (Vasilescu 2015), the hijacking of a passenger ferry (L. F. Vasile 2015), and widespread, violent resistance to collectivization (Potra 2015) are other examples of opposition. It is the armed resister in the mountains, however, that constitutes the first avatar of the hero type, according to the post-Communist mnemonic hegemony.

While benefiting from important support networks in local communities—which scaffolded their hopes in destabilizing the post–World War II settlement—armed resisters' groups were gradually decimated by the Securitate (Dobrincu 2007b). Interestingly for this book, their members' aspirations were embedded within certain socioeconomic and professional positionalities, political experiences, and relational identities that fueled their commitment to national independence. Most of them belonged to communities that had been at the center of national liberation struggles in the nineteenth century and therefore had very strong affective investments in Romania not becoming a Soviet satellite (Ciobanu 2014). Some had built military careers within the Romanian army (Dobrincu 2006); others had paramilitary experience as part of the 1930s extreme-right death squads. For these fighters, ideology, military honor, and martial camaraderie constituted strong animating forces (Dobrincu 2007a). Certain group leaders were part of deeply respected local economic elites, who saw their authority and privileges threatened by the Communists' nationalization plans. Regional socioeconomic interests were paramount: armed resisters' support networks in the villages were animated by a strong aversion to their traditional structures' being undermined by the national plan of collectivization and urbanization (Ciobanu 2014). Greek-Catholics joined the struggle because of the regime's aggressive policy against their church, but religion was also a broader motivator against communism's perceived atheism. Members of the extreme-right movements of the 1930s and 1940s—who embraced a form of mystical Orthodoxy—withdrew into the mountains to avoid persecution and conceived of themselves as defenders of the faith (Dobrincu 2007a). Village intellectuals, students, disgruntled Communists, and members of the parties banned by the new regime were also well-represented in these groups.

Depending on their ideological position, some groups were pro-German, others pro-American. At the time, there was a shared and deeply held belief that the Communist takeover was just another brief episode in the country's history and that a cataclysmic conflict between the USSR and the United States was imminent. This belief fueled the fighters' hopes and motivated them to endure hardship, perpetually harassed by the regime's forces, keenly preparing to liaise with the American troops they so anxiously waited for. The United States' position in relation to the Greek Communists, some encouragements from the British Embassy in Bucharest, and a (failed) paramilitary mission supported by the United

States in 1953 led resisters to believe that the Iron Curtain had not been permanently drawn. The year 1956 permanently quelled that dream. As the Hungarian revolt was brutally suppressed, armed resisters began to lose faith in the possibility of reversing the state's takeover (Petrescu and Petrescu 2007). Gradually but surely, the Securitate forces disabled the last bastions of the "resistance in the mountains."

Throughout the entire duration of the regime, dissident[6] artists and intellectuals took a variety of critical positions. Some contributed to the "drawer literature"—too dangerous to publish in Romania but potentially publishable abroad, if successfully smuggled out of the country—while others embraced a coded language to pass censorship. Visual, avant-garde artists produced performances and installations, mainly for private consumption (Preda 2017a). Not many publicly denounced the abuses of the regime: Doina Cornea and Paul Goma are the most celebrated—despite some problematic aspects of their political biographies. Cornea was a French professor, whose symbolic acts of dissidence were fueled by her devout Christianity, Europeanism, and a romanticized view of the pre-Communist past. Goma engaged in repeated public acts of resistance and solidarity with other Eastern European dissident movements, which led to his imprisonment and years of home arrest (Neubauer and Török 2009). From Paris, the exiled intelligentsia helped put international pressure on the regime, thus protecting some of its targets. Monica Lovinescu and Virgil Ierunca played a key role at Radio Free Europe (Neubauer and Török 2009), an experience narrated in Lovinescu's diaries (Lovinescu 2010). While canonized as a resistance saint by official memory "gate-keepers" after 1989, her positions were not uncontroversial. As in Cornea's case, Lovinescu's views on some of the intellectuals of the 1930s who had been associated with the extreme Right, as well as her indiscriminate anti-communism, betrayed a certain historical and ideological thought-lessness about the subsequent ultranationalist colonizations of the Romanian intellectual space, in the 1930s, under communism, and post–1989. These figures did, however, help cultivate a hegemonic aesthetics of the intellectual-resister—above petty earthly fears and material concerns, of utmost moral integrity, austere and frugal. As we shall see later, alongside the armed resister, the intellectual became the second avatar of heroic resistance in the official memory regime hegemonized after 1989.

Besides 1956, two more years marked watershed moments in the story of anti-Communist resistance: 1977 and 1987. 1977 ended a period of relative stability, as new generations socialized under communism came of age and many enjoyed the benefits of national welfare policies (Petrescu and Petrescu 2007). The 1970s brought increased home ownership, economic well-being, and relative cultural liberalization (Boia 2016). Various challenges to the regime emerged in the 1970s: the human-rights movement initiated by Paul Goma, the devastating earthquake in 1977 that killed more than 1,500 people and caused great economic losses, and the miners' strike in the Jiu Valley. It is important to note that the strike was motivated by economic concerns and did not have an antisystem character: the miners protested for their pensions and benefits (Petrescu and Petrescu 2007). While the regime caved in to their demands, a slow process of repression was set in motion: up to four thousand miners were internally displaced and many of the leaders were placed under Securitate surveillance (Deletant 1995).

The 1980s brought a deep economic crisis: food and energy rationing became so severe that many despaired. Romanians contacted western embassies, tried to pass critical manuscripts or diaries across the border, painted antisystem slogans on public buildings, spread flyers, held clandestine religious services and opposed the official plan to demolish several churches in Bucharest. One citizen theatrically staged the dictator's funeral in the center of the capital (Floroiu 2015); others disseminated political satire (Pleşa 2015). Actors inserted subversive gestures in theater performances to undermine the plays' approved "messages" (Preda 2017a). Women had illegal abortions in opposition to the pronatalist policies of the regime (Bucur 2008). Many were severely punished, with penalties ranging from "official warnings" to losing their job, imprisonment, and even death.[7] Most of these resistances were politically ineffective, as they pitted powerless citizens against an overpowering state machine, in a country located beyond the Iron Curtain, where many were too afraid or too comfortable to show any sign of solidarity. Resistance was therefore often a response to the collapsing living standards, or of sheer naivety in relation to the state's repressive capacity.[8]

This is why the 1987 workers' strike in Braşov reverberated beyond the factories where it started in response to wage cuts imposed for unmet production targets (Petrescu and Petrescu 2007). Thousands of citizens joined in what soon became an antiregime demonstration. Protesters occupied and vandalized the local headquarters of the Communist Party and the People's Council. Riot police were promptly deployed, and participants quickly dispersed. In the immediate aftermath, sixty-one workers were arrested and given sentences of up to three years in prison (2007).

The deepening dissatisfaction of the 1980s, in conjunction with the collapse of Communist regimes in Soviet satellite states eventually culminated in the bloody end of the dictatorship. An estimated maximum of one thousand people died and many more were wounded in the violence surrounding the protests of December 1989. The military leadership quietly sided with a newly formed organization, the National Salvation Front (NSF), which included formerly marginalized top Communist apparatchiks. The NSF took advantage of the popular movement to legitimize themselves as leaders of the revolution and came to power in the vacuum left by the flight, show trial, and subsequent execution of the dictator on December 25, 1989.

THE OFFICIAL STORY

The two erasures at the center of this book can be easily traced in the official story of Romanian communism. To do so, I will briefly reconstruct the stages of its evolution in context.

The 1990s faced Romanians with several challenges (Ciobanu 2015a): Romania's participation in the Shoah, the Communist repression that lasted more than four decades, and its bloody end in December 1989. Because the deaths of the revolution were more recent and the victims mobilized publicly—but also because Romania's participation in the Jewish and Roma genocide had been erased from the national mnemonic doxa—the historical legacies of the 1930s, 1940s, and 1950s were sidelined and the initial criminal proceedings dealt with the killing of peaceful demonstrators in December 1989[9] (Stan 2013). The lack of political will and the reproduction of political elites eventually stunted reflective processes of memory-making. Beyond the show trial of the Ceaușescus in December 1989—a trial that violated principles of legality and laid all responsibility on the ruling couple, obscuring the institutions, practices, and publics that supported them (Mihai 2016a)—legal obstacles to penal justice (amnesty decrees and the expiry of the statute of limitations for crimes committed before 1975) led to very feeble institutional efforts to "work through the past" in the first decade (Grosescu and Ursachi 2009; Stan 2013). The victims fallen or wounded during the public revolt were recognized and special welfare provisions were institutionalized for survivors and their families—though, as time went by, the category of "revolutionary" was used abusively to claim material and symbolic compensation as a market in false "revolutionary certificates" developed. An emphasis on national reconciliation dominated the state discourse in the 1990s, aggravating center-right civil-society actors and public intellectuals, keen on a robust reckoning with communism—often captured in individualizing, moralizing vocabularies that demonized Communists and made everyone else a victim (Bădică 2010; Rusu 2017).

The state's position slowly began to change in the 2000s. The opening of the Securitate archives was a sinuous, incomplete, and frustrating process, marked by political interference, illegalities, and lack of cooperation by the relevant branches of government (Stan 2004, 2012; Stan and Turcescu 2017). The National Council for the Study of the Securitate Files (CNSAS) and the Institute for the Investigation of Communist Crimes and the Memory of the Romanian Exile (IICCMER)—the two main institutions meant to articulate the official memory—got embroiled in numerous controversies, especially regarding their legal powers, ideological positioning, and role in making and breaking political careers and reputations. The files' political instrumentalization by various powerbrokers dented the public's trust in the "truths" emerging from the archives. IICCMER was founded as a research institute whose findings were supposed to support the state's prosecutors in their efforts to try crimes committed before 1989. It produced impressive amounts of research—some of it underpinned by reductive anti-communism, some of it sophisticated and nuanced. It was only in 2016—because of important changes in jurisprudence related to the import of international legal categories (Grosescu 2017)—that the director of a political prison the IICCMER helped indict was sentenced.

In 2006, the Presidential Commission for the Analysis of the Communist Dictatorship in Romania was founded by the president of the republic, in a strategic self-legitimation maneuver (Rusu 2017). The Commission was supposed to give the final, official verdict on the Communist past—which it did, causing great discontent. From the beginning, the final report was mired in controversy: the text betrayed a highly moralistic, individualizing approach to systemic violence.[10] It focused heavily on the party's elites, on their psychological profile and their power to dictate policy, most likely because of the expertise and methodological commitments of the report's main authors, but especially because of their ideological stance. The text is uneven, due to coauthorship. Throughout, however, it is written in a dramatic tone, presenting communism as demonic and alien to the Romanian people, while anti-Communist resistance is depicted as a "national reflex" (Comisia Prezidențială 2006, 158). The USSR's interference is highlighted throughout, Romanian communism being labeled "an occupation regime" (2006, 167)—a distancing move meant to signal Romania's readiness to reintegrate with the capitalist, European "civilization," where it had supposedly always belonged. The authors take the moral high ground and write intransigently, in a retributive vein, depicting communism as a "black hole in history" (Bădică 2010), a criminal, evil system, and a "disease" that traumatized an entire country (Comisia Prezidențială 2006, 166).

Such visions made possible what Tileagă (2017, 16) calls "the operation of social repression, the suppression of the socially inappropriate thought that communism may have been historically part and parcel of national identity." The report obscures the specific and resilient form communism took in Romania, Romanians' involvement with and support for the regime, the benefits they accrued from it, and their contribution to the system's reproduction. In deploying the aesthetic of a "penitentiary colony, populated by délateurs, collaborators and Securitate Officers" (Comisia Prezidențială 2006, 19), the report avoided uncomfortable truths about collective responsibility, the reproduction of toxic nationalism, and various and widespread forms of cohabitation, collusion, and involvement with the regime's repressive institutions—effectively collapsing the vast space between the evil perpetrators and the saintly victims. The vituperative conclusions sat uneasily with the authors' proclaimed scientific credentials, which they invoked to shore up their own authority to tell "truth": a heroic, ascetic image of the intellectual is invoked and juxtaposed to the imbecilic, uneducated, and evil apparatchiks who had derailed the country's history.

The reactions to the report were vehement, yet they remained mostly confined to the intellectual sphere. Some pointed to the report's lack of scientific reliability and incongruities. Others offered ideologically over-determined criticisms. The report itself had very limited resonance within the broader public. Surveys consistently show, however, anti-communism as not dominating the population's attitudes—understandably given the bitter disappointments related to the socioeconomic costs of the wild capitalist liberalization inaugurated in the 1990s (Abraham 2012).

A similar conception of Communist history—as external to the nation, demonic, criminal[11]—emerges from the most important memorializing project, the Sighet Museum. Formerly a prison where numerous political prisoners were exterminated, Sighet was until 1997 privately funded by an NGO and heavily promoted by prominent anti-Communist intellectuals and artists. Initially a museum about the prison, it gradually became the de facto main museum of communism in Romania, and the state started funding it. As in the Presidential Commission's report, an apolitical, hypermoralist, Manichaean, and unique narrative is imposed: communism was a foreign aberration, while political prisoners are presented as saintly martyrs (Bădică 2010).

The alignment between anti-communism and the Christian Orthodox Church is essential for understanding this narrative. After 1989, the Church made great efforts to downplay its own involvement with the regime and put significant pressure on the state to block access to the secret police files that incriminated it. Most importantly, it sponsored a narrative of resistance through religious spirituality against atheistic, imported communism—capitalizing on former prisoners' accounts, which highlighted the positive role of faith in their enduring horrific detention conditions (Ciobanu 2017). The Church's cohabitation with the Communist regime (C. Vasile 2017) and the clergy's deep involvement with the Fascist movements of the 1930s and 1940s was mystified (Stan and Turcescu 2005). Christianism, anti-communism, and patriotism got fused in a version of the past that revived the anti-Semitic ultranationalism that preceded communism (Ciobanu 2017), silencing the voices of other religious and ethnic groups. Thus, the problematic political biographies of the political prisoners were obscured by renewed monovocalism: civil-society actors and public intellectuals unreflectively embraced the idea of resistance to communism as a Christian phenomenon. Many authoritative voices participated in the prisoners' martyrization, decontextualizing their struggle, obscuring their less palatable motivations, and attributing to them a unified plan to resist communism, conceived as an alien imposition on the authentic *national* body (Ciobanu 2014).

The most widely viewed documentary about the Communist political prisons shown on the public national television, *Memorialul Durerii*[12], directed by Lucia Hossu-Longin, contributed to the institutionalization of this hegemonic vision by aestheticizing "national history as Christian martyrdom" (Popescu 2017, 269). It homogenized the nation and obscured the anti-Semitism and the Orthodox version of fascism endorsed by many political prisoners and anti-Communist resisters, whom it symbolically canonized as "prison saints" (Ciobanu 2017). Sanitizing their political biographies, the documentary presents them as avatars of Christian endurance and dignity, who could not be cowed by the regime's demonic violence. Undoing the damage of communism required, therefore, a return to a highly romanticized vision of the interwar period, whose ultranationalist, anti-Semitic violence was rendered invisible. Thus, Christian ideas of the nation as a victim of foreign intervention by atheist Communists prevented any reckoning with the regime's stability for over four decades.

This dichotomic, pathologizing, and exteriorizing narrative about communism was strongly supported by several self-appointed "gate-keepers" (Stan 2014) of the Romanian intellectual world. Identifying with the center Right and the Right, they endorsed and gave public prominence to this virulent anti-communism, while simultaneously fabricating for themselves a specific form of resistance: "resistance through culture," the form of struggle suitable to those of a "contemplative nature" (Pleşu 2010). While acknowledging that this was not a form of active resistance, the main promoters of this concept—Gabriel Liiceanu and Andrei Pleşu—argued that it constituted a refusal of the Communist dissimulation of language and meaning. They withdrew into philosophical research during the 1980s, under the mentorship of a former political prisoner, Constantin Noica—himself a former sympathizer of the extreme Right. Critics pointed out that privatization was in fact a form of shirking responsibility, mere therapy for the soul, a self-centered dodging and a bending of the head in search for a private, isolationist form of normality, which left the public order untouched. As it turned out after 1989, the only reason the group could do its work was the mentor's compromise with the Securitate, whose informer he was. Before this aspect of his biography became publicly known, "resisters through culture" enjoyed considerable moral capital, which they mobilized to their own advantage for cultural and political purposes.

The case of "resistance through culture" throws into sharp relief the effects of reading the past in morally uncompromising, aestheticizing, and individualizing ways: on the wrong side of history sit the evil, anti-Christian Communists, on the other, the ethically unwavering intellectuals and the prison saints, who had (supposedly) traversed the dictatorship unsullied. Individualizing blame and virtue, this narrative obscured the broader national and international forces at play and the complex social positionalities Romanians inhabited and reproduced through their very actions.[13] It is only very recently that nuanced, complex analyses began to emerge, written by a new generation of historians, social scientists, and legal scholars—on whose work this study relies. Some of these critical analyses come out of the work of the IICCMER, others were authored by scholars associated with various universities, from within or outside Romania. The temporal distance from the dictatorship as well as the looser connection with the traumatic experience of the 1980s allows these researchers to shed a more impartial light on history's cast of characters. These sophisticated accounts track the complexity and heterogeneity of the *in-between* in a temporally dynamic way, highlighting the social underpinnings of the regime's endurance as well as the effects of its resilience on various groups' horizons of expectations and action. They also criticize the self-serving narratives institutionalized after 1989 and the limits of the hypermoralizing, demonizing perspective on Communists and their supporters. Their contributions can thus be read as the labor of a hermeneutical caring refusal, which nonetheless had little effect on the public space of memory, colonized as it still is by anti-Communist trumpeting and hagiographies of prison saints. To look for alternative, more effective sources of mnemonic friction that can trouble the automatism of the collective mnemonic imagination in this case, I now turn to several artists and their caring aesthetics.

SABOTAGING MYSTIFICATIONS

The same imperatives that drove me in selecting artworks from France guide me here as well. Without any ambition to offer a comprehensive account, I looked for films and novels that refused—or at least problematized—the double erasure of widespread complicity and non-heroic, unsaintly resistances from the official records of suffering and valor. In proposing unassimilable visions of the past, these works recover complexity and illuminate the interplay between structures and relationality. For these reasons, I propose to read them as examples of aesthetic mnemonic care.

The first section discusses a novel and a film created before 1989, for their makers' historically acute lucidity about the temporal resilience of the regime over four decades and the palette of opportunities it opened for both colluders and resisters. The novel *Plicul negru (The Black Envelope [1986])* by Norman Manea, a Jewish-Romanian intellectual who lived through both extreme-right- and extreme-left-wing dictatorships in Romania, offers a complex and unflattering picture of the ecology of violence, highlighting how societies often replace one monolithic, uncompromising form of dogmatic univocality with another. Dan Pița's film, *Concurs (Orienteering* [1982]) is an allegory for the Communist regime that foregrounds the heterogenous *in-between*, problematizes "percepticide"[14]—the practice of unhearing and unseeing violence—and highlights the not-so-negligible role of nonheroic resistances.

The following section delves into the world of the relational underpinnings of hope and their fragility when confronting instances of proximate betrayal. I select two novels by the same author, Herta Müller, the winner of the 2009 Nobel Prize for Literature [15]: *Heute wär ich mir lieber nicht begegnet (Astăzi mai bine nu m-aş fi întâlnit cu mine însămi; The Appointment [1997])* and *Herztier (Animalul inimii; The Land of Green Plums [1994])*, both of which thematize the relationality of both complicity and resistance and thwart any temptation to pass harsh judgments on betrayal: when prosthetically inhabiting Müller's gaze, readers enter neither a historical "black hole", nor a captive society, but a complex universe of fear, complicity, and violence that is not, however, completely devoid of love, friendship, and solidarity. Moreover, her intellectual resisters—with their ineradicable flaws and weaknesses—offer a persuasive alternative to the "untainted intellectual" model canonized after 1989.

Last but not least, I look at two films whose directors are considered stars of the Romanian New Wave—a label applied to an internationally acclaimed group of filmmakers who embrace a realist style characterized by documentary-like shots and minimal editing and who are thematically preoccupied with the recent past via marginal characters (Pusca 2011). *Medalia de onoare (The Medal of Honor [2009])* by Călin Peter Netzer seduces us into entering the world of a mild-mannered yet stubborn rhinoceros—who, post-1989, hesitantly yet surely embarks on a journey of self-reinvention as a hero-elect. The film thus magisterially comments on the personal *and* collective need for fabricating a redemptive past. In contrast, Corneliu Porumboiu's *A fost sau n-a fost? (12:08 East of Bucharest [2006])* focuses on a provincial community's yearning for a glorious revolution. Like Netzer, Porumboiu problematizes the confiscation of memory but also makes space for dissenting voices to reconfigure mnemonic spaces.

"ORDINARY BEASTS IN THE SWAMP CALLED THE PRESENT": INTERSTITIAL VIOLENCE, PERCEPTICIDE, AND INESCAPABLE CONTAMINATION

Plicul negru: Coping, Thriving, Exiting

Manea's novel *Plicul negru (The Black Envelope)* took a long time to appear in press, heavily censored, three years before the end of communism.[16] Because of the circumstances of its production, the form is hermetic yet highly engaging. The story needs reconstructing from disparate allusions and bits of information provided by various characters at different points in the novel. The text keeps the reader guessing, full of innuendos and clues, never transparent, enveloping them in the viscous reality it seeks to capture yet simultaneously shedding light on its rich texture. Published in its uncensored form after the institutionalization of hegemonic anti-Communist memory, the novel sabotaged the Manichean and externalist narrative that colonized the Romanian hermeneutical space after 1989 by offering a complex picture of the structural and historical underpinnings of violence. The style was specifically crafted to avoid the ideological scalpel of the censor, with felicitous effect on the aesthetic experience of reading the text. Black humor, metaphorical dexterity, lyricism, burlesque perorations, and philosophical reflections on history—all come together to provide an atmospheric novel that transports the reader into the last decade of the dictatorship. In this section, I zoom in on three themes that speak to this book's central concerns: the relationality and temporality of the multifaceted *in-between*, the complex positionality of traitors, and the historical continuities—as opposed to the radical break—between the interwar Fascist authoritarianism and its Communist successor.

The main character is Anatol Dominic Voinea-Voinov, nicknamed Tolea, an erudite high school teacher who lost his job in dubious circumstances—unclear whether because of his bisexuality or a setup by the secret police. He is fifty and works as a receptionist in a hotel in Bucharest. Tolea is Jewish on his father's side, and we learn that his family had been persecuted by the Fascists in the 1930s and 1940s. His father—a philosopher who became a wine merchant to become socially less visible—died in ambiguous circumstances, after he received a letter containing anti-Semitic death threats. Tolea suspects the letter had been sent by one of his sister's admirers, whose love was unrequited. The novel centers on Tolea's unsuccessful efforts to solve the mystery of his father's death, against the background of the fears and frustrations specific to the 1980s.

And yet, the novel is only seemingly a detective story. The characters constitute a diverse moral fauna, each located at the intersection of several vectors of identity and immersed, to a greater or lesser degree, in the duplicitous mire extending beneath the closed horizon of expectations. Tolea appears to be on the verge of a nervous breakdown. Tormented by nightmares from his family's past, he seamlessly treads the boundary between his memories, his dreams, and the unsatisfactory reality. He perorates in Latin and French and lectures his colleagues about ancient history, World War II, and the similarities between Argentine (Fascist) and Romanian (Communist) dictatorships—a not-so-veiled allusion to the ideological continuities between the Romanian fascism of the interwar period and communism. His monologues are replete with abstruse metaphors, alluding to generalized ideological and moral contamination at all levels of society.

In themselves, these metaphors constitute humorous, incisive, yet indulgent observations of "the swamp" and its inhabitants. The experience of the dictatorship is like that of "quarantine," a "desperate somnolence," or "the great feast of the apocalypse," which has its source in indigenous factors. Under such circumstances, "improvisation is salvation"—an allusion to widespread social accommodationism; those who refuse to adapt are "colorful extras in the great farce," inhabiting "truth's waiting rooms." Comedy abounds: informers are "experts in reality" who may sometimes experience "unremunerated remorse," while their reports to the secret police are "folk studies in human behavior." Troubling clean moral distinctions between perpetrators and victims, Tolea's musings recall Ionescu's play: "Yesterday, the disease had only reached the neighbor or the neighbor's neighbor, today it is already in you and it is too late. The premises of evil, in each captive, not only in the executioners?" (2015, 12).

This brings us to the novel's first insight—into the interstitiality, relationality, and structurality of involvement. Manea uses allegorical tropes to capture the experiential dimension of widespread duplicity, which cannot be traced to an external force. Given the assumed omnipresence of informers, all citizens bear the physical marks of dissimulation, a wrinkle-like scar under the left eye, caused by too much winking: while everyone speaks, speech is meaningless. Therefore, winking becomes the only form of reliable communication. Reality itself is dissimulated: everyone is pretending in order to exist socially and attain a modicum of happiness. Romanians live in "a world of surrogates, this circus of ours" (2015, 21). Communism is thus introduced not as an alien, diabolical imposition but as an order sustained by a people of winkers.

Not everyone winks, however: some are deaf. While doing his detective work on the fateful letter, Tolea visits a deaf people's association. The association is an allegory for the ideologically committed, and humor is deployed effectively to evoke the atmosphere in it: "Nothing distracts them during work. They don't speak, they don't hear, they don't listen, they cannot gossip or joke. They don't waste their thoughts on trifles. They work concentrated, all the time. They are orderly, disciplined, loyal. Loyal, the most important characteristic" (2015, 139). Tolea wonders if the members' "amputated life had maintained any resource of ambiguity" given that they were "armored in their own isolation, in which there was no room for deviation, detours, delays, naughty jokes, gossip and controversies, hesitations and dilemmas" (2015, 149). The Association's director, Orest Popescu, is a specialist in the art of survival: having fought on the German side in World War II, he reinvented himself as a Communist after 1945. Manea thus misses no opportunity to remind us of *the long durée* and the ever-present recalcitrant aftermaths of rhinoceration.

The third category of citizens Manea discusses are the mentally ill. Dr. Marga, Tolea's friend, runs a psychiatric hospital. He lost an eye, which leads the reader to think that, unlike other dissimulators, he refuses to wink—that is, to accept the hijacking of language. He dedicates himself to scaffolding those around him, friends and patients alike, offering medical succor to "men, women, children, soldiers, priests, vagabonds, peasants, sex workers, ministers, undertakers, masks and surrogates, the great army of the defeated, the last remnants of normality, thunderstruck by destiny, incapable of becoming indifferent, refusing health and indifference and normality" (2015, 100). Mental illness is the realm of true freedom: the ill are those who cannot reconcile themselves with the present, yet are too powerless or too cowardly to do anything about it. They are "capable of sensing the world's going off the rails, the rupture and the screeching ignored by all those who toil to keep up the comedy that's looking for an end" (2015, 100–101). Isolated, they support each other, clinging on to their savior, Marga, who signs off early-retirement applications and hospitalizes those who cannot endure reality. Thus, he enables practices of political exit: his work is merely palliative, as there is no "cure," and so his therapies, which transform the patients into calm bodies, are complicit in the reality they cannot change.

Thus, the in-between emerges not as a uniform group of victims but as displaying complex layers of involvement and passivity, opportunism and political withdrawal. Time is used as a trope throughout the novel and a prism through which Manea highlights, first, generalized yet internally heterogeneous, acquiescence. While the mentally ill opt for sedation outside politics and the deaf work away with docility, others more cynically take advantage of the existing "opportunities." Ştefan Olaru, one of Tolea's brilliant university mates, becomes an engineer and joins the ranks of the Communist Party, thus receiving all sorts of benefits forbidden to the more principled. He has no qualms admitting he had sided with the parvenus and rationalizes his decision: "It is more interesting, believe me. I don't like the losers, the *déclassés*. It is much more interesting on this side of the divide. Not just more useful. Much more interesting." He delimits himself from those "who frown" and who "don't wear watches"—that is, maladjusted people such as Tolea, who subscribe to an ethical view of posterity. For him, the "here and now" is the only time, the only "correct code" for living:

to exist socially given the regime's stability, one must become duplicitous. Aware of his mortality, Ştefan hopes to live as well as he can, as intensely as he can, in the present, keeping busy, painfully aware that no radical political change was imminent. About forty years earlier, during the rise of fascism, Tolea's father, Marcu, had similarly said: "The vain possession of a moment, that is all we can wish for" (2015, 74). Because the past is officially erased and a different future unimaginable, "we are present, just present" (2015, 169). Communism is therefore not a "black hole" but a resilient present that people live differently, depending on the resources they can muster and the hopes they can nourish in navigating its murky waters.

Reflections on time are, secondly, a formal means for problematizing the regime's indebtedness to the ideologies that preceded it—that is, for highlighting the structural and discursive reproduction of absolutist univocality. The letter Tolea's father received had on it a picture of the Cerberus—the three-headed beast who guards the gates of the underworld. The beast is also featured in Titian's painting *The Allegory of Prudence*, which depicts three male heads—a young man, an adult man, and an old man—under which one can symmetrically see a dog, a lion, and a wolf. Tolea discusses this paining with Titian himself in one of his reveries. He lectures out loud feverishly: "The Hungry wolf devours memories. The dominating, all-powerful lion, is the present. The future is hesitant, like a servile dog" (2015, 372). The painting also features an inscription in Latin, "ex praeterito / praesens prudenter agit / ni futura actione deturpet" (from the experience of the past / the present acts prudently / lest it should spoil future actions). Tolea becomes obsessive about the dictum and interpellates Titian: "The present acts prudently. Pru-den-tly, that's what you wrote. Prudently, not carelessly. With prudence, not indifference. The present acts prudently, not to harm the future" (2015, 371). The text on the painting stands in great contrast with Tolea's racialized experience of historical time: the Fascist past infects the Communist present and cancels his future, which is no longer imaginable outside self-sustaining cycles of intolerant nationalist monovocality. Tolea's breakdown is inevitable, leaving him incapacitated, but also ultimately free, in Dr. Marga's hospital.

The third theme worth highlighting is Manea's balanced portrait of the traitors—the secret police informers. In tension with the official story, in Tolea's words, they are ordinary "beasts of the swamp called the present, that's all," and not "the Devil's servants, they don't enjoy such a high rank" (2015, 44). Toma, the main informer in the book, has an elusive presence, at the limit between reality and reverie. We know he is a xenophobe who recruits Tolea's landlady, Ortansa—code name "Pick Lock"—whose character he humorously captures in his reports: "Ortansa embodies our national qualities. The close collaboration, inseparable, between the good and the evil" (2015, 253). An artist in moral haziness, Toma inspires fear, though he is not as knowing and dangerous as others imagine. From his reports, however, we learn that he is an orphan, raised by his uncle, a former liberal politician, now old and relying on Toma's superiors' mercy to receive medical treatment and lodging in the deaf association's residence. The uncle had turned "mad" (on the novel's code) and consequently had two brain "surgeries." The surgeries have affected his hearing and capacity to speak—he is becoming "deaf," that is, compliant—and have induced in him a permanent state of euphoria. Toma cannot exclude the possibility that the uncle will have another fit of "madness"—that is, lucidity—so he pleads with his superiors to secure the much-needed medicine to keep him docile. We understand that Toma truly loves his uncle and sees the "therapy" as preferable to other, more "drastic" measures his superiors could take toward a former liberal. In exchange, he commits to faithfully informing on Tolea.

The ambiguity of Toma's position and the relationalities that underpin his vulnerability exemplify Manea's refusal to cast stark moral judgments on his characters and, implicitly, on his fellow citizens. The novel poignantly captures temporally and intersubjectively the lived experience of life under the dictatorship. All characters have a history that positions them in various locations within the dissimulated reality. Their identity— ethnicity, ideology, gender, cultural capital—frames and constrains their life trajectories and opens up different horizons of hope and action. While the deaf are loyal, the psychiatric hospital enables withdrawal and the refusal of dissimulation—yet therapy does nothing to disrupt the system. Some take advantage of the opportunities opened by the regime and prefer not to think about posterity—understood morally. Others reinvent themselves, swapping right-wing ideologies for left-wing ones, opportunistically. All this while, the majority winks, simultaneously captives and active participants in the mystification of reality, crossing the ideologically porous boundaries between fascism and communism. In prosthetically enabling the reader to visit the deaf association, the psychiatric hospital, and Tolea's apartment, Manea interrupts the automatism of fervent anti-communism and the political hagiographies institutionalized after 1989. Under his metaphorical quill, the avatars of masculinist and intellectual resistance dissolve to reveal a shadowy—complex and ever shifting—swamp, whose beasts fail to conform to the prescribed script.

The Temptation of Percepticide: *Concurs*

Dan Piţa's career spans decades and is punctuated by several international awards. However, his work was not always aligned to the Socialist Realist principles of artistic production imposed under the dictatorship. Therefore, some of it was banned and the director was put under surveillance. The film included here, *Concurs* (*Orienteering* [1982]), follows a group of workmates who spend their Sunday participating in an orienteering competition, getting lost in a dense forest as well as in personal relationships and morality itself. Workplace hierarchies, petty rivalries, romance, acerbic competitiveness, and jealousy are all at play. Humor, surrealist apparitions, an eclectic soundtrack, and colloquial dialogue are Piţa's stylistic means for ushering the viewer into a world full of dangers that test the group's fragile bonds of solidarity and capacity to respond morally to a crime.[17]

I propose to read the film as an allegory of the tiresome *in-between* occupied neither by perpetrators nor by victims, showing its internal diversity, its temporal dynamism, and the—limited yet significant—spaces and modalities of impure resistance. Like Manea, Piţa offers a sophisticated, critical, yet compassionate account of how various people enter into and slide between various positions on the spectrum of involvement, pulled by various forces and with devastating consequences, against the background of continuous political surveillance and harassment. Most importantly, the film seduces us away from the convenient certainties of generalized victimhood and sovereign heroism, thematizing the self-serving occlusion of moral failures and public participation in systemic violence. It does so not only by illuminating percepticide, but also by showing how authority can be pierced effectively, even under apparently hopeless circumstances.

Metaphorical references to the Communist regime abound. The forest is dark and dense, and, from the beginning, the ominous music creates an atmosphere of mystery and danger. Long shots of the participants' fog-enveloped bus signal the entry into a confusing and perilous situation. The officials in charge of the competition arrive in a car equipped with a siren and dressed in the anonymous clothes of the apparatchiks. The deafening sound of a helicopter—perpetually heard but never shown—adds to the tension, hinting at permanent surveillance. An authoritative voice is heard shouting instructions and lecturing over the megaphone, but few pay attention to its tired clichés—an early allusion to the limits of authority. All participants know that "anything can happen in the forest"; this is why they abide strictly by the rules of the competition, hoping to stay out of trouble—Pița's gesture to the benefits of accommodationism and quietism. Enigmatic men dressed in black warn participants to leave the forest before nightfall, lest a "catastrophe" befall them. All characters look tired and often unthinkingly repeat typical party slogans—for example, the principle of "order and discipline." The director confessed to having purposefully tired his actors so as to get them to look drained—an allusion to the generalized state of emotional exhaustion characteristic of the last decade of the regime (*Dan Pița* 2015).

The diverse cast and their interactions constitute the best key to understanding both patterns of involvement with the regime and resistance to it. Bărbulescu, the overweight boss dressed in a tracksuit yet carrying a briefcase—the very stereotype of the petty party official—tries to keep everyone together. His unfaithful wife bails out of the contest, pretending to be ill. She is replaced by a young man who happens to cycle by, "the Kid." Vasile, second in command, is in charge of the compass and tries to assume leadership, though his authority is permanently disputed by Sandu, his workplace rival. The group also includes a "councilor"—an intellectual fond of Latin and botany—and the reluctant Mitică. Two women are also part of the team: Lavinia, who is romantically involved with Panait, the group's macho photographer, and Tatiana. They all know each other well, except for the Kid, who joins them last minute. Throughout the film, the team meanders through the woods, overcoming a variety of obstacles (a swamp, a deep ravine, a snake) with the help of the Kid, who keeps them safe.

At some point during their tortuous journey, they hear bloodcurdling cries for help. A long shot at the beginning of the film had shown a woman being harassed by four men while suntanning. The viewer immediately associates the cries with that image. Initially, the team tries to find her, spontaneously running in various directions, without success. Vasile is unhappy about the disruption and tries to persuade them to give up the search. He initially claims this was a prank. Then he argues that they should not interfere in police business—a ridiculous proposal given they had no means to call the police. Later, he denies having heard anything and insists that they were all suffering from "aural hallucinations." The others contest Vasile's judgments and confront him—accusing him of having pretended to be deaf so as not to have to fill in a report of the event. And yet, as the cries stop, one by one they all sit in the grass, exhausted and sweaty. The Kid alone persists in his search, but he, too, fails and eventually gives up. It is only at the end of the film, when the competition is over and everyone has gone, that the Kid, forgotten and left behind, discovers the woman's body and is disconsolate.

The characters occupy different dynamic positions in the nebulous area of complicity. In Pița's apt hands, they become key tools for sabotaging any fantasy about generalized victimhood and moral purity in relationship to the dictatorship. While everyone is implicated and responsible, the film does not position them as a uniform mob of innocent witnesses or impotent victims.[18] While all feel drained and harassed, not everyone takes the easy way out: the social alienation induced by decades of authoritarianism has heterogeneous effects. Different levels of dissent emerge at various points in time, and nobody—not even the Kid—fits the noble hero profile.

Vasile is inflexible and thoughtless. His attitude toward the unexpected betrays a deep fear of losing control and a callous insensitivity. He is determined to complete the route and gets ragingly furious every time his authority is challenged. When the Kid is more effective as a guide, he suggests that they "get rid" of him. His refusal to acknowledge the woman's cries is symptomatic of percepticide, motivated by a desire not to take responsibility and assume the costs of intervening. Vasile is morally disconnected from other human beings and oblivious to their suffering or disagreement—and, as we shall see in the analysis of Herta Müller's work, this is one of the most pernicious effects of stable repressive orders. In making his choices, he allows the murder to proceed unchallenged.

While Vasile becomes hostile to the Kid for the threat he poses to his command, Panait is driven by romantic jealousy and aggressive masculinity: Lavinia is impressed with the Kid's agility and physical strength, which put them all to shame. Threatened, Panait insinuates that the Kid is a party spy, an informer. The generalized paranoia regarding the all-seeing state is instrumentalized to slander him. Panait speaks like a policeman-rhinoceros, effectively conjuring a cloud of suspicion. However, while some fall for his plot, others resist and ironize his "investigation," protecting the Kid's reputation. Refusal is shown as effortless: thus, Pița makes it conceivable that some abusive practices can be opposed and that solidarity with potential victims is nonetheless possible.

Bărbulescu's character is interestingly ambiguous, a comic mixture of self-aggrandizement and noble gestures, despite his being a rather weak leader. He has a deep—preposterous and thereby comic—sense of his mission and is driven by a deluded idea of manly honor, which sometimes helps him make the right moral choices. When Mitică disappears in a deep sewer, he wants to singlehandedly climb down on a rope into the dark tunnels—a suicidal action given his very poor physical form. When Vasile threatens to file a complaint against Sandu, Bărbulescu surprises everyone by forbidding it and dismissing Vasile as a "bureaucrat"— something that sits uneasily with his own party role and the briefcase he carries at all times. At the end of the film, when the team members realize they had left the Kid behind, it is Bărbulescu alone who gets off the bus to search for the young man, displaying an exemplary sense of responsibility. The caricatural vision of the apparatchik is here replaced with a nuanced, humorous figure, who sits uneasily within official memory's ankylotic investment in a demonic vision thereof.

Mitică and the councilor take the most radical actions to dissociate themselves from the group and the mindless chase. The former hides in a sewer. When the Kid finds him, sad and tired, enjoying the silence, he pleads to be considered dead—this is how badly he wants to escape the mad chase through the forrest. Pița renders filmically Mitică's longing to get away: the sewer's otherworldly calmness is translated musically, and Mitică's figure is shot from afar under a ray of sunlight that penetrates the darkness, thereby signaling his entrance in a space of peace and serenity. The sewer matches Manea's psychiatric hospital—a dark yet soothing space of withdrawal and self-preservation, that leaves, however, the world outside untouched. Similarly, overwhelmed by the endless bickering of his colleagues, the councilor puts himself into a trance-like state, blocking everyone sensorially. Both these characters enact individual, self-protective withdrawal that, however good for their own psychological well-being, does nothing to disrupt the group dynamics or help the murder victim.

However, the film does go beyond withdrawal and introduces more effective—though not heroic—modalities of resistance, thus pluralizing viewers' mnemonic and resistant imaginaries. Fighting periodically erupts between the conformists and those who see through their petty megalomania and insensitivity. The challenges to the fragile authority of the absurd Vasile culminate in a moment of heightened confrontation, when Sandu accuses him of formalism, incompetence, and an unhealthy desire to win at all costs. Sandu acts out of sheer acrimony, lambasting Vasile, but, irrespective of his not-so-noble motivations, his actions have beneficial effects, undermining Vasile's efforts to muddy the waters of responsibility for the crime they witnessed aurally. While Vasile perorates defensively, Sandu pulls down his pants, a moment of physical comedy that follows one of tension, the effect of which is to show that the emperor is, indeed, naked.

This is not a singular example: the film repeatedly shows that solidarity is possible, and "small resistances" (Greco 2019) can succeed even under hostile circumstances. When Bărbulescu promises a "meeting" to assess the team's performance for after the competition, everyone scoffs—exhausted and bored—rendering his authority vacuous. Similarly, when Vasile claims the cries were not real and when he suggests they "get rid" of the Kid, almost all deride him, defending the Kid's merits in bringing them safely to the finish line and insisting they had heard the calls for help. While the unknown woman was never rescued, the Kid—somebody they got to like for his help at crucial moments—is protected by the group. The permanent squabbling and fighting, however irritating, shows how easy it is to oppose repressive and percepticidal dynamics and prevent their catastrophic effects. Impure resistances—many of them not even intended as such—are recuperated and valorized by the film, highlighting how one can, without too high a risk, disturb the more mundane workings of the authoritarian habitus in mindsets, emotional registers, and practices. While the system stays in place, life under its auspices can be rendered more humane, more dignified, and less fragile.

The Kid has been interpreted as the outsider, the moral actor par excellence, the one who insists on the truth and eventually distances himself from the group as too corrupt (Nasta 2012, 41–42). The film's opening images set up these expectations: he is shot cycling alone, on the road that leads to the forest, wearing a golden raincoat—a modern knight in shining armor. Throughout, he is predominantly presented as principled, helping everyone in need, even if he is not fully respected or integrated. However, he is no unsullied hero. He, too, eventually gives up searching for the woman. When Panait interrogates him aggressively, he cowers and fearfully admits that the woman's cries might just have been an impression. Afraid, even he backs off from his intransigent "truth"—thus contributing to the silencing of the victim. Through his capitulations, the film disrupts the temptation to read the Kid as an unrelenting force of the good, thereby injecting a healthy dose of plausibility into the character.

Concurs serves as a powerful meditation on what is seeable and hearable and the political and moral implications of not seeing or not hearing. The original soundtrack and shots of surreal apparitions cast a shadow on the viewer's perception of reality—an emaciated white horse, a classical quintet, a wedding party, and a truck full of live chickens make improbable appearances in the forest—prosthetically enabling the viewer to experience the disorientation caused by the ideological colonization of reality. The debate over whether the members had indeed heard the woman's screams highlights the ways in which convenient doubts get hold of people in a climate of fear, suspicion, and exhaustion, with devastating consequences. Over and over again, Pița shows how percepticide is always a temptation, given the alienated forms of sociality typical of repressive regimes, how it is enabled structurally, and how even the most morally sensitive give in to it under duress. However, not everyone succumbs. At the end of the film, as the members ride the bus back to the city, they realize the Kid has been left behind. Unwilling to return for him, some insinuate he had never been on the trip, casting doubt on his very existence. Sufficient people, however, contend that he did participate, and it is because of their refusal to unsee the Kid that the bus eventually turns around. Collective insistence on undeniable evidence prevents self-interested distortions of reality.

With the exception of Vasile, the characters shift position over time. They oscillate between courage, cowardice, and laziness. Deploying sympathetic, caring humor, the film takes us on a compassionate, prosthetic journey into the wearied, divided, yet highly relatable group. Professional advancement and recognition, sexual and romantic interests, interpersonal enmities, and envy—push in different directions, often with unexpected results. Thus, moments of compliance and complicity are interspersed with moments of efficacious resistance. The film skillfully reveals what it takes to pierce through the veneer of authority and respectability that the leaders struggle to enact, thus disrupting homogenizing victimization narratives and revealing that the in-between need not be permanently and irredeemably compliant. Crucially, it enriches the repertoire of resistant action, highlighting the important effect of small, impure resistances: insisting on having seen or heard something is sometimes sufficient to thwart violence.

INTIMATE BETRAYAL
Heute wär ich mir lieber nicht begegnet:
"Wouldn't you go crazy?"[19]
Herta Müller's novels on the Romanian dictatorship are inspired by her own biography, located at the borderlands between the Romanian and the German cultures and marked by her having been under the Securitate's surveillance—for her writing and for belonging to critical cultural circles. In both works discussed here, her genre of choice is autofiction: autobiographical details, which she introduces in essays and interviews, also emerge in her fiction, so much so that a rich intertextuality defines the relationship between the autobiographical publications and her novels (Marven 2013). Pace some of her interpreters, the point of her fiction is not to provide an accurate, "true" picture of the past but to make it imaginable for those who have not—or at least not fully—shared that past: by closely capturing sensorial, emotional, and material details, the fictional text makes the situation conceivable and palpable to the reader,

potentially triggering "a mad rush through the head" (Müller 2017, 98)—
her metaphor for the cognitive, emotional, and sensorial effect the aesthetic encounter with her text would ideally inspire. Therefore, her novels
support this book's project at the level of intention.

The novels discussed in this section deal with proximate betrayal from
the perspective of the victim, in particular its corrosive effect on the
basic armature of hope. They both feature Müller's innovative uses of
metaphor—that bring her close to the surrealists—as well as her twisted
temporality, lack of a clear plotline, and the blurring of the border between the imaginary and reality (Eddy 2013)—all of which are meant to
facilitate the reader's trip into her disjointed world. Given the mystify-
cation of reality and the subversion of language characteristic of authoritarianism, metaphorical language is, for Müller, more apt at capturing
the truth of her experience.

Both novels discussed here are written in a sharp and urgent prose,
made of short, tempestuous sentences that are often poetic and sometimes
aphoristic, congealing Müller's learning to cope with her circumstances.
In both books, she moves back and forth between two tasks. On the one
hand, she chronicles the effects of fear and betrayal on hope, and in particular the narrator's obsessive examination of herself and her surrounding
objects as a survival mechanism. Via her plurisensorial analyses, Müller
induces the reader into a world where those who had experienced betrayal
and were subjected to police surveillance need to develop a hypervigilance:
once interrogations start, both novels' protagonists—modeled on Müller
herself—can no longeer live mechanically, unreflectively, distractedly,
naturally. Once betrayed, her perceptions had to be deautomatized, and
thus the "alien gaze" was born. This metaphor refers to the habit of scru-
tinizing oneself, everything, and everyone compulsively, out of the fear of
being caught or betrayed again.[20] The effects of the radical contriction of
hope's prospects are thus captured in their complex penetration of both
the psyche and the body: fear becomes integral to the victim's cognitive
functioning, emotional responses, and bodily hexis. On the other hand,
Müller records everyday conversations, behaviors, fragments of songs,
graffiti, petty fights, and mundane details of life in student dorms, factories, post offices, hairdressers, apartments, and streetcars—to appre-
hend life under normalized, long-term ecological violence, including the

everyday complicities and indifference that made it both possible and bearable. Against this ordinary background of alienated sociality and widespread, pragmatic accommodationism, she foregrounds the specific experience of proximate betrayal, as experienced from within the positionality of an ethnic (German) minority woman.

Heute wär ich mir lieber nicht begegnet (*Astăzi mai bine nu m-aș fi întâlnit cu mine însămi*; *The Appointment*), published in 1997, is one of her most accessible novels. It accounts for a morning in the life of a woman, who is also the narrator, who had been summoned for an interrogation by the Securitate. The reason is her trying to smuggle abroad marriage proposals addressed to Italian men, by hiding little notes in the pockets of trousers produced for export in the textile factory she works for. We learn that this is one in a series of interrogations, which have taken a heavy psychological and physical toll on her. The title in the original German and in Romanian translation—roughly translated as "Today I Wish I Hadn't Met Myself"—hints at the extreme distress she experiences in facing her own terror.

Readers accompany her as she prepares for the appointment and travels to the Securitate headquarters. Müller takes us on a tram trip in the Bucharest of the 1980s, via the emotions, sensorial responses, and memories of the horrified narrator. The text's power to simultaneously evoke the ordinary and register the maddening fear of the main character seduce the reader into her lonely reality and into learning, alongside her, various coping strategies. The novel thus offers a prosthetic experience of entrenched anxiety that feeds a permanent state of alertness and suspicion and that, in undermining hope, reduces the potential for solidarity and resistant action.

Carefully observing and accounting for the surrounding materiality gives the hunted woman some measure of control over her own life. The protagonist superstitiously wears the same green blouse and eats a walnut before each interrogation. She always carries a toothbrush and a towel to interrogations, a precaution in case she is arrested. Her preparations for the interrogation are gender-specific, given that the humiliations to which she is normally subjected by her tormentor are also gender-specific. She obsessively counts the telegraph poles and houses between her home and the police station and closely observes the other passengers on the tram, what they wear, how they move, what they say. Müller thus reveals how objects anchor and channel her thoughts and emotions: the character inhabits a materiality that is not inert. Clothes, makeup, food, plants, animals, and landscapes assault her senses, exacerbating her worries, though sometimes they soothe the mind and bring temporary relief: focusing perceptively on the surrounding matter keeps fear under control and sustains a meager hope that she will survive the interrogation.

Traced against this background of unbearable tension, the devastating effects of various proximate betrayals—by neighbors and lovers—are brought to the fore with full force, in a simultaneously captivating and perturbing story. Via flashbacks, we learn how the protagonist ended up in this situation: she had been betrayed by an office mate, Nelu, with whom she had a brief affair, but whose love was unrequited. The narrator confided in him about her—preposterous—plans to marry an Italian and leave the country. Soon after, the interrogations begin, the result of Nelu's betrayal, who, out of sheer jealousy and sexual frustration, informed the authorities. All emigration fantasies are swiftly and permanently smothered. As we shall see, this experience of a lover's betrayal will influence how the narrator reads reality from then on.

The only consolation for the bitter disappointment is Paul, a man she meets by chance, falls in love with, and marries. Their love story enables both to temporarily suspend fear, driving about the town on the back of his red motorcycle. He works in a factory, from which he steals materials to illegally manufacture TV antennae, which he sells on the black market. Because of this, he has a run-in with the police, but nothing seems to follow. As the narrator attends her regular Securitate appointments, Paul shares her anxiety and supports her psychologically, though he resorts to heavy drinking to cope. The only other source of psychological support is Lili, the narrator's best friend, who is eventually killed while attempting to cross the border illegally. When this happens, Paul remains the narrator's only anchor—the man with whom she shares a delicate aspiration: that the future will not get worse.

The negative psychological effects of surveillance are aggravated by the realization that it is deeply embedded in the protagonist's immediate lifeworld. Of all the betrayals that dot the novel and undermine the protagonist's trust in the world, one is particularly striking because of its routinized character. An elderly neighbor—a man caring for his ill wife—one day approaches her to say he had been asked to report on her comings and goings by the Securitate. When she suggests that he could have refused, he is deeply surprised that she could even consider such a thing. One gets the impression that informing gives some meaning to his otherwise monotonous, unhappy life. Self-importantly, he even reproaches her for the hassle of having to write daily reports and is particularly upset that he must buy, at his own expense, the necessary notebooks—he had already finished two. At no moment does it occur to him that his concern for the cost of the notebooks is petty, a definitive proof of complete alienation from his neighbor. Given the stability of the political order, all thoughts of solidarity and resistance appear to have been banished, and complicity develops interstitially and habitually, in ways that sabotage the possibility of imagining a different future.

To throw him off, the narrator buys him a new notebook—sure that she would morally "paralyse" him (Müller 2014, 215)—that is, force him to see right from wrong. She gets a large math notebook, which she delivers to his door. Her gesture turns out to be painfully naive: he refuses her "gift", not because it induced a moment of lucidity or shame but because the notebook was too big to fit in his pocket, and was therefore inconvenient while he was haunting the building, watching her. The naturalization of complicity and the moral estrangement between neighbors is reliable, insensitive to shaming gestures. Betrayal thus penetrates the intimate layers of the protagonist's life, leaving her isolated and depending on an ever-smaller number of people to nurture and support her already fragile trust in the world.

The narrator's resistance to her interrogator's pressures to admit her "guilt" has negative repercussions on Paul. He is involved in an accident— his motorcycle was hit by a truck and the only person who came to his aid was a passerby, an elderly man. Analyzing the event in the apartment, the narrator remembers that one of her interrogator's generic threats was that "road accidents often happen." They decide to only use public transport to avoid unnecessary risks. Paul takes the damaged motorcycle to the scrap-metal market, where he sells it to the same elderly man who helped him when the accident happened—a coincidence that raises some passing suspicion.

As the tram approaches its destination, the woman's anxiety intensifies. Because of a trivial incident, the tram cannot stop at the right station and she cannot get out. Looking through the window, struggling to make her way to the door, she sees Paul and his red motorcycle in a courtyard, sharing a laugh with the elderly man to whom he had supposedly sold it. The sight petrifies both narrator and reader. Had Paul been lying and betraying his wife all this while? Had he been in cahoots with the new owner of the motorbike? Was the elderly man a Securitate officer? Why was Paul in that courtyard, shining his motorcycle? The novel gives no answers and ends with the narrator's tense laughter and a question: "Haha, wouldn't you go crazy?" (2014, 233).

Müller centers the theme of proximate betrayal, its multiple agents, and their various motivations—ranging from petty jealousy to thoughtlessness—as well as the debilitating effect it has on victims' experiences and actions. Nelu informs on his colleague's plans to emigrate out of romantic disillusionment, oblivious to the repercussions this will have on her life. The neighbor is driven by a misguided sense of duty and respect for authority—but also sheer boredom—at a time when political change seemed unimaginable. In Müller's novel, traitors are located at different degrees of proximity to the main character, and, while betrayal by lovers is life-changing in its devastating effects, the matter-of-fact complicity of her neighbor leaves her despairing.

Perhaps most importantly, The Appointment invites the reader to grapple with how much more terrifying the anticipation of betrayal is under conditions of alienated sociality. It is not clear whether Paul had betrayed her or whether the narrator merely imagined it, panicking on a particularly stressful day. Having lost her friend, Lili, she kept clinging to Paul as the only scaffold for strength in her otherwise hopeless life. Was he fed up with how her interrogations obliterated their chances of happiness and endangered him? Was he angry at how her refusal to cower to the Securitate condemned them to a life in terror, that only alcohol could make bearable? Had he given up on her? Or was he in that courtyard just to see how his beloved motorcycle had been refurbished? Was he even there at all? Whether seeing him was a fear-induced hallucination or an accurate perception, the effect was certain: a horrific, sharp pain that makes the narrator—as well as the reader—struggle with doubt, wondering how she could still remain sane. When intimates become informers, it is a life-shattering experience, that cannot but inform all future relations, infusing them with suspicion and a complete severing of the anchors of hope: when fear structures one's habitus, one learns perhaps to always expect betrayal.

However, even if betrayal brings one close to madness, the second work by Müller analyzed here shows that it does not necessarily extinguish love.

The Thicket of Love and Disappointment: *Herztier*

Herztier (*Animalul inimii*; *The Land of Green Plums*), first published in German in 1994, accomplishes several objectives for this project. First, it highlights how even the most reflective resisters fall prey to complicity, cowardice, and despair, while beneficiaries of the system can sometimes be reliably solidary with its opponents. Second, it short-circuits any temptation to moralistically demonize intimate traitors by revealing their ambiguous motives and changing behavior over time. Perhaps most importantly, Müller also compels us to see how hate can never fully erase the love that precedes proximate betrayal—and in this sense, as I show below, this novel takes off where *The Appointment* ended. Third, while *Herztier* helps us understand the role friendship plays in scaffolding the hopes of impure resisters, it also reveals its vulnerability: Müller induces us into a world of tension, illuminating how fear can produce extraordinary—and unwanted—levels of intimacy.

Narrated in the first person, the novel features two women friends, the same unnamed narrator modeled on Müller herself and her colleague Tereza; three male artists who are the narrator's friends—Kurt, Edgar, and Georg; a secret police agent; and a few other minor characters. The narrator and her artist friends engage in a variety of cultural activities that get them in conflict with the authorities. Müller's characteristic choppy, short sentences help the reader enter a life lived *à bout du souffle*, in terrifying fear and hyperlucid introspection. The juxtaposition of lyrical reflections about suicide, suspicion, and happiness and the naturalistic reconstruction of mundane details simultaneously highlight resisters' loneliness and their longing for an ordinary normality. Snippets of Romanian folk songs and poems[21] are deployed throughout to capture thoughts, emotions, and memories in flashback, or to reconstruct the atmosphere of a specific place and time. Lastly, the original verses that Müller attributes to the four artists who cryptically express dissent perhaps best exemplify her own caring mnemonic labor, aiming to recuperate language from its ideological colonization.

The narrator and her three male friends are brought together by their politics and artistic practices of resistance and critique, their German ethnicity, their disdain for their fathers' shared past in the SS, and the suicide of one of their dorm mates, Lola. Lola's death is triggered by an unwanted pregnancy following a liaison with one of the local (married) party leaders. To cover up for him, the Communist leadership expulses Lola from the party postmortem, under the pretense that suicide was incomprehensible in a country where happiness was guaranteed under the ministration of the supreme leader.

The general meeting organized to exclude Lola from the party prompts a crisis in the narrator: she is shocked by the unanimous standing ovations the party leaders got from the audience when they announced the expulsion. The absurdity of this collective acclamation—in which she herself participated mechanically—leads her to reflect on everyone's complicity with the regime, all frantically applauding, out of fear, opportunism, or cowardice: "The mind cannot grapple with something like this," concludes Georg, as they struggle to make sense of this event that exposed everyone—including themselves, as critics of the regime—as living variably complicitous lives.[22] This revealing event rendered visible resisters' ongoing struggle to find a balance between a powerless, raging indignation and a competing, voluptuous desire to enjoy a meaningful private life—a struggle rarely legible in heroic accounts of self-sacrifice.

The narrator shares a personal but also intellectual and political friendship with the three men, and a close, loving relationship with Tereza, a Romanian colleague whose father's importance and prestige as "official" artist is hinted at from the beginning. Georg, Kurt, Edgar, and the narrator write poems and songs, document instances of political repression, and read banned books—all in a hopeless attempt to at least marginally irritate and antagonize surveillants, whom the narrator labels "the cemetery makers."[23] Aware of their own impotence, the four nonetheless feel a compulsion to stay true to themselves. All three are surveilled, harassed, interrogated, and assaulted by the secret police, though their punishments and humiliations are gender-specific.

To enable the reader to grasp the acute fear they lived with and its effects on their friendship, Müller uses the metaphor of "heart's animal"—which is the novel's title in German and in the Romanian translation. The narrator's senile grandmother had taught her that everyone's heart was an animal and that hers was a mouse, one that ran all day long, always tired. Reflecting in her essays on the unadulterated joy of surviving another interrogation, Müller argues that this metaphor was best equipped for capturing "the lust for life inside the fear of death" (2017, 64). The narrator learns that the frightened heart's animal must be held under control and that, in general, it could be handled better in friends' company:

> Because we were afraid, Edgar, Kurt, Georg and I were always, everyday together. We sat at the table, but fear remained so personal, in each of our heads, the fear we had each brought within us to the meeting. We laughed a lot to hide it from the others. But fear is uncontrollable. When you keep a straight face, it sneaks in your voice. When you manage to keep a straight face and a steady voice . . . it sits somewhere, just outside your skin. It lies about you, you can see it in the nearby objects.
>
> We could see whose fear was where, because we had known each other for so long. We often couldn't stand one other, because we depended so much on each other. We felt the need to exchange insults. (2016a, 76–77)

Friendship nurtures their small resistances and the hope in a meaningful political change, but also—and perhaps especially—enables them to stay sane. And yet, the text vividly emphasizes the toll fear took on friendship and on a group of resisters that fell radically short of both the intellectual and armed avatars of heroism that colonized the Romanian mnemonic space after 1989. In sharing fear, each of them became fully transparent to the others, in ways that threatened the integrity of their selves: "Through that fear we had seen, more than was permissible, inside each other" (2016a, 77). Such exposure could only be made manageable with difficulty. All four friends lucidly admit the role the others played in nurturing their hopes, derisory as they were. They acted for each other, often motivated by love—rather than a commitment to a lofty and abstract idea of freedom—contrary to what the regulative ideals prescribed. Yet anxiety put a painful strain on the relationship, especially since friendship could never be a surrogate for their lost jobs, for material comfort, for being unable to express themselves artistically in freedom—things that these impure resisters also longed for, their "lust for life inside the fear of death."

A specific episode captures this double-edged nature of friendship for the resisters: following his betrayal by a lover, Georg is brutally beaten by the police.[24] He shuns his friends and goes straight to the passport service to submit an application—longing for an exit, which would inevitably constitute a different type of betrayal. He tells them afterward: "I did not want to hear your words, meant to calm me down . . . I did not want to hear those soothing sentences coming out of your mouths. I hated you then, tormented as I was, I could not have possibly seen you. Even the thought of you drove me mad. I wanted to vomit, to expunge you and myself from my life, because I knew how much we depended on each other." (2016a, 202)

In including Georg's desire to give up, his moment of cowardice, his affirmation of himself outside resistance, his wish to be free of all political commitments and of the friendship that bound him to those commitments, Müller disrupts implausible investments in ideals of steadfast, courageous opposition, but also, perhaps most importantly, perceptively qualifies our trust in the nurturing power of relationality under radical conditions of repression.

Tereza's ambiguous character contributes to Müller's resisting a different temptation: to demonize betrayal. Tereza is no self-conscious resister, and yet her actions offer respite and support to the four who assumed a more openly critical stance. She enjoys life, is passionate about fashion, and talks incessantly about anything but politics. She resists joining the party, sarcastically telling local leaders that her political consciousness had not yet developed fully. Under her father's protective shadow, Tereza enjoys great material benefits, reserved for the notables of the regime. She has breast cancer, which she decides to ignore, out of a sheer incapacity to deal psychologically with the disease.

The narrator loves her company, as the moments spent with Tereza constitute a reprieve from her heightened anxiety. While she knows little about Teresa and has a hunch her father might be collaborating with the Securitate, she trusts her to keep their antiregime poems and banned books in hiding. She tells Tereza the story of her interrogations, the humiliations and cruelty with which the political police treated them all. The narrator is fearful for Tereza, lest she should be punished for their friendship. When she is fired for refusing to collaborate with the police, Tereza proves loyal. While a beneficiary of the regime, Tereza is thus reliably solidary: she violates the interdiction to have any contact with the "suspect," mobilizes her contacts to find her an alternative source of income, and, when pressure is mounting on her to join the party, she showers the assembly with sarcasm. While not politically motivated, Tereza's actions effectively pierce the structure of authority in ways that have important positive effects on the four friends' chances of survival. Needless to say, there is no space for Tereza's small resistances in hegemonic mnemonic imaginaries.

The narrator, Georg, and Edgar eventually leave for Germany. Georg and Kurt die soon after. Tereza obtains the right to visit the narrator in Berlin. We learn she eventually summoned the courage to get treatment for cancer and is as vivacious as ever. However, upon arriving, she admits she only managed to travel because she agreed to spy on the narrator at the behest of the secret police. This confession is experienced as an instance of world-shattering treachery. Tereza suggests that they fabricate together a story for the surveillants. The narrator is torn between her deep love and commitment to Tereza and her utter disappointment. It is only upon finding out that Tereza's betrayal had gone much further—she had copied her apartment's key to hand it over to secret agents active in Germany—that she sends her away. The sense of loss, however, is doubled by an incapacity to fully let go of the friendship: "I wanted to tear the love out of my chest, throw it on the floor and trample on it. Then, I would have quickly lain there, next to it, so that it could sneak back into my head, through my very eyes" (2016a, 148).

Müller thus refuses to read disloyalty moralistically. Her affection for Tereza, Tereza's prior friendship, and the knowledge of her impending death makes it difficult to pass uncompromising judgment. Six months after this fateful visit, Tereza dies.[25] Her death is no relief to the narrator, for love had never fully given way to hatred, despite the betrayal. Müller captures the women's relationship over time and via the metaphor of the "thicket," a complex, ambiguous organic growth, from which friendship could not be fully banished, despite everything: "Tereza's death hurt me as if I had two heads, bumping into each other. One was full of the severed love, the other full of hate. I would have liked the love to grow back. It did, like a thicket of grass and straws mixed together" (2016a, 232).

Müller thus disturbs the automatism of any stark condemnation by following Tereza's actions over time: the love and faithfulness preceding the betrayal cannot be forgotten and erased, no trenchant verdict is possible. The imagery of a thicket of love and hate possibly provides us with the most powerful evocation of the beliefs, feelings, and sensations invited by proximate betrayal, given the complexity and temporality of human relationships. In introducing the thicket, Müller invites her readers to approach betrayal ethically but always allowing for ambivalence and inconclusiveness.

'When we are silent, we are unpleasant . . . when we speak, we become ridiculous"—these are Edgar's words that end the novel. Having survived the dictatorship and their own suicidal thoughts, the remaining two friends mourn and remember their losses. Trying to capture in words their experience is ridiculous, for words are painfully insufficient. At the same time, silence is impossible, for it alienates the survivors from each other, rendering their connection even more fragile. Müller thus helps us calibrate our faith in the power of relational scaffolding: friendship is vulnerable to fear and, on its own, sometimes insufficient to sustain resistance. However, even when radically imperiled by proximate betrayal, love's tendrils can—and often will—endure, wound around the human heart.

YEARNING FOR HEROES

Medalia de onoare: Mnemonic Pliability

Călin Peter Netzer's films won several important international prizes—including the Golden Bear in 2013—consolidating his international reputation as a key voice in the Romanian New Wave, in which Corneliu Porumboiu, whose film I discuss below, is also included. The filmmakers subsumed under the New Wave enjoyed extraordinary international success and acclaim on the festival circuit. Their stylistic staples are "a cinema of duration, contemplative hyperrealist visuals, slice-of-life plots, loose causation, bold (hand-held) camera, and scarce musical commentary" (C. Pârvulescu 2013, 367). The choice of realism by the New Wave auteurs after decades of regimented Socialist realism puzzled critics and viewers alike. The minimalist aesthetics (resulting also from economic constraints) and the thematic "miserabilist" focus on ordinary individuals' social suffering (be it in relation to the Communist dictatorship or the wild capitalist experiment that followed) cemented their reputation as refuseniks: their efforts to record ordinary, difficult, and ambiguous experiences and wrest them from forgetting sat uncomfortably with a collective longing to move on and start anew. Romanian viewers found the films too depressing, too close to home, alienating and even antinational (Uricaru 2012; Şerban 2010). *À contre-courant*, the New Wave "redeems realism on the basis of its revolutionary potential, proving that realism at its best does establish a relation between experience and memory" (Ieta 2010, 24). As we shall see, as aesthetic refuseniks, both Netzer and Porumboiu resisted the temptation to center "'great men in crucial moments of history' narratives and experimented with more artistic approaches, in which the protagonists' agency, sense of history, and bravery were called into question" (C. Pârvulescu 2013, 365). Treating their characters compassionately, "warts and all", while navigating everyday life, these directors caringly constructed alternative vistas on the complexities of action, responsibility and memory.

In *Medalia de onoare* (*The Medal of Honor* [2009]), Netzer deploys this aesthetics to tell the story of Ion I. Ion, a seventy-five-year-old retired doctor, whose life is dramatically changed when he receives—mistakenly—a medal of honor for his supposed military exploits in World War II. The film provides a powerful reflection on the vulnerability of memory to individual and collective mystification, foregrounding the mnemonic double erasure driving this book's inquiry via its main character, his betrayal, and his fabricated heroism.

The plot is set in the winter of 1995, six years after the fall of the Berlin Wall. Establishing shots of Ion's dark, crammed, and cold apartment transport the viewer into the turbulent first years of the transition, marked by severe economic instability. Ion is struggling financially. He lives with his wife, Nina, who has not spoken to him in years. The viewer gradually learns that this is due to Ion's having delivered his own son—Cornel—to the Communist miliţia because he was planning to leave Romania illegally. As a consequence, Cornel did time in prison. Upon being released, he eventually emigrated to Canada, where he built a successful career as a doctor.

Hit by the social costs of the brutal transition to capitalism, the couple barely make ends meet—a typical situation for the 1990s. They are shown moving mechanically about the small apartment, alienated from each other, suffering from cold, in a darkness barely pierced by the screen of the TV. The main character's name—Ion. I. Ion/ John J. John—hints at his ordinariness. Their lives are joyless and hopeless, the economic difficulties amplified by the conflict in the family. Ion has a bottle of alcohol hidden in the bathroom, from which he drinks secretly. Cornel calls his mother regularly, but refuses to speak to his father, despite the latter's continuous insistence—an exclusion powerfully captured cinematically by Netzer's intelligent use of camera angles.

Everything changes when, one gray morning, Ion receives a letter asking him to collect a medal from the Defence Ministry. He is initially puzzled and thinks it a mistake—he could not remember committing any acts of heroism, something he confesses to his silent wife. He goes to the Ministry to make inquiries but fails to get an explanation. Ion takes the medal to a pawnbroker to have it assessed—more interested in how much money he would get for it, understandable given the couple's precarious situation. Next, he undertakes an investigation at the War Veterans' Association, hoping for some edification. There he meets a retired general who had also received a medal for having destroyed a large Russian pillbox at Sevastopol in 1941. It is important to note this took place while Romania was fighting on Germany's side. Hearing the general's story, Ion decides to write a letter of complaint, asking for the medal to be revoked.

However, sleepless at night, he reminisces about the war. He digs out the letters he sent his wife from the front, looking for clues as to any potential heroic acts. While Nina disdains his searches, he reads old missives, recalling his youth, their love, and his camaraderie with fellow soldiers. He gets stuck on a story he narrated in a letter, according to which he and two other soldiers chased some German soldiers and took over their tank. The story is told ambiguously and does not support any clear case for heroism. Ion is undeterred: he becomes determined to find evidence of his merit—along clear masculinist militarist lines. This newly developed conviction takes him to his former comrades' homes, who, however, also fail to provide any corroborating evidence.

Ion rehearses the story in his head over and over until gradually, it becomes a true story of heroism. Ambiguous details become certainties: he can even visualize the tank's takeover. His courage becomes increasingly evident in his mind, and shots of him looking at the city's war memorials with teary eyes through streetcar windows mark his transformation into a hero, ready to tell of his "exploits" to anyone who would listen: the kids in the neighborhood, the heating engineer, his wife's rummy partners.

The culmination is an invitation to attend a commemorative ceremony and meet the country's president. The local community is very proud, their contagious sentimentality betraying a strong yearning for heroism—a much-needed analgesic for the disappointing post-Communist present. Ion is extremely happy, his insipid life suddenly turned exciting: the director catches him in head shots, rehearsing his address to the president in the intimacy of his bathroom, deeply emotional, watching himself in the mirror. Things get even better when Cornel unexpectedly announces that he would visit with his family for Christmas—the stars appear to be aligning for Ion.

Catastrophe strikes when the postman delivers a letter that confirms his initial suspicions: the medal was not his. A typo was involved: the correct name of the recipient was Ion *J*. Ion and not Ion *I*. Ion. Ion is devastated as he had pinned all his hopes—including that of reconciling with his son—on this medal, which, he thought, would have redeemed him in everyone's eyes. By now heavily emotionally invested in his own heroism, he visits Ion *J*. An antimilitarist who had lost an arm in the war, Ion *J*. condescendingly renounces the medal and even provides Ion *I*. with a letter confirming he could keep it. The Ministry—to Ion's despair—does not accept this letter. Panicked, he threatens to go on a hunger strike, but to no avail, as the medal is confiscated. Despairing, he buys a fake medal from the pawnbroker.

The film can be read in two interrelated keys. First, foregrounding Ion as a social type, this is a story of a family drama against the background of the wild capitalism of the 1990s in Eastern Europe. Ion is recognizable as a rhinoceros: while courteous and mild-mannered, he displays entrenched patriarchal attitudes within his family, is unreflective about his own betrayal, has a great capacity for self-delusion, and is ultranationalist—he disapproves of his son's newly acquired Canadian citizenship, of his grandson's being called Joshua, and of his poor Romanian, and he votes for a far-right party. Through characterization, Netzer gestures toward the rabid nationalist doxa that marked both communism and the fascism that preceded it, and that continued to colonize the mnemonic and political space after 1989. Ion had surrendered his son to the Communist authorities to prevent him from leaving the country—a decision that could have cost Cornel his life. Six years later, Ion seems unable to understand the gravity of his deeds and thinks his wife's silent treatment is disproportionate punishment. Even without this painful episode from the past, the conflict between Ion and Cornel is very typical of the time and the place, translating the differences between the liberal, cosmopolitan youth and the older, nationalist generation. Cornel judges his father harshly, accuses him of having collaborated with the secret service—and while Ion initially denies it, he eventually proudly admits: "of course, they approached me." He seems to be unaware that he is thus vindicating the son's ire and confirming the viewer's impression that he is, indeed, an unreflective accomplice of the repressive apparatus. When he reprimands Cornel by saying "you have learnt nothing in prison," not for a second doubting that Communist prisons were places of instruction, the viewer is left perplexed.

Gradually, however, we understand that love had also played a part in his denouncing Cornel. The film refuses reductive demonologies and avoids the temptation to scapegoat Ion: similarly to Müller's novels, it highlights complicity's multiple determinations. Thoughtless, cruel, and selfish, Ion acts within a shrunken horizon of hope, despairing at the thought of losing his beloved son for good: nobody suspected that the Eastern Block would collapse a couple of years after Cornel's attempted escape. Ion is shown empathetically, as an old father, punished relentlessly by his wife, rejected vehemently by a son whom he misses dearly, a looser of the political transition. Netzer thus contextualizes Ion's betrayal, making it less horrific. Cornel seems to eventually forgive his father's actions—though the medal does not appear to play any role in it. The end is redeeming as a possible reconciliation is hinted at in the awkward embraces of the reunited father and son.

The film can also be read as an allegory of the political mystification of the past for the purposes of the present. Ion embodies the double erasure at the core of this book: he had been an accomplice of the regime, he denounced his own son to the authorities, and, in the disappointing present, he fabricates a biography of a hero-elect, in which he invests heavily for self-interested reasons. His personal journey reflects the institution of public memory. The medal is for heroism displayed during World War II—and Ion's ambiguous story takes place in 1945—after Romania switched sides and joined the Allies. Official memory is, however, indiscriminate: the government awarded medals for heroism tout court, irrespective of the context in which it was supposedly shown. "Heroic" fighting on Germany's side[26] is equivalent to fighting on the side of the Allies: an empty and blanket vision of "heroism" guides the policy. Ion's voting for a far-right party—as well as his disdain for his son's Canadian life—constitutes another hint at the continuation of patriarchal hypernationalism into the 1990s. Being awarded a medal by the former Communist apparatchik–turned–democratic president, Ion Iliescu, does not faze him; no ideological incompatibility disturbs his pride. Netzer's nod to Bérenger's forewarning could not be clearer.

These details set the stage for the film's tackling the mechanisms of mystification. Netzer aptly shows how, if the stakes are high enough, the past becomes flexible and can be deployed for various purposes, by the individual and the community alike. He illuminates the need for a certain—heroic, clean, spotless, radically abstracted, and thus noncommittal—"version" of history for individuals and communities to emotionally and cognitively invest in, when the present is unfulfilling. Less cynical than Friang's Gérard, Ion is deeply touched when the president hands him the medal. His neighbors see him in a different light once he is invited to the presidential palace: they are willing to forget about his lapsed utility payments and even entrust him with passing a petition to the president. The neighborhood kids listen to his stories as if hypnotized. On the basis of scant and unreliable evidence, a whole edifice is built, and its creator begins to sincerely believe in its veracity. Provided he speaks confidently of his exploits, everyone believes him: his story sticks because it is yearned for.

Thus, avoiding both lamentation and moralistic indictments, *The Medal of Honor* adopts a complex multifocal lens to foreground heroism's powerful and dangerous lure. At the same time, nonetheless, Netzer reveals its emptiness and limited power when it comes to true reconciliation:

Ion's family's forgiveness has nothing to do with his medal. The film therefore amounts to an invitation to its viewers to take direct and honest responsibility for the configuration of their community's space of memory and actively nurture inclusive, welcoming relationships in the present.

The Elusive Revolution: *A fost sau n-a fost?*

Corneliu Porumboiu's work has received numerous international awards, including Cannes' Caméra d'Or for his 2006 *A fost sau n-a fost?* (*12:08 East of Bucharest*). Shot in a minimalist aesthetics—Şerban called it, "a type of auteur film with ready-made installation" (2010, 18)—the film powerfully tackles the processes by which an idealized image of heroic resistance colonizes communities' imaginaries, in ways that blind them to the much more complex realities of political transformation. Like Netzer's *Medal of Honor*, it illuminates the malleability of memory and the mechanisms through which history can be revised. However, Porumboiu pushes his caring aesthetics further: he foregrounds the inescapable plurivocality of political memory as the key obstacle to the satisfaction of an irrepressible yearning for clean slates and patented heroism. Through humor and a formal cinematic device, he compassionately records his ordinary characters' lives and shows them bickering, ranting, drinking, swearing, and lying—but also being honest, self-reflective, and humble. In doing so, he exposes mnemonic slippages, decelerates the spectators' socialized memory, and relativizes the official framework of remembrance by foregrounding dissension.

Based on a real experience and set in a provincial city in the country's northeast, the film chronicles a talk-show broadcast on the local TV station, on the occasion of the sixteenth anniversary of the fall of communism. In the first part of the film—filmed with a fixed camera—we follow the station's owner and talk-show host, the vain Jderescu, struggling to recruit participants for his "special edition." Porumboiu offers long, still shots of streets lined with uniform, modest apartment blocks, then cruises from one meticulously reconstructed dark, austere apartment to the next, in search of the ordinary individuals to be featured on the show. Jderescu ends up with two guests, Pişcoci—a lonely, retired widower— and Mănescu, a history teacher and notorious alcoholic. He packs them both in his car and heads to the studio under the gray, snow-heavy sky.

Jderescu is contoured as a typical patriarch, cared for by his obliging wife. A former textile engineer, he appears to be a nouveau riche with a penchant for petty authoritarianism. The TV station is his vanity project, in which he invests effort and emotional energy, harassing his staff, keeping a tight control on everything, and cutting off callers who disagree with him. He cultivates an intellectual image, pompously citing Hesiod and displaying busts of Plato and Aristotle on his bookcase, which also features a mythological dictionary—an early hint of the artificiality, arbitrariness, and ultimate absurdity of the theme at the center of the upcoming talk show. He has a young lover and harbors nationalist beliefs—he strictly forbids the playing of South American music on his station.

In contrast, medium, sustained closeups of Mănescu and Pişcoci reveal their loneliness and misery. Mănescu, severely indebted because of a serious drinking problem, is kept on a short leash by his wife. He borrows money from the local Chinese shopowner, with whom he has a good relationship, despite his racist drunken rants. He is very lenient with his pupils, and, before the camera starts rolling at the beginning of the talk show, he gulps some wine because "he is nervous." Pişcoci is an elderly widower who struggles to make ends meet. He longs for social contact and therefore jumps at the opportunity to play Santa at the school's Christmas show, spending some of the little money he has to buy a new costume from the Chinese shop.

While the first half of the film is dedicated to contouring the main characters and getting them in the TV studio, the second reconstructs the talk show itself, modeled on similar shows that debated the character of the Romanian "revolution" for many years after 1989: Did Romania experience a revolution or a coup? Was the revolt authentic or orchestrated from abroad? Were there genuine revolutionaries or only dupes and secret agents? These questions translate a deeply felt, enduring longing for clarity, courage, and a recovered sense of historical agency after decades of dictatorship—a longing the film masterfully reveals and sabotages at the same time.

To the Romanian viewer, the fictional talk-show's guiding question—whether the town's inhabitants participated or not in the 1989 revolution—is not ridiculous, nor is the participants' investment in it. The subordinate question at the center of the show—"Where were you on the 22nd of December, 1989?"—was obsessively asked post-1989, out of an irrepressible collective desire for a clear distinction between those who fought the dictatorship and those who conveniently watched the events on TV, between those who benefited from the regime and those who suffered because of it.

To decide whether there had been a revolution in their town, the talk-show participants had to establish that the town's folk came out to protest in the town's main square *before* the dictator's escape from Bucharest, at 12:08 on December 22, 1989—the exact date and time his helicopter took off from the government's building. It is the host's firm belief that, if they came out after 12:08, they merely celebrated freedom, as opposed to bringing it about—as authentic antiregime, heroic resisters, who assumed the risks of political struggle.

Mănescu rises to the occasion and tries to embody the heroic avatar: he claims that he and three colleagues—two of them conveniently dead, a third an emigrant to Canada—went to the square at 11:30, to fight against the "communist nightmare," afraid but driven by a strong sense of purpose. Porumboiu makes Mănescu the voice of the standard anti-Communist narrative. He claims they shouted antiregime slogans and threw rocks at the party headquarters, trying to break in and occupy it, but the secret police fought back. When asked how he could tell they were secret police, he says he knew one of them—named Bejan—because his child was a pupil in his class. Jderescu specifies that Bejan is a successful businessman—the film's allusion to the conversion of political capital into economic capital after 1989. Mănescu concludes the redeeming, emotion-ally satisfying story by claiming "we defeated them" just as the square was beginning to fill in with townsfolk, celebrating the dictator's flight. The town's reputation is saved: they were not mere witnesses, but active, heroic participants in the national drama.

The sense of relief is short-lived: Mănescu's claims are contested by a series of callers who, one by one, reject his narrative, some in neutral, others in unflattering language. The callers pluralize memory, reveal-ing its artificiality and its fragility to contestation. A woman claims she saw him drunk in the neighborhood bar at that crucial time. The party headquarters' doorman claims he saw nobody in the square until 12:30. Bejan, the supposed secret agent, calls to threaten Jderescu with a libel trial for allowing a drunkard to taint his name on TV. His tone is calm, authoritative, and paternalistic, calling the show's discussion "fairy tales to put kids to bed with"—simultaneously capturing the fictional aspect of memory-making and its vulnerability to naked power. Mănescu's only supporter is the Chinese shopowner, who confirms his trustworthiness, calling him "honest," the "kindest man in town," while admitting he had his flaws. Like Ion I. Ion, Mănescu becomes more and more somber, visibly disappointed that his credibility is challenged, as if his self-esteem depended solely on there having been a revolution in their town, with himself cast in the hero role, first on the "barricades."

When Pişcoci's turn to speak finally comes, he undermines all feverish attempts to satisfy the misguided search for the town's authentic, heroic participation in the revolution. He asks everyone to accept human cowardice and recognize that they went out after 12:08, that they watched the revolution on TV. He acknowledges the disproportionate, galvanizing role played by the indisputable popular revolts in Timişoara and Bucharest: he compares the revolution spreading from these two cities to the rest of the country to the Christmas lights that are gradually turned on all over their city, starting at the center and moving toward the periphery. He is completely frank about his own behavior that day: he had had a fight with his wife and spent his time trying to reconcile with her. He admits to feeling frustrated with the revolution, since the dictator had promised a large pay raise to appease the protesters. The raise was never implemented, to his deep regret, depriving him of the chance to take his beloved wife on a holiday. He admits to coming out after 12:08, and only to prove to his wife that he "could be a hero" and "wasn't afraid of communists." He invites everyone to admit they were in no way at the forefront of the struggle. As Pfeifer writes, "It is not contradictory for him to assume that a revolution can still be a revolution, even if not every revolutionary fought for freedom in the face of immanent tyranny" (2018). While the Chinese shopkeeper makes a compassionate plea for tolerance toward the self-certifying hero's sins and imperfections, Pişcoci's monologue injects him with a lethal dose of historical lucidity and reflexivity.

Throughout, humor—tender and humane, compassionate, not biting—is Porumboiu's weapon of choice for scoring important points about reductive, heroizing myths, their magnetism and radical distance from ordinary people's lived experiences of the revolution. While this is a "tough kind of film-making, that does not mince words" (Șerban 2010, 18), the director's aesthetic refusal is caring, not moralizing and cruel. The setup is theatrical: the three share a rectangular table, and a picture of their town's city center—so typical of Romania's Socialist architecture—serves as background. The actors are crammed in and look uncomfortable, rubbing shoulders and interrupting each other, to great comedic effect. To suggest the unreliability of political memory, Porumboiu has Jderescu pompously preface his show—in a stern and self-important voice—by discussing Plato's myth of the cave, wondering if 1989 marked a true exit from the cave or perhaps the entrance into a bigger one, where Romanians mistake a hay fire, once again, for the sun. The affected peroration is hilarious for its gratuity, but it also casts a first shadow on the determined yet impossible search for the unique truth/sun.

To reinforce this point, Porumboiu's diverse cast of idiosyncratic characters, both petty and noble, offer a multitude of perspectives on what happened—or didn't happen—at 12:08 in the town's main square. Their humorous bickering essentially illustrates a healthy plurality of political memories among ordinary people invited to confront a complex question. The partiality, heterogeneity, and instability of memory-making is also reflected in the shooting style of Jderescu's young and undisciplined cameraman, the object of his boss's permanent ire. In the second half of the film, the characters are static, seated in the studio, while the cameraman keeps playing with various frames, shifting arbitrarily and abruptly between wide and very narrow shots, refusing to use a camera stand, working at awkward angles and distances, as if in search for the elusive truth. He resists Jderescu's insistence on close-ups on his face—an attempt to dominate the conversation in typical rhinoceritic mode—and instead produces an image that is erratic, shaky, fragmented, and incomplete, as are the participants' certainties and claims to authenticity.

Deploying absurdity and laughter effectively, the film subverts the intransigence of heroic narratives and opens up the hermeneutical space to alternative, though less reassuring, truths. Notwithstanding the strong romantic pull of heroization, Porumboiu seductively sabotages its power, undermining all claims to glory. Pișcoci's deadpan, concluding words— "We each lived the revolution in our own way"—invite cognitive and emotional friction between the yearning for redemptive heroism, on the one hand, and less comforting yet more plausible accounts of historical agency, on the other.

CONCLUSIONS

In one of her interventions, Herta Müller stated: "In art, beauty is the thing that gets under the surface of things and that does not deceive, that does not conceal how complicated they are, but shows us how uncertain and unfathomable, and even how intolerable things are. Beautiful is the opposite of shallow. Aesthetically speaking, beauty and ugliness are the same" (Müller cited in Eke 2013, 99–100). Located within different genres and enjoying different degrees of international recognition, the works analyzed in this chapter have tracked the complicated, the uncertain, the unfathomable and the intolerable, serving as props for us to prosthetically inhabit—intellectually, but also affectively and sensorially—a resilient ecology of violence and its many disappointing aftermaths. A rich political, psychological, and material tapestry of the spectrum of involvement emerges from the six works discussed here, all of which relativized the standpoint from where official history is written and tried to pull us away from predictable scripts. In one of his interviews, Corneliu Porumboiu insightfully stated, "After the revolution, history textbooks featured two-three heroes, two-three villains, but never the view from below" (2007). This chapter will have provided multiple views "from below," diversifying the historical cast of characters and offering a kaleidoscopic picture of experienced history, thereby illuminating a range of interstitial, dynamic complicities and impure resistances.

Moreover, because of the specificity of the case, the caring refuseniks discussed in this chapter rendered my theoretical framework more complex by shedding important light on several aspects of the double erasure. First, the alienated sociality—social atomization coupled with moral disconnect—brought about by enduring systemic violence fed routinized practices of complicity, so much so that we can perhaps speak of a habitus of dissimulation, which had, of course, devastating effects on the possibility of solidarity. The role surveillance played in the Romanian repressive apparatus and its sophisticated control strategies make this aspect stand out in contrast to the other two cases. The most deleterious effect of alienated sociality was perhaps the normalization of an expectation of betrayal, which structured the experience and psyche of the victims in ways that led to a second level of alienation—from oneself, via the development of an "alien gaze." Sustained practices of self-monitoring and hypervigilance, of mind and body training for safety became essential in light of the constant administration of fear.

However, second, the works analyzed here concretize the ways in which minor resistances and refusals can sometimes successfully pierce the structure of authority and prevent the normalization of percepticide. While their effect on the system is limited, they can save lives or at least make the everyday more bearable and more humane at the micro level. For this reason, they are important to recognize and remember, even if—or perhaps especially if—they are sometimes undertaken by individuals associated *with* or benefiting *from* repression.

Third, artistic renditions of intimate betrayal—the most painful type one could experience—highlight the limits of reading complicity in an intransigent moral key. By revealing that disappointment does not necessarily erase the love that preceded it and that both emotions can coexist sabotages any punitive, act-based, and temporally static framework for reading even the most shocking forms of complicity.

Lastly, the "lust for life inside the fear of death" powerfully articulates perhaps the key aspect of resisters' impurity—their all-too-normal desire to survive and to lead meaningful, rich private lives. As Müller (2017, 56) writes in her essays: "An impetuous pity for those it [death] had touched, that spontaneous compassion that lasts for a while, then goes away. That petrification, fingers curled, nails painfully stuck in your palm, lips tight while you watched some unknown being arrested, beaten, crushed, in plain sight. Then you go away, your mouth dry, throat burning, walking fast, as if somebody had pumped fetid air into your stomach and your legs. You feel a languorous guilt that you cannot stop anything bad from happening to the others and a wicked happiness that you had not been the punished one." Making such desires vivid aesthetically suspends the collective and individual yearning for superhuman exemplars of courage, patriotism and self-abnegation and redirects it toward a vision of resistance that is more tangible, more relatable and therefore more inspiring.

As in the French case, this chapter did not exhaust the rich artistic production about this period and cannot recognize all its caring refuseniks.

Films such as Cristian Mungiu's *4 luni, 3 săptămăni, şi 2 zile* (*4 Months, 3 Weeks, and 2 Days* [2007]), the collective *Amintiri din Epoca de Aur* (*Tales from the Golden Age* [2009]), and Radu Muntean's *Hârtia va fi albastră* (*The Paper Will Be Blue* [2006]), as well as Cătălin Mitulescu's *Cum mi-am petrecut sfârşitul lumii* (*The Way I Spent the End of the World* [2006]), would have opened alternative vistas on the "ordinary swamp" of the dictatorship, its multiple inhabitants, and its memory. In literature, Norman Manea's collections of short stories, Daniel Bănulescu's *Cel mai bun roman al tuturor timpurilor* (*The Best Novel Ever* [2008]), or Herta Müller's *Der Mensch ist ein großer Fasan auf der Welt* (*Omul este un mare fazan pe lume*; *The Passport* [1986]) could have similarly been mined for the ample resources they provide for reorienting the mnemonic imagination. Nonetheless, while incomplete, the selection of works included in this chapter will have exemplified various instantiations of caring aesthetic refusal in a way that also enriches our theoretical matrices for understanding historical responsibility.

5 The Spectrum of Apartheid in South Africa

Against the background of settler colonialism, between 1948 and 1994 the principle of white-supremacist apartheid organized South Africans' sense of reality, perceptions, fears, and hopes and the material armature of their lives. The National Party (NP) won the elections in 1948, in coalition with the Afrikaner Party. Capitalizing on Afrikaner resentment in relation to the Anglo-Boer War and the two World Wars, NP deployed racist discourses foregrounding the Black "threat" to Afrikaner identity. While the entire political spectrum presupposed white supremacy, and segregation preexisted apartheid, it was NP that institutionalized a radical version thereof: supported by its cultural-ideological arm, the Afrikaner Broederbond (AB), the party whipped up white fears about the economic integration of Black labor into the economy and cities' texture, presenting itself as the guardian of white domination and purity. It swiftly abolished white representation for Black Africans and keenly translated white nationalism and religious particularism into legislation (Welsh 2010).

NP remained in power for forty-six years, facing only weak opposition from the United Party (UP), the Liberal Party (LP, from 1953) and the Progressive Party (PP, from 1959). All prime ministers and state presidents between 1948 and 1994 belonged to the racist AB (Fobi 2014, 81).

Newspapers such as *Die Burger* and *Der Volksblad* served as key propaganda vehicles. Initially, NP focused on consolidating its power through a series of electoral reforms that disenfranchised what it categorized as "Coloured" and "Indian" people and increased the white electorate by lowering the voting age (Welsh 2010). The Population Registration Act of 1950 entrenched racial lines, while the Group Areas Act regulated racial segregation in all administrative units, gravely affecting families and businesses catalogued as "Indian" and "Coloured." Black people had already been segregated geographically in townships since 1923. Subsequent Pass Laws—traced by Mahmood Mamdani (2015) to North American settler colonial policies—balanced white needs for "security" with white needs for cheap labor (Posel 1991; 2001). The legal infrastructure of white supremacy was thus laid out. Simultaneously, cultural apartheid was promoted under the guise of a return to traditional African political structures, the "bantustans," whose chiefs were subordinated to the state (Welsh 2010). An ecology of violence, apartheid determined every aspect of South Africans' life: access to public space, housing, work, public services (including education, health care, and transportation), sports, leisure, and family and intimate life.

Although the idea of a "master plan" for apartheid is contested (Posel 1991), as "Minister for Native Affairs" and then prime minister, Hendrik Verwoerd implemented increasingly strict policies of enforced segregation and disenfranchisement and relentlessly repressed Black resistance. After Verwoerd's assassination in 1966, John Vorster took a more pragmatic position (Welsh 2010, 84). His inviting white immigrants to the country aggravated the extreme Right, fearful for Afrikaner supremacy. Foreign investors were encouraged to open factories in the homelands, trying to limit Black presence in cities, not very successfully. The demands of the economy triggered many concessions, given that the majority of the workforce was Black.

Vorster was followed in 1978 by P. W. Botha, a meek reformer, who legally recognized trade unions in 1979, removed the prohibition of interracial marriages and sex in 1985, and abolished the infamous Pass Laws in 1986 (Welsh 2010, 217). Transportation, hotels, amenities, beaches, and cinemas were slowly desegregated. In 1983, a tricameral parliament was proposed, with representation for whites and individuals classified as

"Indians" and "Coloured." This institutional setup—approved through a referendum—alienated both hard-core Afrikaner nationalists and the Black resistance. Public unrest intensified throughout the 1980s, against the background of international isolation. When F. W. de Klerk came to power in the last white elections in 1989, he faced massive mobilization, economic turmoil, and increasing international pressure. Against the background of widespread violence in the early 1990s, he finally reined in the security forces, liberated political prisoners—including Nelson Mandela—and entered complex and protracted negotiations with the ANC, which by then had become the key resistance organization. The Truth and Reconciliation Commission (TRC) was established soon after the first free elections and became an internationally renowned institutional experiment.

While a thorough account of complicity with and resistance to apartheid cannot be offered here, symmetrically to the other cases in this book, I highlight several faces on the spectrum, recognizing their complex social positionality. I start by sketching the structural, institutional infrastructure of complicity as part of an ecology of violence, in ways that confirm the limits of the hegemonic individualizing model.

The legislature and the judiciary translated the doxa of white supremacy, backed by an overblown security apparatus: "Whether it was the denial of fundamental rights of movement, expression, assembly, residence, association and so on; or the forced relocation of millions of dispossessed people, or the creation of 'independent states' recognized by no one, all such actions were clothed in the respectability of formal legislation" (Coleman 1998, 28). According to Motlhabi, laws could be classified as regulative laws constituting apartheid, punitive laws targeting those who violated regulative laws, and preventive laws making potential violations of regulative laws costly and difficult (1984, 29). Dissent was criminalized and emergency rule was liberally deployed (Madala 2000). Thus, Steve Biko's remarks on the legal underpinnings of the white supremacist order could not be more precise: "No average Black man [sic] can ever at any moment be absolutely sure that he is not breaking the law" (1987, 75).

Courts duly implemented apartheid laws and most judges supported white supremacy—despite ample opportunities to resist. Liberal judges were exceptional, and overall, the legal system was dominated by an arbitrary executive. Political trials, detentions without trial, and banishments were legally authorized (2000). The police had the legal right to break up public gatherings by force. Torture was institutionalized, the death penalty widely used, and basic rights irretrievably eroded. The Supreme Court supported the legislature and the executive in their agenda. The few jurists who refused appointment did so out of political conviction, whether antiapartheid or anti–death penalty; most preferred the more lucrative business of lawyer (Welsh 2010).

The term "securocracy" is used to describe the security apparatus, especially in the 1980s, when the fabricated myth of an imminent Communist attack justified its expansion (O'Brien 2010; Worden 2012). The "total strategy"—devised during Botha's administration—mandated extraordinary repressive measures, authorized intervention in neighboring countries, and garnered the support of western democracies in the fight against communism (Coleman 1998). The army participated in this "existential" fight (Worden 2012), and its mission was to destabilize anticolonial struggles and destroy exiled resistance cells, within and without South Africa. In the South African Defence Force (SADF)—the conscripted white military and anti-insurgency branch—the majority of soldiers were right-wing nationalists. Recruited already in schools and inculcated with a highly romanticized idea of protective masculinity that centered on aggressive armed fighting, white men underwent a hyperracialized process of training for combat (Cock 1991). White women were also important promoters of this ideology, within families but also as members of the SADF's support organizations, of the civil defense and commando units: seeking career opportunities, they accounted for 14 percent of the forces by 1991 (1991). In contrast, the "End the Conscription Campaign," which started in 1983 but got banned in 1988, gathered mostly English-speaking whites who criticized the conscription's role in exacerbating the conflict. Exile, conscientious objection, and suicide were more radical ways of resisting conscription, at a time when only a university degree offered a temporary reprieve.

Seventy percent of the members of the South African Police were thought to harbor white nationalist commitments (Coleman 1998). The Security Branch—an elite force within the police—often used torture and committed extrajudicial killings. The police developed networks of

informants who often helped disable resistance cells. In retaliation, resisters killed policemen, especially Black ones, seen as traitors. To understand the police's ideological outlook, it is useful to remember that the
extremist white supremacist Afrikaner Weerstandsbeweging (AWB) was
founded by an ex-policeman, Eugène Terre'Blanche, and included many
of his former colleagues (Welsh 2010). A culture of impunity and excess
flourished in the force, exacerbated by the repeated use of emergency
rule (Pauw 2017a). Death squads unofficially operated, dedicating themselves to the extermination or turning of antiapartheid activists (Pauw
2017b). Some of the squad members were documented psychopaths with
criminal records. The Vlakplaas—the most infamous squad, led by Eugene de Kock[1]—turned Black activists into agents for the regime (Jansen
2015; Binckes 2018), while the Civil Co-operation Bureau focused on the
elimination of ANC leaders and supporters, and the destruction of their
bases (O'Brien 2010).

Ideologically, the AB gathered key intellectuals and played a central
cultural and ideological role (Bloomberg 1990). AB started off as an all-
white, all-male, and all-Protestant (Calvinist) Afrikaner secret society
in 1918, and, notwithstanding important internal divisions, it grew to
shape education, politics, media, and religious practice. Its main function
was to preserve a unified, dominant Afrikaner culture and articulate the
relationship between nationalism and Christianity in a way that marginalized English influence (Dubow 1992). Throughout apartheid's history,
it enjoyed variable levels of autonomy from the NP. In the 1970s and
1980s, the organization was working on alternative racial constitutional
arrangements, meant to preserve white supremacy. However, gradually,
they came to see the need to abolish legal racial discrimination as crucial
to white interests (Welsh 2010).

Apartheid censorship was enabled by legislation and relied on collaborationist publishing houses and writers' groups. The AB shaped the
remit and power of the censorship machine. Intellectuals, writers, and
academics served on the relevant monitoring bodies. Some worked assiduously; others tried to protect what they considered to be valuable
literature. Most censors belonged to the male, educated, and ideologically
committed Afrikaner cultural elite, though by 1992 a few Black censors
had joined (McDonald 2009). Many publishers, avid for financial gain,

observed the imposed constraints. Some white authors who cherished the British colonial idea of an idealized independent republic of letters were critical of censorship—but not necessarily of apartheid. More broadly, the white monopoly of the publishing world had crippling effects on African-languages writing.

Works by local and foreign dissident authors were systematically banned. Afrikaner writers were not spared either, since, as the nation's bards, they were expected to nurture the relevant mythologies. Not everyone complied: the Sixty-ers, a group of young Afrikaans writers that included Adam Small, André Brink, Etienne Leroux, and Breyten Breytenbach, were critical of the regime. Several of their works were banned, not without resistance from cultural institutions (Welsh 2010). Breytenbach's open defiance got him imprisoned (Dubow 2014). While some works by white writers were permitted on appeal, no banned Black author ever got a second chance (McDonald 2009).

The press was controlled through legislation and intimidation (Hachten and Giffard 1984). The Black press bore the brunt of state interference: publications got suspended and journalists were banned regularly. Official radio and TV were subordinated to the state, and the AB oversaw their programs. While the English press fashioned itself as the opposition press, its staying within the legal limits effectively legitimized the regime. Lists of banned publications were disseminated regularly, while newspapers did not have the right to cover police brutality and prison conditions. The Newspaper Press Union—which gathered the owners of commercial newspapers—reached an agreement with the police to report only on certain aspects of the security policy. Covering incursions in neighboring states, civil unrest, and repressive "counterinsurgency measures" during the time of the "total strategy" was closely monitored. The press even created its own code of conduct, encouraging self-censorship and fining journalists who violated the code, in an effort to stave off further state interference (Coleman 1998) and protect its financial interests (Hachten and Giffard 1984). Critical reporting did exist, but its effect was overall limited: sufficient media outlets sustained the ideological atmosphere wherein white supremacy could flourish.

In general and especially before the 1980s, Afrikaans-speaking universities ideologically legitimized official policies and trained the apartheid bureaucracy (Hugo 1998). Stellenbosch educated several prime ministers. Unlike many researchers in the English-speaking universities who produced critical work, most Afrikaner intellectuals were nationalist loyalists (Welsh 2010). Their loyalty was expressed in active ideological work, at one end of the spectrum, and silence, at the other. Open dissenters faced difficulties with career progression, and sensitive appointments were screened, especially under Verwoerd and Vorster, but no severe political and personal repercussions faced dissenters, unless they had associated themselves with organized resistance (Hugo 1998). Afrikaner intellectuals often articulated political criticism in private but shied away from going public for fear of losing their comfortable positions. Liberal, English-speaking academia took an ambivalent position, tolerating protest but also conforming to apartheid laws and enjoying a safe elite status (Dubow 2014, 128–29).

Moving along the spectrum, Afrikaner businessmen were unlikely to dissent, since they enjoyed direct access to ministers. Businessmen's varied degrees of commitment to Afrikaner nationalism came into tension with their interest in open markets and economic growth. Anglophone corporations de facto sustained the apartheid order (Dubow 2014). In a presentation at the TRC in 1997, the main business organization recognized their ethical failures (Welsh 2010). Beyond the national market, international businesses made fortunes violating the sanctions against South Africa (Ellis 2013, 272). It was only in the mid-1980s that international sanctions and divestment were reluctantly implemented (Dubow 2014, 223–24).

Complicity was also the game played by the medical profession: in its report to the TRC, its representatives acknowledged that health care provision was racialized and that doctors had colluded with the security apparatus. Certain psychiatric hospitals were integrated into the prison system, where they pathologized dissidence and deployed inhumane "methods" on Black patients. The very practice of setting a psychiatric diagnosis was racialized, reserving more "complex" mental illnesses for white patients (Filippi 2016). Most troubling, doctors issued false postmortem reports and lied in court, refused to treat or mistreated detainees, and hid evidence of torture or abuse (Wildschut and Mayers 2018). Ideological commitments, the fear of losing a job, a culture of obedience to authority, and lack of training in medical ethics and in the identification of torture—all contributed to the moral disengagement from victims (Gready 2007).

Everyday, ordinary complicity with the apartheid order was enabled by a "contract of ignorance" (Steyn 2012)—the social construction and normalization of a racially hierarchical reality and its relevant subjectivities according to what social epistemologists call "a need not to know," for knowing would trigger a crisis of identity. On the one hand, whites were cognitively and affectively constituted by a metanorm that put them in charge. White complicity in apartheid involved "indifference or callousness, cowardice or dishonesty, the failure of imagination and empathy, or just plain laziness" (Vice 2010, 327), which were simultaneously psychically and somatically anchored in individuals' habitus. All these attitudes, emotions, and beliefs are symptoms of a recalcitrant, naturalized, doxastic ignorance that rendered inaudible dissident and victims' voices. As Ndebele writes, "the psychology of habit . . . made prejudice a standard mode of perception" (1998, 23). Thus, Black people were "denied any chance of accidentally proving their equality with white men" (Biko 1987, 88).

On the other hand, "survival" and "protective" ignorances were embraced by Black South Africans to make life bearable and shelter their children from the most humiliating encounters with apartheid: "Not only do the oppressor populations need ignorance to shield them from knowing the realities of the injustices that undergird their privileges for their psychological well-being and for the perpetuation of privilege to remain unquestioned, but the oppressed also need to construct their own systematic ignorances to manage their condition within unequal power relations and keep body and soul together. Ignorance thus provides an important "insulating medium" for the reproduction of a hierarchical racial order, both a consequence and cause of non-relationality, of living past each other" (Steyn 2012, 21). Black ignorances were sometimes at the margin of consciousness; other times they were fully internalized: the ideological apparatus of the regime succeeded in constituting docile subjects (Subreenduth 2006). However, prudence also played a key role: staying alive meant staying out of trouble, which also meant staying out of politics. This is what explains a lot of Black parents' forbidding or discouraging their children from enrolling in resistance, out of sheer fear for their lives.[2]

Thousands of Black police officers and soldiers fought for apartheid and, "for most black South Africans, the face of apartheid was black. From the clerks who staffed government offices, the teachers who taught Bantu education, the 'elected' and non-elected officials who ran townships, to the policemen and -women who enforced apartheid laws, the average bureaucrat was black" (Dlamini 2015, 12). The Bantustan system ensured a degree of Black allegiance to the regime by securing civil jobs and enabling the creation of profitable patronage networks (Dubow 2014). The multiple crippling economic and political constraints the Black population faced made it impossible to sustain continuous and effective mobilization at all times, especially given the high costs of resisting, the internal divisions between resistance groups, and the regular closing of the horizon of political hope by sustained—and often spectacular—repressive state violence. In particular, the massacres that punctuate the history of the regime served as heavy curbs on political aspiration and hope.

The case of the impimpi, or askari, is a painful one for the memory of the resistance struggle. Black resisters sometimes turned state witnesses under torture, out of political disillusionment, resistance fatigue, or a desire for a "normal" life, for fear of capital punishment or for money. By 1990, the Vlaakplas had three hundred askaris in its ranks (O'Brien 2010, 187). Askaris were instrumental in the strikes against the armed resistance within and outside South Africa, in obtaining information about resistance structures and their leadership, and in orchestrating political trials against captured resisters. Because of the real threat they posed to antiapartheid groups, real and suspected askaris—as well as police informers within townships—became the target of gruesome exemplary violence at the hands of the ANC.

Regime-supported and police-enabled Black vigilante groups—such as the Witdoeke—compounded the spiral of violence that characterized the mid-1980s. These groups of Black fighters were invested in the state-established Black Local Authorities, which they were paid to protect against the antiapartheid forces seeking to destabilize them. Within these groups, desperately poor, and even formerly convicted, young men acted brutally with the covert support of the state. The vigilante leadership was made up of local homeland chiefs and bureaucrats—middle-class Black people who had a vested interest in the stability of the homeland apartheid structures (Coleman 1998). Some of the vigilantes were incorporated in the state formally as community guards. While funded and incited by the regime, their activities remained largely outside any form of state control.

English-speaking whites positioned themselves ambiguously, de facto reaping the benefits of white supremacy while vociferously—yet mostly ineffectively and unevenly—expressing political disapproval. As Dubow explains, by the 1960s, English-speaking whites had adjusted to the apartheid order, notwithstanding their feelings of cultural superiority over the "uneducated" Afrikaner (2014). Pop-cultural products in English satirized apartheid institutions, without posing any serious threat. English-speakers cultivated a delusional and hypocritical sense of moral superiority and separateness from apartheid, from which, however, they benefited. Literary figures such as Alan Paton, Nadine Gordimer, and Athol Fugard wrote critically—though not uncontroversially—about apartheid, and their work attracted the attention of both international publics and domestic censors. Lawyers such as George Bizos and Sydney Kentridge won some important victories in the courts. Helen Suzman embodied the liberal antiapartheid voice in the legislature, while newspaper editors such as those at *Rand Daily Mail* investigated police abuse. In general, however, English-speaking South Africans did little to threaten the system and when they did contest it, they adopted paternalistic positions, traceable to a white habitus. Thus, Njabulo Ndebele comments that the story the English-speaking whites could tell at the end of apartheid was set "in the interstice between power and indifferent or supportive agency. In that interstice, the English-speaking white South African has conducted the business of his life. Now he [*sic*] was indignant and guilty; now he was thriving. This no-man's land ensured a fundamental lack of character. With a foreign passport in the back pocket of the trousers, now they belong—now they don't" (1998, 27).

Moving into the resistance area of the spectrum of involvement, important Black resistance organizations targeted the processes that preceded and culminated in NP's victory. Political opposition to apartheid developed against the background of the Cold War and was channeled via important class- and race-centered organizations. Unions had resisted since the 1920s, while the South African Native National Congress—renamed the African National Congress (ANC) in 1925—was founded in 1912. Throughout its history, the ANC adopted a variety of positions in relation to the state, initially favoring legal protest but later embracing armed struggle because of relentless state brutality (Juckes 1995). The foundation of its Youth League (ANCYL) in 1944 marked the shift to a more assertive form of African nationalism, often in tension with the agenda of the Communist Party, with which the ANC collaborated. Nelson Mandela and Oliver Tambo were key theoreticians and activists in the ANCYL. A broader alliance with the South African Indian Congress (founded in 1919) and the Coloured People's Organization was formed in 1947—the Congress Alliance—structured around racial pillars and a common pursuit of equality (Everatt 2009).

Organized resistance evolved in relation to the changing shape of repression and the geopolitical opening or closing of the horizon of hope. A broad repertoire of strategies developed in the 1950s, animated by various political projects. A Gandhian campaign of passive resistance was organized in 1952, in which few whites participated (Welsh 2010, 111). Women protested the Pass Laws, while boycotts and sabotage acts dotted the mid-1950s (Motlhabi 1984). Adopting a more radical Black Nationalist position, the Pan-African Congress (PAC) split from the ANC in 1959 (Broun 2012). The multiracial, redistributive principles of the programmatic Freedom Charter authored by Z. K. Matthews in 1956 were approved by the ANC (Motlhabi 1984; Juckes 1995), triggering the state's arrest of 156 activists, including the ANC's leadership. What became known as the "Treason Trial" proved an embarrassment for the state: the court took five years to dismiss the charges as unfounded, bolstering political solidarity among the accused.

White support for Black resistance was limited to organizations committed to universalistic forms of humanism. Several English-speaking churches, Communists, the South African Congress of Democrats (CD), LP for a short while, displayed variable degrees of solidarity. In the 1950s, the very few antiapartheid whites were ideologically divided between liberal gradualists, who argued for progressive reform and qualified franchise for "advanced" Black people, and the white Left—Communists, Socialists, and other Marxists—who favored immediate general enfranchisement and endorsed extralegal resistance (Everatt 2009). CD was formed at the ANC's invitation to institutionalize white representation within the Congress Alliance in 1953. Unlike the other, much more cohesive components of the alliance, however, CD had an NGO-like framework and was only superficially united under the umbrella of resistance against fascism, the only thin basis on which various whites could agree.

The Communists and the liberals were nonracialist, while the ANC adopted a multiracial perspective and structure. ANC's stance therefore sat uneasily with liberal individualism and Communists' unilateral focus on class. Before going underground in 1950, the Communists articulated a "two-stage" theory of social transformation, prioritizing Black empowerment over socialism. These ideological tensions meant that it took many years before the ANC and the Communist Party started collaborating clandestinely in the late 1960s.

Within white antiapartheid organizations, "there were activist and beneficent Christians, Jews and atheists; pacifists and militants; and other variations in world view. They had two common values: they hated apartheid, and they hated each other—though not always in that order" (Everatt 2009, 19). Antiapartheid whites were mostly middle-class, from liberal professions, and predominantly English-speaking. The Black Sash—an organization of middle-class white women formed in 1955 in response to the state's disenfranchisement of "Coloured" South Africans—opposed various apartheid policies from a position of safe privilege until the early 1990s (Burton 2010). The Torch Commando is an exception to the bourgeois profile in that, for a short period in the early 1950s, it gathered World War II ex-servicemen who opposed the NP (Everatt 2009).

Under Verwoerd, apartheid legislation was met with public protest, which triggered the state's brutality: the infamous Sharpeville Massacre (1960) counted sixty-nine victims who had peacefully protested against Pass Laws (Lodge 2011). The ANC and the PAC were banned in 1960—making this year an important turning point within resisters' political horizon of hope, as it marked the end of trust in peaceful protest and constitutional politics.

Given the use of emergency rule in the 1960s, the leadership of the ANC and PAC created a United Front abroad, establishing headquarters in various African capitals and in London (Juckes 1995, 103). MK—the military wing of the ANC—was founded in response to the inefficiency of peaceful protest. The USSR, Sweden, the GDR, Bulgaria, Czechoslovakia, and China supported the exiled fighters financially and logistically, against the background of the Cold War (Ellis 2013; Dubow 2014). Mandela served as MK's commander and led the international quest for political, financial, and military-training support. He was arrested in 1962 and charged, together with several other resistance leaders, under the Sabotage Act (Broun 2012). To understand how ecologies of complicity function, we must note that western governments did not respond to the UN General Assembly's call to impose economic sanctions on South Africa when Mandela was captured (Juckes 1995, 105). The infamous Rivonia trial (1963–64) featured as defendants ANC and MK members and Communists. Mandela and the Black resistance leadership were sentenced to life imprisonment. A conditional release was offered to him in 1985, provided he renounced violence—something he refused: he remained imprisoned until 1990 (Juckes 1995, 108).

The trial had a negative impact on Black fighters' motivation, especially given the feeble international reaction. Black resistance needed time to regroup. Surveys reportedly registered growing apathy in the late 1960s (Juckes 1995, 115). A period of calm followed because of the closing of the horizon of hope, aggravated by the reform of the security system into an abusive repressive force and the proportional augmentation of Afrikaner wealth and Black poverty. Moreover, gradual changes in citizenship laws and the status of "bantustans" entrenched apartheid: Black people were given "bantustan" specific citizenship, while their South African citizenship was annulled (Motlhabi 1984). The state thus empowered compliant chiefs who provided the white economy with cheap Black labor, in exchange for an artificial and constrained "national autonomy." Some chiefs contributed to apartheid's stability, personally benefiting from the system and inviting often exploitative foreign investors to their areas. While critical of the regime's strategy to "tribalize" the country and fragment the resistance, the ANC hoped the bantustans would create opportunities for localized resistance. In 1975 Zulu chief Mangosuthu Buthelezi, the state-recognized leader of the KwaZulu Bantustan, founded the Inkatha Freedom Party (IFP) with the support of the ANC—as a cultural-nationalist organization. However, later, the relationship between the two organizations deteriorated, as Buthelezi sought to consolidate his power autonomously from the ANC and within the apartheid order, relying on state support to do so.

It was during Vorster's premiership that the Black Consciousness (BC) movement developed in Black universities in the 1970s, with Steve Biko as its key figure (Pityana 1991; Cloete 2019). Biko argued against the antiracialism of existing resistance groups. However, his understanding of Blackness focused on the experience of powerlessness and political consciousness, and he argued for psychological emancipation from white values (Juckes 1995; Cloete 2019)—and thus made it possible to recruit those the state classified as "Indian" and "Coloured." Influenced by Black Power in the United States and decolonial thinking in Africa, Biko articulated a philosophical-political vision that appealed to those disenchanted with liberal gradualism and the sidelining of Africans in multiracial organizations (Biko 1987; More 2018). The emphasis on Black unity—broadly understood—went directly against the state's administrative and political fragmentation of the Black population into "bantustans" (Motlhabi 1984).

The movement faced similar challenges to those facing the ANC and PAC: the leadership comprised educated, middle-class intellectuals. BC started in the universities, among students, and its constituency did not share their profile. It implemented social-assistance programs (Brown 2016) and did ideological work, tapping into African Socialist thought and a rather romantic view of precolonial culture. Dominated by educated men, it integrated women in supportive roles and thus reflected the patriarchal order—something that some BC women fiercely contested (Magaziner 2011). Apartheid was read as the emasculation of Black men and the struggle as one between white and Black men (Gqola 2001a; Desai 2015). The connection between "masculinized memory, masculinized humiliation and masculinized hope" (Enloe 1990, 45) transpired from the articulation of BC ideology and, as we shall see, it informed national mythmaking after 1994.

Simultaneously, labor conflicts intensified: 1973 brought widespread strikes, which targeted low pay and appalling work conditions. The Soweto uprising started in 1976 as a culmination of previous years' mobilization. After the heavy repression of the early 1960s and the period of relative calm that followed, the workers' strikes and BC activism of the early 1970s prepared the ground for renewed struggles. Thus, by the time the Soweto uprising erupted, the horizon of hope had been pried open by students and workers engaged in overt conflict with the state. The uprising itself was triggered by the—controversial even among Afrikaners—requirement to teach certain classes in Afrikaans, a strategy for dislocating the English language's cultural domination. This decision was merely a spark, given the abysmal living conditions. In response, the state killed between five hundred and one thousand protesters. The violence spread beyond Soweto, forcing the state to retract the controversial policy.

Biko was arrested and killed in police custody in 1977—marking another watershed moment in the struggle's history. His death reverberated internationally and emboldened resisters. In response to the public outcry and protests, the state banned several BC-related organizations. While the relationship between the ANC and BC had been tense because of their different positions on race, many BC supporters joined the ANC and the MK (Welsh 2010) but also PAC (Brown 2016). The ANC thus slowly but surely became the main opposition force. Students—many of whom were women—crossed the border to join its training camps (Ellis 2013).

Throughout the 1980s political mobilization increased, triggering the state's repeated resort to emergency rule. In response, militants attacked local authorities but also Black police and informers. The government sought to control unrest in townships via strict curfews, armed occupation, and extralegal killings. These measures were, however, unsustainable: they triggered capital flight, and several banks withdrew from South Africa, rendering it financially vulnerable (Coleman 1998).

By 1989, in the grip of a political and economic crisis, the government agreed to start secret negotiations with the ANC. Nearly one thousand detainees went on hunger strike, forcing the state to release many of them. De Klerk came to power against the background of an extensive Defiance Campaign, met with large-scale reprisals. Cycles of horrific violence ravaged the most densely populated, poor areas. Conflicts over the role of local Black authorities, power, and scarce resources; the advancement of the ANC into IFP homelands territories; and the secret financing and training of IFP fighters by the state fueled a spiral of violence (Ellis 2013; van Baalen 2014). The security forces, ANC, IFP, Azanian People's Liberation Army, AWB, and many other actors were responsible for the bloodshed (Dubow 2014). An estimated sixteen thousand people died between 1990 and 1994 in a state-sponsored "low intensity war" that hindered the negotiations.

The talks brought together a fragmented opposition and a government who initially had no intention of ceasing to hold power. Dialogue collapsed at various points, in response to acute violence. Given the negative effect this strategy had on de Klerk's popularity rates, in 1992 he reined in the security apparatus, whose generals were reluctantly retired. Violence, however, continued till after the 1994 elections, which the ANC won in a landslide.

THE OFFICIAL STORY

The centrality of the TRC within South African official memory-making cannot be overestimated. Its message was clear: without the amnesties associated with the political negotiations that led to the end of the apartheid era, "we would have been overwhelmed by the bloodbath that virtually everyone predicted as the inevitable ending for South Africa" (Tutu 1998, 22). As "both live event and as an archive produced from oral testimonies" (Y. Hutchison 2013, 23) the TRC "script" invoked African normative traditions and values to advance a hegemonic narrative that foregrounded truth and reconciliation over justice, promoting—not uncontroversially— both a dominant perspective on apartheid and an aestheticized vision of a "rainbow nation." The Promotion of National Unity and Reconciliation Act instituting the TRC was signed into existence by President Mandela on July 19, 1995. The purpose of the commission "was the establishment of a complete picture of the nature, causes and extent of gross violations of human rights" (Office of the President of South Africa 1995). Both perpetrators' motives and victims' perspectives were to be accounted for as thoroughly as possible. Most controversially, the document provided for "the granting of amnesty to persons who make full disclosure of all the relevant facts relating to acts associated with a political objective" (1995). Out of a total of 7,115 applications for amnesty (of which over 60 percent were submitted by ANC members and only 17.8 percent by the security services) only 1,674 were successful, a rather modest figure, especially since around forty thousand human-rights violations were reported by survivors. Of the applications submitted by state officers, seven were by

Black operatives and five by Black askaris (Foster, Haupt, and de Beer 2005, 13–15).

From the beginning, the Commission was shrouded in controversy and its promises were soon betrayed. Its institutional and normative limitations, problematic relationship with the Prosecutorial Office, lack of a robust structural evaluation of the apartheid regime, and limited attending to the victims' needs left many dissatisfied and angry. The truths that the commission promised and claimed to have delivered—forensic, narrative, dialogical, and healing (2005, 22)—were in tension with one another and failed to meet different parties' political expectations. In nuce, the aesthetics of the rainbow was not reflected institutionally and materially.

The Commission makes the object of an immense scholarly literature, to which I cannot do justice here. Its narrow definition of "political motive"; its genealogy in colonial institutions; the choice of an individualist framework; the equivalences it established between the various sides to the conflict; its neutralizing, moralistic, and legalistic language; the homogenization of women's voices; the failure to address mundane and ecological oppression under apartheid—these are just some of the contentious issues foregrounded in the critical literature.[3] Instead, I focus here on two aspects, of central concern to this project: that of structural complicity and impure resistances and that of the hegemonic official narratives that rendered both invisible.

First, while the report touched on some of the contextual factors that fostered human-rights violations, its embrace of the human-rights paradigm led it to focus mainly on victims and perpetrators, thus reproducing dichotomic and individualized ways of thinking about violence (Gready 2011; Leebaw 2011). These categories were understood apolitically, uprooted from the contexts where the individuals subsumed under them acted. Moreover, the idea that all South Africans had been victims—often proclaimed by Archbishop Tutu—let beneficiaries of apartheid off the political and legal hook of responsibility: the moral victory against white racial supremacy displaced more radical ideas of political restructuring and economic redistribution (Meister 2010). This was compounded by the TRC's focus on visible, easily recognizable crimes, leaving almost completely untouched mundane practices of colluding with and benefiting from systemic dispossession and disenfranchisement. With few exceptions—for example, the medical profession, businesses, and the judiciary being the most prominent—its individualized, Christian confessional mode left mostly untouched the complex forms of sociality and relationality that made abuses possible and the cultural, economic, and social underpinnings of the violent ecology. Thus, the report did not thematize "the complexities and ambiguities, rich in the lived experience under apartheid, of collaboration and complicity with apartheid, of the murky terrain of spies, crossovers and informers, or of the role of bureaucratic functionaries in a long chain of authority. It passes over questions about the producers of doctrines, ideas, plans and policies—not least the policy of apartheid itself—that lead to conflict and violence. It skirts around issues of social structures and processes, including poverty, oppression and domination" (Foster, Haupt, and de Beer 2005, 3).

Second, scholars have problematized its obscuring narratives about the past and the propagation of new, reductive national mythologies, whose political effect was to preclude a more discriminate engagement with the murky zones of complicity and resistance. Verne Harris observed that "narratives of a noble struggle ('the struggle') against oppression, of heroes and heroines versus villains, of 'the people' or 'our people', of truth and reconciliation, of nation-building, reconstruction and development, the 'New South Africa', 'Madiba Magic', the 'rainbow nation', and so on, have been dominant" (Harris 2011, 6), eliding the reverberation of past exclusions into the present, as well as resistance's own violence. While understandably driven by a sense of political urgency to mark a new beginning, such metanarratives failed to illuminate the complexity of apartheid and its resistant other, sidelining heretic voices in favor of another totalizing colonization of the hermeneutical space by noncommittal memory.

Joining the growing chorus of voices that reject the notion of "postapartheid" as historically inaccurate and as presupposing a progressive view of history, Pumla Gqola offers one of the most incisive critiques of the idea of the reconciled "rainbow nation" and the nationalist masculinism that underpinned the imaginary of the "New South Africa." The rainbow nation is for her merely a "farce of sameness and colour-blindness" (2001b, 103) that, through its redemptive narrative, absolves the white beneficiaries of apartheid of important responsibilities in the present.

While a "rainbow" symbolizes unity and equality and celebrates cultural differences as a key feature of the refounded polity, difference is superficially interpreted, while unity is merely a fantasy that masks enduring grave inequalities in the "not-yet": "It becomes possible thus, hiding under rainbowism, to dismiss the effects of history on the contemporary . . . It reinforces the illusion of pervasive equality and negates the need for equity endeavours to rectify the effects of the interlocking systems of apartheid, patriarchy and capitalism, among others" (2001b, 103).

The resilience of systemic racialization, recalcitrant internalized categories, and their material, symbolic, and affective repercussions are made light of by the abstracted vision of rainbowism and its featuring of Mandela as "Forgiver-in-Chief" (Msimang 2018). Thus, the TRC's self-authorized imposition of the unique redemptive framework though which the past could be discussed—built through a pragmatic selection of voices—falls into the temptation of intransigent monovocalism, suppressing more radical voices concerned with ongoing structural oppressions. As Michael Rothberg insightfully put it, "At the limit, such a vision becomes a form of narrative fetishism, its version of progress built on disavowal of the ongoing production of trauma and inequality in the present" (2019, 95). It conceals the deep and ongoing effects of racialization, politically, economically, and culturally. Thus, Pumla Gobodo-Madikizela correctly suggests that the wailing of witnesses testifying at the TRC can be read retrospectively as prophetic with regard to the inequalities and violence of the present, a sort of "lament about the future" (2020) that highlights South Africa's remaining trapped in "the temporality of the *in the wake*" (Adebayo 2020).

Yet this is not the only aspect of the past that the hegemonic narrative excised from the community's mnemonic fabric. Gqola (2009, 66) also examines how the "widespread reading of ANC masculinities as exclusively, or predominantly, assertions of political agency, codified as heroism" allowed for both uncritical narratives of gender in the liberation struggle and for continued patriarchal domination after 1994. In other words, she argues that the interpretive association between the claiming of manhood and the claiming of political freedom should not distract us from analyzing patriarchal domination's continuation in the "new South Africa": "Heroic nationalism evokes the triumph of a just struggle over slavery, colonialism and apartheid through the disavowal of fear. The courage and activism of the liberation movements is signaled as heroic masculinity in a multitude of ways: through the masculinist embodied spectacle, the foregrounding of men's activism, and the narrative of national founding fathers Mandela, Tutu and De Klerk. Even the contestations of founding father narratives often posit a different set of inadequately recognised 'fathers of the Nation': Sobukwe, Tambo and Biko" (2016, 66). Indeed, the memory of the ANC and BC are dominated by masculinist tropes that foreground the imprisoned men, obscuring women's role within the movement (Desai 2015). Moreover, sexual violence against women within the antiapartheid organizations was glossed over by the TRC (Coombes 2011). Such narratives reinforce problematic conceptualizations of the public–private divide, of the political, and of victimhood and perpetratorship and help mythologize a purist, morally intransigent, and politically problematic vision of virile, heroic resistance.

This view of masculine heroism consecrated in national mythologies and deployed conveniently in the present, is most clearly present in autobiographies published by former male fighters (Unterhalter 2000). Masculine heroism is centered around autonomy, political work, courage in thought or deed, and loyalty. Political work is constitutive of the hero's subjectivity, it presupposes full dedication and emotional involvement in the project of building the nation and entering history. The hero is autonomous from the private sphere and the women and children who inhabit it: it is male camaraderie that makes physical and psychic suffering bearable under harsh circumstances. A high level of self-confidence, trust in the rightness of one's cause and in one's comrades exudes from these autohagiographies—in ways that resonate with similar narratives elsewhere.

These masculinist forms of nationalism often erase from registers of honor the thousands of women who marched in the Defiance Campaign of the 1950s, who were involved in the ANC, the PAC, BC, various unions, the Democratic Front, and the Women's Congress. Many were arrested and tried for treason, imprisoned, and tortured—yet the official narrative's focus on Robben Island renders their suffering invisible (Hiralal 2015). While several autobiographies and diaries detailing the gendered nature of women activists' repression have been published—by, among others, Winnie Madikizela-Mandela, Zubeida Jaffer, Pregs Govender, and Amina

Cachalia—they have rarely gotten the attention that men's autobiographies enjoyed. Notwithstanding the fact that militarized motherhood was ideologically mobilized by the ANC propaganda and that, by 1991, 20 percent of MK forces were women (Cock 1991, 162), women were often pushed into subordinate roles and subjected to sexual harassment in ways that reflected the broader gender order (K. Miller 2009). Women served as combatants in armed organizations, as persistent protesters in the township uprisings of the 1980s, and as protectors of the young at all times. And yet their status as veterans was rarely acknowledged (Magadla 2015). In the BC, university-educated women were well represented, though leadership positions were accessible to them only as "honorary males" (Ramphele 1991). Noncombatant work—such as community-support work, including medical-clinic work, tutoring, and construction work, in which women were well-represented—is overshadowed by the armed struggle (Hadfield 2013). And, as elsewhere, so are the stories of resistance's abuses and excesses. The political memory of the resistance against apartheid is thus armed and gendered male and aesthetically dominated by the figures of Mandela, Biko, and Tambo.

In parallel, discourses of "whiteness in distress" flourished after 1994. Given the embeddedness of white ignorances in the Afrikaner habitus, their resilience beyond the transition is not surprising (Steyn and Foster 2008). The difficult search for a reconstructed Afrikaner identity led to exile, political withdrawal into zones of comfort and privilege, or the articulation of a new form of white minority nationalism that whitewashed the past (Van Zyl-Hermann 2018). Having lost political power but enjoying enduring economic advantage (Msimang 2018), "an Afrikaner identity based on racial exclusivity, racist notions of inherent black inferiority, and out-group threat" (Verwey and Quayle 2012, 553) fed parochial, racialized imaginaries—reminding us that repair could never have been a one-off event, but a process of radical and sustained affective attunement, political reconfiguration and material redistribution in a country with "segregated temporalities" (Brendese 2013).

SUBVERTING THE DOUBLE ERASURE

Mirroring the previous chapters, I now turn to six artists who illuminated the limits of official memory and the chimera of "clean slates," in ways

that vindicate and extend various aspects of this book's theoretical contribution. The first subsection deals with *the unassimilable*—that is, events,
actors, and voices that sit uneasily with the vision of the past fashioned
through the double erasure. While novels of the 1970s and 1980s featured
mostly positive visions of the resistance, the works I discuss here shed a
critical light on it. Zoë Wicomb's *David's Story* (2001b) tackles women's
resistance and the sexual violence committed against them in MK training
camps. Via an ingenious formal setup, Wicomb reveals memory's vulnerability to self-interested fabrications, but also the possibility of caring for it
aesthetically, via the insertion of dissenting voices and perspectives. I then
read *Bitter Fruit* (2003) by Achmat Dangor as an account of what must
be denied for rainbowism's martyrs to preserve their honor and dignity.
The novel centers on a former resister, Silas, an MK operative and ANC
politician who struggles to reconcile his triumphant reputation as hero
with his wife's rape at the hands of the apartheid police.

The two works discussed next address the costs that the norm of
masculinist heroism inflicts on individuals, both in the everyday practice
of resistance and at the level of political memory. *The Innocents* (1994)
by Tatamkhulu Afrika sheds light on resisters' betrayals and complicities in their multiple determinations, rendering implausible any morally
intransigent, individualizing, reductive ascriptions of blame. The novel
simultaneously problematizes the oppressiveness of heroic models in relation to complex identities and the vulnerabilities they underpin. In
contrast, John Kani's film *Nothing but the Truth* reveals the hypocrisy of
political hagiographies. Most importantly, it seduces us into considering
a crucial yet neglected aspect of the fight for racial emancipation: the
need to relativize cultural whiteness and give due recognition to African
traditions in institutionalized spaces of knowledge is subtly proposed as
an alternative arena for unsung "impure" heroes.

Last but not least, I turn to a novel and a film that both use the geography of Johannesburg to reveal the afterlives of apartheid. Ivan Vladislavić's *Restless Supermarket* features a rhinoceros—a retired proofreader,
Aubry Tearle—whose daydreams in the early 1990s betray his refusal to
accept the end of white minority rule. The novel constitutes a lucid reflection on the resilience of exclusionary ideologies and their stability in
institutions, practices, and materialities, in ankylosed minds and bodies.

Meanwhile, Ralph Ziman's *Gangster's Paradise: Jerusalema* (2008) focuses on the bitter disappointment triggered by rainbowism's betrayed promises and innovatively instrumentalizes Johannesburg's urban tissue to offer a hyperrealistic view of hopeless deprivation and racial inequality. Via a rather conventional gangster story, the film scores important critical points about both ideological and material continuities, as well as new political challenges.

OFFICIAL MEMORY'S OTHER: THE UNASSIMILABLE
Unassimilable Agencies: *David's Story*

Award-winning writer Zoë Wicomb is the author of novels, essays, and short stories that critically engage with nationalism, masculinist memory, and complex identities. Her book *David's Story* (2001b) is an inexhaustible source of insight and reflection, to which I cannot do justice here.[4] In this section, I unpack Wicomb's problematization of the challenge that *the unassimilable* poses for founding narratives, given what is usually erased from them: cultural difference, in the case of nationalist community-building processes, and women's resistance and violence against women, in the case of all political mythologies, the TRC's included. Like Dangor below, Wicomb foregrounds a former male fighter and his tortuous attempt to make sense of his past, only to illuminate the disingenuousness of his story and decenter his authoritative voice.

Wicomb problematizes memory's imprecision and pliability via both narrative and form. The novel contains multiple plotlines, set in different temporal and geographical locations—a formal choice gesturing toward the impossibility of any precise accounts that could underpin clean political slates. Wicomb pushes the reader in a maze of styles and competing narrative vistas: as Graham explains, for her, "narrating the past must always be an inductive enterprise, one of decoding meaning through absence, loss, and rupture" (2009, 5). Thus, readers embark on an identity quest alongside an MK fighter, David Dirksee, who is struggling to come to grips with what can and cannot be told about the antiapartheid struggle and his own participation in it. To write his memoirs, he contracts an amanuensis. Her role turns out to be simultaneously radically critical and creative, for it is she who ultimately writes the story, on the basis of a few fragments he provided and their conversations. It is she who helps

readers make sense of the omissions in David's story. The label "amanuensis" is therefore misplaced since her role is not limited to copying or
taking dictation (Dass 2011)—in fact, Wicomb hands out the historical
authorial voice to her,[5] a transfer of voice signaled in the first sentence of
the novel: "This is and is not David's story" (2001b, 1).

The collaboration between David, a fighter classified as "Coloured"
by the apartheid regime and his amanuensis, an educated woman who
remains unnamed throughout, is set in 1991, in the dying days of apartheid. Already in the "Preface" of the story, the amanuensis tells her readers
that David had been "unable or unwilling" to clarify certain aspects of
his biography—despite her repeated probing—and that he seemed to be
searching for the middle ground between "necessary secrecy and a need to
tell" (2001b, 2). She hints that the multitude of starting points in David's
tale, all vying for selection, and the fragmentary nature of his writing
reflect his wanting to distance himself from his own past. She also warns
the reader about her having rewritten large parts of the manuscript, parts
that David did not get to reread before his suicide. The fictional preface
therefore sets the stage for the entire novel, cautioning the reader that
David's story will not provide the "truth and nothing but the truth"
and that other voices—and bodies—will compete for recognition. Using the palimpsest as a narrative strategy (Graham 2009, 166), Wicomb
sabotages the clear vision of "truth" the TRC embraced and promoted—
the truth of testimony as transparent, reliable, and unquestionable and
as instrumental to healing and reconciliation—and seeks to illuminate
memory's fragmentary nature, contestability, vulnerability to forgetting,
and self-serving fabrication and erasure, as well as plurivocality. The interplay between memory and the imagination, inevitable in any narrative
about the past—collective and individual—takes center stage through
the amanuensis's deletions and insertions, whose aim—I suggest—is to
correctively incorporate what is unassimilable from within the confines
of both David's masculine habitus and the doxastic rainbowism of the
new South Africa.

From the various bits David does reveal—via indirect speech—we
understand that he had a difficult relationship with his father, who
disapproved of his political solidarity with the antiapartheid struggle.
We get the impression that David's frustration with his father's racism,

complicity, and apoliticism leads him to start a research project into the history of the Griqua people, to whom his family belonged. The Griqua are descendants of the Khoi, an important indigenous people of South Africa. Wicomb inserts real historical figures in David's genealogical quest: he focuses on tracing the positioning of the Griqua leaders in relation to white colonialists, only to discover painful points of convergence regarding the institutionalization of the racial order. His project shows how political memory had been instrumentalized, distorted, and reinvented by one of the Griqua chiefs, Andrew Le Fleur, David's supposed ancestor, for the purpose of articulating a robust collective identity. This involved erasing two interrelated aspects: the community's internal heterogeneity and the history of enslavement that partially underpinned it. The version that Le Fleur wrote as a basis for his political claims was compatible with colonial ideas of racial separatism and hierarchy, leading David to see his ancestors as accomplices of white supremacy. The longing for nationhood and for a distinct identity drew the Griqua very close to the roots of apartheid. Thus, via David's inquiry, Wicomb problematizes the value of nationalism and its embrace of various forms of "purity" as the basis for any project of community building.

David presents this research to the amanuensis, who tries to write it as a story. In the process, she operates with a sharp mnemonic scalpel. First, she leaves out some of the less credible aspects of David's genealogy, in particular his take on Sarah Baartman, hinting that his writing reproduced the colonial gaze that objectified her (Negri 2017). Second, she inserts many women's dissenting voices, conjuring them as repressed yet authoritative sources of knowledge and opposition, to David's chagrin: she performs a caring labor of hermeneutical refusal and mnemonic insertion that seeks to redress his exclusions and erasures. The amanuensis uses her imagination to reinscribe women's agencies and enable readers to prosthetically hear women's voices, but also to see their traumatized and objectified bodies; in the process, she realizes that David's research on Griqua history is merely a psychological diversion strategy.

What is it a diversion from? From a reckoning with the unassimilable violence the ANC committed against its own women combatants. From David's truncated and mysterious testimonies, we learn he had been himself suspected of treason and tortured by the ANC in the Quatro

Camp in Angola. He bears the marks of torture on his body—he has a limp and suffers from tinnitus. David is married to Sally, herself a former activist and fighter, whose political involvement stopped once she became a mother, something for which she is deeply resentful. Via Sally's reminiscing, we learn that women's "initiation" in guerrilla techniques in training camps outside South Africa included sexual abuse by ANC comrades. Her "retiring" to the role of mother at the end of apartheid constitutes a second violation, which she deeply begrudges: in conversations with David, she displays sharp political acumen and historical insight. It is not exclusively through Sally's character that the unassimilable violence the ANC committed against women comrades is thematized: the mysterious Dulcie, about whom we learn very little throughout the novel, stands in for the uncomfortable systemic gendered violence in the training camps and, as I will show, for the erased agency of women fighters. Through David's unwillingness to talk about this mysterious character, Wicomb problematizes the threat that recognizing women's resistance and the widespread sexual violence they suffered would pose to the stability of rainbowism and its sacred pantheon of male martyrs.

David provides very little information about Dulcie. She is a comrade, a well-trained fighter who is not afraid to "get her hands dirty," a politically charismatic orator who can woo a hostile crowd, someone who does not care for her appearance, a tough resister, and a commander of an ANC cell. Sally is deeply jealous of her, though David insists that they were never involved romantically. When the amanuensis presses David about Dulcie, he becomes deeply troubled, his discomfort is physical. Cornered, he finally discloses that Dulcie had got "too big for her boots" and had become inconvenient to "the big men," especially since she knew "too much," including about the "fabrications"—false accusations—against her (2001b, 204). Dulcie's tortured body emerges as a mysterious presence throughout the novel—an unacknowledged archive of violence—haunting David, who cannot in*corporate* it into the story he yearns to tell about the struggle: we don't know for certain if she was tortured by the apartheid police or by her ANC comrades. We do not know if David had anything to do with her death. However, his repeated chastening of the amanuensis for being a soft liberal and his stubborn defense of the elemental role of violence in any war—against the enemy and against traitors—as well as his drawings of a dismembered female body in his notebook leave us uneasy: "Look, he pleads, I've trusted you with a delicate job. The struggle is sacred; it's been my life. It must not be misrepresented. You know, as all sensible people do, that the fight against oppression is just one, that it has been managed as justly as possible in politics" (2001b, 197).

Given what she hears in David's testimony, the amanuensis cannot help but think that his past was like "a stack of so many dirty dinner plates that will not come unstuck as each bottom clings to another's grease" (2001b, 197). Through his image, Wicomb undercuts any romantic investment in heroic biographies and clean refoundings, highlighting the occluding processes that must take place for there to be only one single story. And Wicomb hints at how it is that women's bodies and lives get stuck between the dirty slates of political memory.

In the book's afterword, Driver convincingly argues that, throughout the novel, "Dulcie remains at a stage of unrepresentability, not least because certain aspects of her treatment cannot be faced, since facing them would force him to confront his own past not only as victim, but also as victimiser" (2001a, 232). And yet, as Sakiru Adebayo (2020) suggested, "the body keeps the score of violence" in a way that makes it undeniable. While Driver's diagnosis is correct, I suggest that Dulcie remains unrepresentable not only as a tortured body but also as fighter and as a voice, as a historical agent. As Gqola and Msimang demonstrated, women were erased from the South African panoply of saintly heroes and, to the extent that sexual violence was addressed, it confined women to the status of passive victim. Drawing parallels between the erasure of Griqua women in David's genealogy and Dulcie's and Sally's erasure from his memoirs of the antiapartheid struggle, Wicomb divulges the intergenerational colonization of a community's hermeneutical space by masculine heroes and the occlusion of women's resistance, as well as of the violence committed *by* and *against* them. Thus, even within resisters' memory, temporalities are segregated by gender.

Through the character of the amanuensis—herself a woman—Wicomb relativizes David's research on the Griqua and the narrative of the resistance by inserting women and their dissent, their exasperation, and their knowledges, including the knowledge that "fucking women was a way of preventing them from rising in the Movement" (2001b, 179). David, "hope-lessly addicted" to "boy's stuff" (2001b, 187) is irritated at the presence of so many "grandmothers" in his story. He asks, "Who would want to read a story like that?" and unthinkingly suggests that at least some of them be replaced by "grandfathers" (2001b, 200). He does not want Dulcie's voice represented, out of a supposed concern for her "safety" when, in fact, it is because Dulcie, as well as the other women in Griqua story and in his life, refuse to be overdetermined by patriarchal ideas of their gender, as either carers or victims. Dulcie is an active combatant; she herself inflicts violence, is tortured, and is killed. David's masculinist, militarist habitus reduces her to a haunting presence that cannot be recognized, for she sabotages his investment in a paradigmatic vision of the warrior-gendered-male.

David's attitude toward Sally betrays the same patriarchal habitus: he is surprised that she—a former fighter—can articulate complex political positions on collective identity, national "purity" and the priorities of liberation. Sally's voice—her memories of training in Angola and of her political work—troubles images of women as essentially weak and in need of male protection. Her demotion and relegation to the private sphere erases her past and denies her a role in the new political dispensation.

In response, the amanuensis's writing of women back into the story, however fragmentarily and uncertainly, invites hesitation in the automa-tism of reductive memory—David's and the readers'—and opens up the possibility of refusing their erasure. In recuperating the unassimilable for an intergenerational story, Wicomb thus seduces us away from male martyrologies and makes women's voices audible and their bodies visible, but also takes heroes down a peg or two. Moreover, highlighting the problematic character of racialized nationalism as a basis for political identity, she aesthetically cares for the mnemonic space by rendering more complex—and more uncomfortable—histories of indigenous leaders' positioning in relation to colonialism and white supremacy, as well as uncritical invocations of the nation in the present.

Unassimilable Traumas: *Bitter Fruit*
Achmat Dangor's work spans three decades of South African history and received important international critical acclaim. Because of his political opposition to apartheid, he was banned between 1973 and 1978. Published

in 2001, *Bitter Fruit* thematizes certain occlusions in the politics of truth and reconciliation by telling the story of a family's unravelling, the Alis', as the TRC is preparing to publish its report. The novel touches on a variety of themes: the lack of acknowledgment regarding women's sexual abuse under and after apartheid, the burden of trauma, enduring poverty and marginalization in the "new South Africa," racial (Frenkel 2008) and sexual identity (A. Miller 2008), and the critique of the TRC in relation to gendered violence (Propst 2017). In this section, however, I focus on how the novel refuses the image of the masculine heroic freedom-fighter that dominated the national mythmaking in the wake of 1994 via a perceptive account of traumas *unassimilable* to it.

Dangor sets the plot at the end of Mandela's presidency, in the tense atmosphere of the Ali household. Silas Ali is a former counterintelligence operative of the underground MK. As the novel starts, he is engrossed in his work liaising between the Ministry of Justice and the TRC, occupying an important political position alongside former comrades. Lydia, his wife, works as a nurse and is estranged from Silas, who had been unfaithful during his militant days and had recently taken to drinking heavily and neglecting his son, Michael. Michael is nineteen, struggling to forge an identity for himself. The other central characters in the novel are Silas's MK fellow fighters—Kate and Julian—Lydia's sister, Grace, and her husband, Alec, a close friend of Silas's.

The crisis that precipitates the plot is Silas's running into François du Boise, a white policeman who had raped Lydia nineteen years earlier, while Silas was locked up in a police van nearby, raging helplessly as his wife was assaulted. We understand her rape was a punishment for Silas's political militancy. He is distressed by the encounter and, in telling Lydia about it, reactivates her trauma. To deal with her renewed pain, she engages in self-harm. After this triggering event, the novel follows its main characters as they negotiate their fraught relationships. We gradually learn that Alec, Lydia's brother-in-law, had been present at the scene of the rape and that he had worked for the apartheid police. Michael is the product of the rape, and upon learning about it, he kills his biological father, du Boise.

While Dangor experimented with fantasy in other works, his style here is straightforwardly realistic. Formally, he deploys free indirect speech—third-person narrative that interlinks the inner thoughts of the characters with the authorial voice of the narrator. The only place where he uses first-person narrative is in Lydia's hyperreflective diary entry on her own rape—a formal reflection of the ethical need to allow her to speak for herself. The reader prosthetically inhabits several traumatized perspectives, all embedded in gendered and racialized relationships and profiled against the background of the new doxastic order that the TRC sought to inaugurate. These perspectives sit uneasily with each other, and Dangor masterfully illuminates their incommensurability via powerful, confrontational dialogues and long introspective passages that trace the characters' contrasting experiences, as well as their alienation from each other. The book's three parts—titled "Memory," "Confession," and "Retribution"—therefore reflect the failure of the linear process of healing and reconciliation on both the interpersonal and the national levels: the story of the Alis can thus be read metonymically as a direct critique of rainbow ideology.

Silas is sketched as a vain resistance fighter with a drinking problem. His main job in the MK was to deal with askaris and impimpi, a difficult and violent task. The text intimates he suffered incarceration, solitary confinement, and brutal interrogations. In the present, however, he is a successful member of the new political elite, who enjoys power and has the abilities of a pragmatic politician, for whom "the rule of law is no longer the keen knife-edge of all meaning" (2003, 165). He displays racist attitudes toward immigrants from Nigeria, Pakistan, and Taiwan; fantasizes about the pleasure of killing comrades with a penchant for speeches that go on for too long; and sexually desires his son's teenage friend. Despite his success and social mobility during Mandela's presidency, he is sometimes nostalgic about the "simplicity" and "clarity" of apartheid, which he counterpoises to the ambiguity and demandingness of the democratic transition. As Michael sees it, Silas belongs to the old generation of fighters who "all have the same brittle air of vulnerability, of souls fallow despite years of feverish cultivation. 'The struggle' sowed the seeds of bright hopes and burning ideals, but look at what they are harvesting: an ordinariness, but also a vanity fed by sly and self-seductive glimpses in the mirrors of their personal histories. In each is born a frantic need for a 'legacy,' a need to be recognised as a 'hero of the struggle.' The world—once more—is full of monument builders and statue erectors"

(2003, 168). This judgment is echoed in Alec's simmering rage at his own still precarious socioeconomic situation under Mandela, "the political saint," which contrasts with the prosperity that top ANC fighters enjoyed: "Now moral zealots were running the world . . . These fucken holier-than-thous have the luxury of jobs and good positions in government" (2003, 85). While the Alis enjoy relative material security, Alec's resentment is triggered by the deprivation that the majority still experiences: Dangor notes naturalistically the putrid smells, the sweltering heat, and the noises bouncing off the walls of township houses—clear markers of the discrepancy between the promise of the rainbow and the lagging reality.

Recalling Friang's treatment of the French resisters' arrogant moral intransigence and self-indulgent need for honors and power, Silas's ego is perpetually searching for validation. While his pain at encountering du Boise is real, he wallows in self-pity and cannot decenter himself. Lydia is bitter at his establishing an undue equivalence between her pain and his. His memories of that night are read from within his masculine habitus—he prioritizes his own hurt over hers, his own helplessness at hearing her cries and especially the humiliation of his virility by the policeman who raped her. He even remembers the shame on the face of the Black policeman who witnessed the rape but not Lydia's face, tears, and suffering. Silas seems incapable of truly hearing her. At a deep, personal level, her assault is unassimilable to his image of himself as a man, a protector, and a fighter. The conversations between them reveal his inability to comprehend her experience, but also the dangers of his conceited belief that he could, as a witness, fully grasp its enormity and master it.

This hubristic assumption aggravates Lydia who confronts him—"You don't know about the pain. It's a memory to you, a wound to your ego, a theory" (2003, 14)—and says later, to herself, "I cannot speak to Silas, he makes my pain his tragedy" (2003, 127). She remembers his failure to console and comfort her after the rape, absorbed as he was in his own shame. In facing her rape, Lydia must choose between a discourse of (dis)honor, imposed on her by the gender doxa, and one of healing and forgiveness, suggested by the TRC. Defiantly, she derides the masculinist, self-centered framework through which Silas reads her suffering, and, in her diary, she recalls how his raging screams aggravated her terror during the rape. Similarly, the redemptive promises of the TRC—which, tapping into a patriarchal imaginary, involve fixing her identity as that of a passive victim—are inadequate. In response, she finds her own, private language of suffering, which she uses to work through and archive her suffering.

The most effective way in which the novel displaces affective and cognitive investments in the goodness of heroes is in depicting Silas's more or less conscious desire to appropriate his wife's rape for the purpose of self-martyrizing and virtue signaling in the political realm—in a way that makes her rape compatible with his manliness. He insists that they need to report it to the TRC, especially since Du Boise was applying to be amnestied for several crimes, including Lydia's rape. She dismisses the proposal as useless, invoking the discordancy between her experience and the TRC's capacity as a forum to address it. When a TRC lawyer brings her the offer to testify in a closed hearing, she sees in his eyes "an evangelist's fervour" (2003, 156), whose troubling sense of moral mission did not match the fact that the rape could not be undone. Moreover, the blind trust in the institution highlights its advocates' incapacity to allow for plurivocality and questioning with regard to its power to deliver on its promise, given its embeddedness within broader patriarchal structures, which set the terms under which Lydia's voice could be heard. As Strauss argues, her silence gives her a sense of control over *when* and *how* her trauma can be dealt with, refusing the limited framework the TRC offered (2008). In deciding to hide the conception of her son through rape, Lydia permanently "crossed over into a zone of silence" (Dangor 2003, 129)—the only way to separate her suffering from Silas's hurt manly honor and to regain a sense of control over her own experience.

Most importantly for this project, she realizes the positive impact that her potential testimony at the TRC could have for Silas's career and reputation as a heroic freedom fighter, and she decides to deny him "the opportunity to play the brave, stoical husband" (Dangor 2003, 156) and to display, as a politician, a saintly impartiality about apartheid's henchmen. Silas's quest for amassing more moral and political capital sheds a critical light on the underlying stability of patriarchal domination beyond apartheid. Realizing his stratagem for incorporating her rape into his martyrdom, she refuses to play along, and in doing so, destabilizes authoritative assumptions about resistance fighters' self-abnegation and unflinching dedication. Her refusal to testify affirms her own agency and her own drive to create an identity outside prescribed frameworks.

Silas's reaction to Alec's confession of betrayal is surprising: while disturbed, he does not get angry, blame Alec, or hold him responsible. On the contrary, he receives Alec's confession with something resembling compassion. While one might interpret this as a symbolic vindication of the TRC and of its injunction of forgiveness, Alec escapes the framework of the TRC—he is not strictly speaking a perpetrator. Silas treasures his friendship with Alec, and he knows the latter worked for the secret police to avoid reprisals, but also to provide his family with some minor comforts before 1994. He also knows Alec still has close connections with the security apparatus, just as the TRC is about to release its report—an emblematic illustration of the continuity of past structures and practices beyond the transition. Silas's compassion is a function of his own disappointment with the present, his resignation to the ambiguity of the political transformation and the compromises it presupposes, but also of his deep affection for his friend, which recalls Müller's "thicket" of love and disappointment.

Via a trauma-centered narrative, the novel joins the chorus of critics of the TRC who argued that it recognized women primarily as victims, whose suffering was subordinated to that of their male family members, who were engaged in the "real" struggle. This framework reproduced patriarchal divisions between the private and the public and safely placed historical agency in masculine hands. Dangor interrupts the gendered, institutionalized trumpeting of limited ideas about reconciliation and foregrounds Lydia's stubborn silence as a form of political resistance to being incorporated into a preset, mythmaking formula that could never capture the specificity of her experience. Silas's approach to Lydia's unassimilable rape—his attempt to deal with it on *his* own terms—remains unsuccessful. Through Lydia's stubborn refusal, Dangor defuses any sentimental attachment to hierarchies of valor: her silence thus inserts a moment of hesitation in the automatism of gendered, hegemonized memory, casting a shadow over TRC's and ANC's *grand récits* and their consecrated protagonists.

HEROIC FRAMES
The Costs of Aspirational Heroism: *The Innocents*
An antiapartheid fighter and prolific writer, Tatamkhulu Afrika was arrested for terrorism and imprisoned in the late 1980s. He is the author

of several volumes of prose and poetry, which garnered a great deal of
attention in South Africa but are little known internationally. Published
originally in 1994, his novel *The Innocents* tells the story of four young
men, three Muslims and a Christian, who seek recognition as trustworthy
members of the antiapartheid struggle. As elsewhere in Afrika's work, the
test of masculinity and one's manly abilities—of living up to a normative
model of masculinity—takes center stage (Dunton 2004): the author offers a realist psychological take on the moral costs and dilemmas involved
in political struggle and on the difficulty of navigating them guided by
absolutist cultural scripts of heroism and valor. I discuss *The Innocents* as a
novel of troubled consciousness, first, for its revealing the heavy weight of
a certain regulatory ideal of virile heroic resistance on resisters' own imagination, its mediation through racialization and religion, and its destructive
impact on their psyches, their commitments, and the actions they take in
pursuit of their political goals. I suggest Afrika helps us see how this ideal
is simultaneously fueled by and in tension with a variety of other aspects
of the resisters' positionality and the relationalities within which they are
embedded. In particular, he foregrounds the role of faith, which nurtures
resisters' sense of injustice but also restricts what they can do in the name
of the struggle. Second, against this complex background, some fighters'
complicity with the repressive apparatus is rendered intelligible not as an
individual moral failure or weakness, but as the result of the competing
pressures that complex identities place on the individual.

The story focuses on Yusuf, a young Muslim man who leaves his
family to join the liberation struggle. Afrika transports his readers into
his tortured psyche and enables them to accompany him on his political
maturation quest, forever doubting himself and his credentials for action. Yusuf is driven by multiple reasons: racial shame—triggered by his
community being spared the worst of apartheid's policies—a religious
commitment to justice, and an aspirational masculinity that seeks validation through political action. A deeply religious man, he is outraged
by the existing racial hierarchy and longs to be accepted as a loyal ally by
the Black liberation movement: a deep sense of racial and ethical inade-
quacy constantly moves Yusuf to invalidate social expectations about his
community's ambiguous stance in relation to apartheid. In approaching
Maponya, the leader of an armed resistance cell, religion provides Yusuf

with a moral compass. As we shall see, it also constitutes an important obstacle to Yusuf's reconciling himself with the violence he must inflict as part of his missions.

In this endeavor, he is joined by his two cousins, Himma and Mailie, two devout young men, who look up to Yusuf, and by Vincent. We learn that Himma is a quiet, sometimes sullen man who could pass as white, while Mailie loves sports and dedicates a lot of time to body building. Vincent, in contrast, is a petty criminal who had done time in jail and who is the only one with "expertise" in sabotage work. Afrika foregrounds Yusuf's battles of conscience as he tries to establish his authority as leader of the "squad," seeking to guide them by example, highly self-conscious, compulsively looking at himself from the outside, constantly unhappy at what he sees. He dedicates a lot of time to thinking through his strategies as a leader who can muster his followers' respect and obedience. He is animated by a masculine idea of valor and courage that he articulates in tune with his religious beliefs. However, it soon becomes clear that he is a novice in the art of political subversion: it is Vincent who teaches everyone how to make petrol bombs and damage property, and it is Vincent who procures a grenade and other explosive materials on the black market.

Maponya is rich in a way that smacks Yusuf as dubious: he suspects him to be embroiled in local networks of corruption. Maponya's wealth is in tension with the ideal of the liberation fighter Yusuf expects and aspires to be. And yet, Maponya is Yusuf's gate into the Black struggle, and so he subjects himself willingly to the required "tests." Maponya has immense authority over Yusuf, whom he confronts with unpleasant truths, such as the guilt Yusuf must feel for not belonging to apartheid's most oppressed category. He taunts Yusuf about his imperfect knowledge of true misery and poverty and doubts Yusuf's squad is ready to be tortured by the police. Consequently, he makes killing the ultimate proof of their trustworthiness and readiness, something that clashes with Yusuf's, Himma's and Mailie's faith. Thandi, Maponya's niece who is an active freedom fighter, is sent to help the "squad" as a stakeout on their missions. She is meant to transfer her knowledge to the less experienced men, but also assess their struggle readiness, on Maponya's behalf.

For the rest of the book, we accompany Yusuf's "team" graduating from simple acts of sabotage with petrol bombs, to using grenades and other explosives to damage garages, stores, and restaurants. Thandi has a hard time being accepted by the men: her gender marks her, in their eyes, for the private sphere, and her actions sit uneasily within the horizon their habitus opens. At the same time, Thandi herself has incorporated the sovereign violent-hero blueprint and often behaves as her uncle's unreflective spokesperson. The men's religion's prohibitions pose serious moral dilemmas, and Yusuf struggles to find ways to live with himself after he violates its injunctions. He is torn between the pursuit of an ideal of justice that his religion prescribes and accepting the revolutionary means such a pursuit requires. Fear is the other challenge, an ever-present companion in their exploits. The members of the group engage in a series of successful attacks, which embolden them and gives them a thrilling rush of power. However, they are soon on the police's radar, and Himma and Mailie are temporarily arrested and interrogated by a duo of security policemen.

Having escaped arrest, Yusuf experiences deep feelings of shame, again paralyzed at the thought that he is not the protagonist of the suffering that the doxastic model of heroism prescribes. He is disconsolate and engages in reckless behavior, hoping to get caught. Luckily, Himma and Mailie's lies add up, and they are released, not before experiencing police abuse and some unwanted sexual advances toward Mailie.

Escaping from this narrow encounter with the police emboldens the squad, leading them to naively fantasize about their likeliness to comic-book heroes. Their camaraderie grows stronger, and Vincent is fully accepted as an equal, despite his criminal record and his multiple "vices," which contravene the others' faith. However, when the reality of the risks involved is made vivid by the time spent in prison, the four men begin to hesitate. The cousins, in particular, seem shaken by their brush with the police, in a way that recalls Müller's "lust for life inside the fear of death." Yusuf's own commitment is shaken: he dreams of a private life, of his family, of going through the rhythms of the religious calendar. Regrets about neglecting the practice of the faith upset him most.

The squad are eventually arrested. True to his vision of sovereign and sacrificial heroism, Yusuf unsuccessfully claims full responsibility for everything, trying to get the others off the hook. He is beaten up and sexually violated in ways that hurt him physically but also insult his beliefs, but he keeps his silence. While in prison, they all long for home and "normality," fully aware they may never enjoy either if they stay committed to the armed struggle. Small acts of kindness by his white jailors confirm Yusuf's faith, though other prisoners might see them as expressions of superficial—even hypocritical—white guilt, that in no way challenge the system that the counterinsurgency police secured.

Of them all, Mailie is suspiciously not beaten or tortured. He is also supposedly transferred to a different prison. By the time they are all released, Yusuf finds out that Maponya had been killed. Thandi expresses doubt that Yusuf could avenge his memory and provides a realist take on the struggle: "You are a good man, Yusuf, and I shall always remember you as that. An innocent trying for the big time. But I do not need innocents now in this matter of my uncle's death. I need those that can handle shit and not care that it smells" (2006, 166).

This short speech articulates the justification of violence in the name of freedom: that political struggle inevitably involves getting one's hands dirty. Realism is mustered to make violence palatable—unsuccessfully so, as we shall see in the novel's denouement. More interesting, however, is Yusuf's reaction to it: having internalized the unnecessary equivalence between heroism and effective armed struggle, he feels dismissed as a fighter and as a man, devastated that even being arrested and tortured could not redeem him in the eyes of the evidently patented fighter that Thandi was. Moreover, the value of the team's missions up to that point is utterly discounted against the definitive standard that colonizes the fighters' imagination.

Soon enough, Yusuf realizes it had been Mailie's betrayal that got Maponya killed. He confronts the traitor, who appears to be thriving once out of jail. It soon emerges that Mailie gave in out of a fear of being sexually assaulted by the policeman who had propositioned him on the occasion of his earlier arrest. His religious beliefs and the care he had for his own body made it impossible for him to tolerate such a prospect. He admits to his betrayal and tries to kill Yusuf, only to be stabbed to death in the physical fight that ensues. Thus, in eliminating a traitor, Yusuf finally passes Maponya and Thandi's ultimate test. Shattered by his deed, he mourns his cousin, no longer sure he cared about the validation that the killing gave him as a fighter: a tremendous feeling of alienation from the struggle and its models overwhelms Yusuf. When Thandi, satisfied that her uncle's death had been avenged, offers to introduce him to the successor cell leader, Yusuf feels only deep bitterness.

In taking the aspiring hero's standpoint and revealing the costs incurred by trying to live up to social norms of glory, Afrika destabilizes glowing saintly images of heroism and invites us to consider what the realist nonchalance about "dirty hands" too easily obscures. *The Innocents* offers us, first, a prosthetic entry into the experience of feeling perpetually inadequate in relation to a regulative idea of virile, violent, and unwavering heroism. With the exception of a few scenes of intense action—the group's missions, their interrogations by the police, and the killing of Mailie—the novel is mostly dedicated to tracing the tension and drama in the protagonist's consciousness. The testing of masculine strength and prowess takes center stage but, most interestingly, the testing both feeds off and impinges on the multiple positionalities of the protagonists' identity and, in particular, on their racialized shame and religious commitment to justice. In problematizing the friction between identity and the prescriptions of the ideal, Afrika inadvertently reveals the latter's poverty and toxicity as a standard, as well as the hypocrisy and dangers associated with arguments about the inevitable necessity of killing: as Mrovlje (2017) shows, embracing the language of necessity in justifying violence can lead to too-convenient mystifications. Once enacted, the relational and personal costs that the ideal's moralist intransigence causes become evident to the protagonist: having murdered his cousin, having finally "proven" himself as a "real man" to the gatekeepers of the People's Army—no longer an "innocent"—Yusuf is disenchanted, aware that a commitment to the fight requires him to compromise on his faith. In response, he takes refuge in his family, in the private, a sphere he so passionately longed to escape at the beginning of the novel, and this is perhaps Afrika's opening up a path toward a reconsideration of masculinity and its entrenched, doxastic scripts.

Secondly, the novel highlights how the normative sources of political mobilization can also feed complicity. Mailie's identity as a religious man and his care for his own body *both* push him into political action *and* make him vulnerable to the threat of sexual violence at the hands of the police. His visceral repugnance toward the policeman who sexually harasses him makes him betray his mates. The novel seems to insinuate that Mailie might be a closeted homosexual and that his repressed sexuality might have something to do with his betrayal—further supporting this book's argument about the multiple social determinants of complicit behavior, which could never be captured by an individualistic, highly reflexive, and temporally static model of intentionality. In problematizing the oppressiveness, artificiality, and hypocrisy of the masculine and sovereign hero model, Afrika disrupts its allure, and firmly embeds us in the messy ground of multifaceted human identities and relationships. At the same time, in disclosing the complex circumstances under which even the brave betray, he asks us to hesitate before passing quick judgments about guilt and well-deserved punishment. Taken together, these narrative operations instantiate a labor of care for both colonized imaginaries and colonized psyches: Afrika pries them open to the readers' scrutiny, possibly a crucial first step toward a revaluation of resistance and the multiple forms it can take.

Nothing but the Truth: Mythological Complicity

John Kani's work spans decades and includes acting, writing, and directing. During apartheid, while enjoying a growing international reputation, he was imprisoned and brutally targeted by the South African police because of his politically critical work. *Nothing but the Truth* (2008) is based on one of his plays[6]—an origin visible in Kani's privileging intense, emotional dialogues between his key characters, often captured in mid-shots. The film can be read as a meditation on the value and limits of reconciliation, at both the interpersonal and the national levels. Set against the background of the TRC, various characters voice familiar critical and endorsing positions in relation to the much-discussed institution. The debates about political forgiveness are then mirrored in a family conflict. My focus in this section lies elsewhere, however: I suggest that the film offers, first, a lucid reflection on communities' retrospective, mnemonic yearning for select heroes and on hierarchical views of courage, with a special focus on the canonization of exiled fighters and the marginalization of the risks, suffering, and struggles of those who stayed behind and bore the brunt of domestic repression. Second, it thematizes the silences that must be cultivated and the mnemonic doxas that must be confirmed ritually for a community's heroes to stay firmly perched on their pedestals. Lastly, Kani sheds light on a neglected yet crucial form of resistance—hermeneutical resistance to cultural marginalization—as a key aspect of the labor of refounding.

The film centers on the funeral of a former ANC exile fighter, Themba Makhaya, whose cremated body is flown in from England for an official ANC funeral. The urn is brought by his daughter, Mandisa, who worshiped her father while alive and plans to have his memoirs published postmortem. Themba's elderly brother, Sipho, a librarian who stayed behind and lived through the last decade of the regime, prepares for this arrival, knowing very well what kind of funeral was expected, given Themba's consecrated-hero status within the ANC pantheon. We see him and his daughter, Thando—a translator who works for the TRC—anxiously awaiting the body and organizing the necessary rituals in Port Elizabeth. Sipho expresses a deep sadness at his brother's death and especially at his not having returned to South Africa while alive. His regret is amplified by the fact that they had not seen each other for twenty years.

The film clicks into gear when, to Sipho's despair, Mandisa produces not a body but an urn full of ashes. Sipho worries that an urn would not serve as the appropriate object for a hero's worship and death rites, given his brother's stature within the ANC. He obsesses about how he could explain to the mourners—who had already gathered at his house, singing and lamenting Themba's death—that there was no body. He consults a priest and a sangoma—a traditional healer—to get around the challenge posed by the lack of a body for mourners to venerate, and they both reassure him, pointing to the type of ceremony they could perform to compensate for the absence of a body.

The funeral preparations take place as Sipho's personal drama unfolds. Despite his long career and dedication to his job, Sipho is denied a promotion as chief librarian. He feels deeply disappointed by the fact that the collapse of official apartheid did not bring any empowerment for him, in this case professional recognition, although he too resisted from inside the country. His failure to secure the post pushes him into despair, and, in a drunken stupor, Sipho confesses his frustrations to Thando and Mandisa. At the climax of his anger, he swears to burn down the library whose director he did not get the chance to be. In the process of expressing his pent-up rage about the disappointments of the present—a present that failed to deliver on the ANC's promise of equality and prosperity—he also tells them "nothing but the truth" about their family's past.

He reveals—via a powerful theatrical monologue—the fraught relationship between the two brothers, always in competition with each other, since an early age. Flashbacks to scenes of the two as children fighting over toys locates their conflict temporally. Themba was their father's favorite son, and memories of their childhood are mostly painful. Themba seems to have always taken advantage of others. As a young adult, Sipho worked to provide for Themba while the latter was studying for his undergraduate degree, which he took a long time to obtain. Moreover, Themba's power to fascinate Sipho's son, Luvuyo, and get him involved in politics led to his death at the hands of the apartheid police. Sipho cannot accept this untimely death especially since, before dying, Luvuyo called him a coward, in contrast with Themba, whose image he sought to emulate. The spell Themba cast on Sipho's son—his risk-taking and involvement with the ANC, his embodiment of the heroic ideal—gets the latter to renounce his own father. This is particularly painful to Sipho, who intimates that Themba never followed through with the actions he advocated, that his heroism was more posturing than action. As Sipho puts it, Themba was involved in the struggle "on his own terms" and got many benefits out of it, material and symbolic capital above all.

Themba's "sacrileges" did not stop there: Sipho tells of how, while he himself did not attend it, Themba transformed his own father's funeral into a United Democratic Front rally. As Themba instrumentalized their father's funeral for political purposes, Sipho felt robbed, once again, of what was rightfully his. The police shot teargas and dispersed the funeral-rally, leaving Sipho alone to bury his father in the aftermath of the confrontation. Last but not least, Themba had an affair with Sipho's wife, from which a girl, Thando, was likely born. Sipho raised Thando as his own daughter and kept the secret for decades. It is because of this betrayal and the conflict that ensued that Themba never returned from exile while alive. The confession makes Sipho's recurrent complaint throughout the film, "people always take things from me," legible to the spectator.

Sipho's breakdown ends with him asking for his own suffering and participation in the struggle against apartheid to be acknowledged, alongside Themba's. Against the background of the personal story, his anguished plea is more than the result of mere jealousy. Sipho admits he envied his brother. And yet, in claiming recognition for his more modest participation in marches and political funerals, for having been tear-gassed and beaten up by the police, and for being part of the thousands who faced the apartheid police and their dogs, he contests the institutionalized hierarchies of bravery that foreground the role of exiled fighters and undervalue the grassroots resistance put up by the many who stayed behind. He points to how the many were yet to reap the benefits of the official end of apartheid. Thus, Sipho's critique of post-1994 politics emerges powerfully from his deep disappointment with the betrayed promises of the struggle: his inebriated rant prosthetically transports the reader into the world of those erased from a community's official story and illuminates the limits inherent in rainbow hagiographies, in a way that echoes Gqola's, Msimang's and Unterhalter's incisive analyses.

And yet, despite all his frustrations, Sipho does not disappoint the ANC mourners who gathered to commemorate and honor their hero. I read the film's powerful soundtrack—made almost exclusively of choral music by Themba's mourners—as a stand-in for the hegemonic story of the sacred struggle. By the end of the film, Sipho joins this choir. The obituary he writes for his brother recognizes his merits and helps consecrate him. Though he cannot really afford it, he buys the most expensive coffin available—one worthy of a hero—and sacrifices a bull. Sipho suppresses his anger at Themba's never having taken responsibility for his actions and their effect on other people's lives so that the mourners' expectations are met. The ANC is well represented at the funeral, which is performed with the required degree of pomp, decorum, and gravity. It is Sipho himself who places the ANC flag on his brother's coffin. He reassures Mandisa when, sober, he tells her Themba was truly a hero and that he would have been killed if he had stayed. Realizing the subversive force of his confessions and everyone's deep emotional investment in that saintly image, he represses his anger and affirms the erasure of his own life in order to preserve Themba's memory. Thus, he eventually capitulates to the imperative of heroic memory, becomes complicit with it, and publicly contributes to the stabilization of its imaginary in the South African space of memory.

In light of Sipho's decision, the title of the film, *Nothing but the Truth*, reveals its irony. The truths of the official story are referenced through historical footage of the hearings of the TRC and images of the ANC representatives at the funeral, bearing banners and chanting. As Sipho's confession revealed, these truths are partial yet politically useful for the movement's securing of moral and political capital. The film helps the viewer into the world of someone who is misrecognized by these truths and who, nevertheless, understands their political use. Like Friang's Jeanne-Claude, Sipho eventually accepts the compromise, a willing accomplice to the national mythology-making and the multiple silences it required.

The film's heretic value is not, however, limited to revealing the silences that need institutionalizing for the hero to remain firmly located in the community's pantheon. At the end of the film, jokingly asked by Thando if he was still planning to burn the library, Sipho tells of his plans to build a new, African library, one where African literature would not be confined to the hidden, bottom shelves but given its proper due. At the beginning of the film, we see Sipho frustrated with African books' relegation to the periphery of the library he worked for, a library that continued to sanction white cultural supremacy and marginalize African knowledges. Through Sipho's dream of getting funds to open a national African library, Kani reminds us that the world is only available to us through the stories we tell about it and that these stories are marked by exclusions and erasures. The closing dialogue thus points to the bigger task of the struggle for emancipation—namely, that of opening and pluralizing the hermeneutical space of the new South Africa. Creating an African library is thus proposed as an alternative—and just as valuable—model of resistance: that of the hermeneutical carer who combats racialized monocultures of the mind.

THE AFTERMATHS OF APARTHEID
Colonial Proofreading and "White
Ululation": *The Restless Supermarket*

A multiple award-winning author, Ivan Vladislavić uses the urban texture of South Africa and its complex materialities as a key element in his fictional work. Published in 2001, *The Restless Supermarket* traces the effects of the momentous political changes on the cityscape through the eyes of an apartheid nostalgic. I propose to read this novel as an allegory of apartheid's residual afterlives in the minds, affective structures, and embodiment of the rhinoceros constituted by colonialism as bearers of "civilization" and who, despite their bemoaning, continue to enjoy significant privileges in the new era.

The plot is set in Johannesburg in 1993, and the protagonist is Aubrey Tearle, a recently retired proofreader, who spends his time in Café Europa, perpetually grumbling about the degradation of the *moeurs*, culture, and social order brought about by the official end of apartheid. Vladislavić incisively tracks colonial white supremacy as a key axis of his individual habitus[7] and, in making the dislikeable Tearle the narrator for most of the novel, the author insinuates readers into Tearle's rigid viewpoint, witnesses to his discomfort and despair as the world changes around him. In the first person, Tearle claims his right to authoritatively impose "order" on a reality that escapes him, and, in this sense, he is the counterforce librarians like Kani's Sipho must face. The depth of resilient and intractable cognitive and emotional investments in hierarchical doxas is powerfully thematized: the elitist, dogmatic Tearle is a prisoner to the automatism of colonial habitus—at the level of thought, speech, feelings, bodily hexis—that nothing can interrupt, and lamentation is his only mode throughout. In this sense, Tearle is the personification of what Steyn and Foster call "white ululation"[8]—a white discursive repertoire that characterized the transitional period in South Africa, in that his perspective

> presents any change to the *status quo* as a threat to the established good that operates in the best interests of all. . . . It is essentially hostile to the new social order and encourages alienation from, rather than rapprochement with, the 'others' in the nation. Fundamentally hierarchical, this discourse is replete with tropes that emerge from the racist colonial imagination, tropes which sap power from Black people and the mechanisms that are being put into place to promote social transformation. (2008, 35)

In the first part of the novel, "The Café Europa," we follow Tearle as he inserts himself in the texture of the city as a privileged witness of "decadence," condescendingly recording all the markers of the white order's supposed collapse and society's "degeneration" in relation to his own set of norms, which he takes to be natural and trumpets continuously. He sees the "signs" in the changing demography of his neighborhood and in the clientele of his beloved café. Throughout, a viscerally racist Tearle experiences both nostalgia for white supremacy and a paralyzing fear at the radical contraction of his horizon of hope: "Our days are numbered!" (2012, 15) he warns, speaking in the name of an imagined white community, because "Silently, while we slept, the tide was darkening" (2012, 131). His complaints recall Hooker's insightful observation about "white grievance" being related to "a specific form of racial nostalgia that magnifies symbolic Black gains into occasions of white dislocation and displacement" (2017, 485). For Tearle—as for white supremacists elsewhere—however modest, Black gains can only be read as white losses and symptoms of white victimhood.

Very little happens in the novel. Via Tearle's reminiscing, which goes back to 1987, we learn that, upon retiring, he made a variety of (white, bourgeois, educated, "European") friends in the café, and started passing the time in their company, doing crosswords, playing board games, reading, going to the zoo, listening to music, and chatting. Tensions sometimes emerged because of his stubborn racism and his insistence on being condescending to everyone, especially people of color or people for whom English was a second language. The group sticks together for a while, as their world crumbles around them. Gradually, however, some peel away, others die. New members join as the café itself changes management and new customers begin to frequent it: people of color, sex workers, migrants from all corners of the world—to Tearle's exasperation. It is in the café that he sees Mandela's televised release from prison, irritated by everyone's excitement and vitalized sense of hope. The beginning of what he calls "ungrammatical years" (2012, 170)—the years of majority rule—eventually leads to the closing of Café Europa: white time had run its course. The now elderly and mostly estranged friends organize a goodbye party on New Year's Eve in 1994, to mark the end of an era, which some more readily accept.

Vladislavić deploys a series of stylistic choices to reveal the aftermaths of apartheid. First, the characterization of his protagonist as a colonial rhinoceros. Tearle is a pedantic, insufferable proofreader who worships the perfection and completeness of grammatical rules—rules that produce unique correct answers to all questions—blind to their being the result of arbitrary human conventions. He is passionate about etymology and compulsively points to spelling and pronunciation mistakes: in restaurant menus, newspapers, phonebooks, letters, commercial labels, and everyday conversations. For a hobby, he collects massive amounts of corrigenda— texts containing all sorts of errors—on the basis of which he wants to organize a proofreading competition in Café Europa, eager to identify those who share his commitment to "purity." He envisages the competition to undo all the errors of recent times, as a moment of radical affirmation of the "truth" and value of the grammatical/racial order, as he sees it.

The degradation he perceives is both grammatical and social and his profession is a metaphor for his visceral racism: he anxiously traces urban desegregation in the phonebooks he proofreads.[9] In the changed Café Europa, he experiences sensorial and emotional discomfort at the unwanted proximity of people of color and immigrants. Vladislavić dexterously reveals the deep and recalcitrant cognitive and physiological anchoring of colonial doxas: Tearle is repulsed by racially encoded smells, voices, skin textures, colors, names, foods, physiognomies, gestures, clothes, tattoos, and accents. He feels physically constrained, sensorially uneasy, and aesthetically assaulted by the shifts in the city's public space. The "mistakes" he sees everywhere are merely the various excluded others that the new political order sought to recognize—a process he laments and experiences as catastrophic. As Marais (2002) points out, Vladislavić's Tearle is a social proofreader as much as he is a textual one: racial integration and emancipation are for him "errors" in relation to the "perfection" of the dying order. Throughout the novel, the protagonist perorates, collapsing the distinction between the grammatical and racial order: "A proofreader worth his salt grieves over an error, no matter how small, in a printed work of any kind . . . Every error matters, not least because admitting even one into respectable company opens the door to countless others. Everyone welcome! the cry goes up, and the portals are flung wide. Only by striving constantly for perfection, and regretting every failure to achieve it, can the hordes be kept at bay" (2012, 98).

Second, on the walls of Café Europa, Vladislavić paints a frieze of Albia, an imaginary white utopian harbor town, on whose streets and wynds Tearle meanders in his imagination, clad in a houndstooth overcoat, his brogues resounding on the cobblestones. An image of an idyllic place that never was, Alibia is safe and bright, a space of nostalgic withdrawal, a sanitized vision of the colonial metropolis. In part two of the novel, "The Proofreader's Derby," however, Alibia becomes Hillbrow—the neighborhood in Johannesburg where Tearle lives. Vladislavić (2012, 191) uses the third person in this section as Tearle imagines himself as Fluxman, his alter ego, who likewise thinks that "the world has become a perilous place, full of pitfalls and eyesores." This second part takes us on fantastic journey into the mural/Tearle's rhinoceritic imaginary, spectators to his restorative, reactionary nostalgia (van der Vlies 2017), which feeds his yearning to undo the present via aggressive grammatical, social, and geographical engineering.

To reflect his protagonist's stubborn attachment to Alibia/old Hillbrow, the author makes the physical environment of the city pliable, geologically unstable: in Tearle/Fluxman's imagination, the end of apartheid threatens not only the discursive order but also the material organization of reality. The neighborhood is flooded, and hippos attack humans, streets reconfigure themselves, skylines rise and fall, parts of the city detach and float away, buildings shift their locations, shantytowns move into the inner city, and "chaos" prevails: the end of minority rule is experienced dramatically as apocalyptic, a sheer violation of Newtonian laws of physics. Invested as he is in the glorified, colonial vision of Alibia/old Hillbrow, Tearle/Fluxman cannot resign himself to these modifications and so, aided by other proofreaders—a hint at the collective desires engendered by intractable racist habituses—he obstinately tries to reverse them, using only a blue pencil and an eraser. Vladislavić (2012, 224) thus conjures a fantasy of restored white power, one that requires a huge effort, but which is eventually successful: "Now the appropriate social distance could be restored between the haves and the have-nots, the unsightlier settlements shifted to the peripheries where they would not upset the balance, the grand estates returned to the centre where they belonged. There was wasteland to play with, and blasted veld, and dead water. The possibilities seemed endless."

When aspects of reality disappoint him, Fluxman deploys his weapon of choice, the proofreader's "delete" sign—the city becomes an unruly text that needs proofreading (Graham 2007) and that eventually yields to his racial ordering principles: "And then it was the human detritus he found in the margins of the city, the erroneous ones, the slips of the hand, the tramps, the fools, the congenitally stupid, the insufferably ugly. They were incorrigible, he reasoned, and doing away with them, at one painless stroke, was more humane than trying to improve them" (Vladislavić 2012, 224). The workings of a racist vision and the desire to expunge inconvenient objects from one's cognitive and emotional but also material reality comes to fore in this second section. Deeply anchored in the nostalgic's affective infrastructure, Alibia stands in for white space and white time. The ululating Tearle, incapable of letting go of his privilege, imagines a society of omnipotent, heroic proofreaders, who, driven by a sense of historical mission, turn back time and reorganize physical space according to racist doxas and their rigid, violent categories.

The last part of the novel, "The Goodbye Bash," restores Tearle's first-person narrative to mark the end of the excursus into white fantasy: readers accompany him back to Café Europa, on its last day before closure, New Year's Day. Tearle is preparing his proofreading competition, with a mixture of excitement and apprehension since, to his mind, "The new year in the offing was black as pitch" (230). The "success" of "corrective" efforts in the space of Alibia cannot, however, be reproduced in the space of the Café: the world had changed irreversibly. The party is a disappointment as it, too, bears the marks of the broader "degeneration." The party atmosphere and the festive excesses are not propitious for the proofreader's derby. What is more, all his old friends turn against him, denouncing his airs and conceits. The night culminates in a terrible brawl, in which Tearle gets stabbed in the chest. He is luckily saved by the dictionary he carries in his breast pocket at all times. Thus, while Alibian fantasies cannot be replayed in Hillbrow, the dictionary—the codex of the white social and linguistic order—absorbs the violence and keeps the rhinoceros—keeper of language, keeper of order—alive beyond the official end of his time. In protecting Tearle with a dictionary while a Black man, Floyd, gets severely wounded and ends up in the hospital, Vladislavić gestures to the continuity of white norms and privileges into the new era: as we shall see in the section that follows, Black bodies continue to be disproportionately marked for violence, even under the bright colors of the rainbow.

To conclude, the book ingeniously discloses the reproduction of the ankylotic racist habitus beyond the official end of minority rule. In centering the resilience of white fantasies and privilege, Vladislavić refuses the optimism of clean slates and rainbows. The Tearles of this world, with their longings and aversions, reveries and nostalgia, remain unable to adjust to the "restlessness" of democracy, its diversity and stubborn resistance to orderly subsumption under racialized, developmental categories. Via the fantastic second section, the author takes readers on a prosthetic trip into the discomfort experienced by the white supremacist Fluxman and helps us see the force of his desire and longing for "order." Any reorganization of the ideological and material space of the city is resisted and reverted in a dream of colonial omnipotence. By the end of the novel, Tearle remains protected by a symbolic and material order that, whether he sees it or not, keeps him alive and well, while a Black man's body gets injured: despite Tearle's relentless lamentation, it is he who goes to bed in safety at the dawn of the "ungrammatical years."

Gangster's Paradise: Jerusalema: Mapping Disappointment
While Vladislavić gives us the white rhinoceros's view of Hillbrow as its political geography changes, Ralph Ziman's *Gangster's Paradise: Jerusalema* (2008) helps us travel in the very same neighborhood through the eyes of two disillusioned Black men, for whom the promise of a "new dawn" failed to materialize. When his dreams of studying at Stellenbosch University are dashed by financial constraint, Lucky Kunene graduates from Soweto high school pupil illegally selling trinkets on the train to carjacker to taxi driver in Johannesburg to real estate fraudster in Hillbrow. Formerly exiled MK fighter, Nazareth, returns to South Africa to find himself poor and his sacrifice unrecognized. Consequently, he, too, embarks on a life of crime, making good use of his military training in violent encounters with other gangsters and the police. Via a class- and race-inflected gangster story[10], the film takes spectators on a tour of a Hillbrow inhabited by the bitterly disappointed, stuck in an impoverished and violent city, having to face the reality of betrayed promises of flourishing and empowerment. Against the background of continuous economic deprivation and polarization, the self-made gangster's crimes appear as the result of a reasonable adaptation—though some are quicker to justify it than others. In parallel, the film also captures the emotional experience of white resentment: via several characters, we witness white moral ignorance and disdain toward a present that is not fully under their control.

The film pairs well with *The Restless Supermarket* because the city of Johannesburg, in general, and Hillbrow and Soweto, in particular, serve as the canvas on which to paint a complex picture of apartheid's after-lives—a picture that foregrounds racialized economic and geographical segregation and systemic violence, against the soundtrack of intertwined Black anger and white ululation. Via the film's title, the director sought to express the general hope "that South Africa post-apartheid was a kind of New Jerusalem. It was a new beginning, a new kind of Promised Land" (Lehman 2011, 122). However, the rainbow fails to materialize since, as Lesley Marx writes, "the brave new world carries not only the scars of the old, but has given birth to mutations of poverty, disease, crime and rampant violence" (2010, 261). The new elite's betrayal of the revolution and the structural reproduction of certain key aspects of the apartheid order give rise to bitter disenchantment and cynicism, and the viewer is left at a loss for clear moral judgments about the two key protagonists.

The plot is simple. The film follows Lucky's life trajectory, starting with his teenage years spent on the eve of the "New South Africa," celebrated as "a new dawn, a new day, a fresh start, a clean page, a new beginning" (Ziman 2008). Everyone's hopes are fed by a radiant vision of equality and prosperity—and the director uses historical footage to capture the sense of euphoria marking the official end of apartheid. Lucky grows up in Soweto, illegally peddling toys and perfume on trains. He applies for admission to an undergraduate degree just as the apartheid regime collapses. The dream of studying at Stellenbosch is shattered, however, when he cannot obtain financial support. In the company of his friend, Zakes, he proceeds to move in and out of a life of crime, under the leadership of Nazareth, a former MK fighter. After a few close encounters with the police, Lucky decides to live an honest life as a taxi driver, but his effort is thwarted when his cab is stolen and he is kidnapped by the mafia, barely escaping by the skin of his teeth. Tired of his dreams being crushed one after the other, he gives up his distance-learning course and comes up with a plan to take over derelict buildings in Hillbrow. Politicizing residents while simultaneously taking advantage of them, Lucky collects their rents and pushes abusive white owners into bankruptcy.

Thus, Lucky slowly becomes a very prosperous "businessman," owner of luxury cars and a house in the suburbs, where he lives with Leah—his

Jewish girlfriend. Throughout, he ironically deploys the New South African language of empowerment and opportunity to describe his activities, thereby revealing them as hollow ideology, with no grasp of the configuration of reality. His wealth draws the attention of the police and especially of officer Swart, who keeps a close eye on him, and of a Nigerian drug lord, Ngu, who wants a share in the profits. Lucky is eventually arrested but manages to escape from police custody. The film ends with images of him walking on Durban's beaches, imparting his street wisdom in voice-over: "After every new revolution, comes a new order. But before that comes opportunity. After all, wasn't it P. W. Botha who said 'Adapt, or die'?" In a country where only a few are reaping the benefits of the dream proclaimed in 1994, where political and economic continuities remain entrenched in the material configuration of the city, where—in Ngu's words—Mandela "did not part the waters" for Black people, Lucky rationalizes his decisions by sarcastically repurposing an apartheid prime minister's injunction.

The characters in the film are drawn unevenly: while Lucky and Nazareth are rather complex and dynamic, Zakes, Swart, Leah, Ngu and the rest of the cast are superficially sketched. Lucky is slow to take up crime, and he does resist its temptation of quick profit and power at several key moments. We see how his own dream of success is slowly eroded, and it is not for lack of trying that he eventually becomes a cynical gangster exploiting the already exploited: though not innocent, his choices are structurally embedded. Eventually, he ends up a purely self-interested fraudster, who takes advantage of the poor in order to get rich: no redistributive action justifies a Robin Hood reputation. Lucky does not redeem himself morally: on the contrary, he stays bent on getting rich and is susceptible to xenophobic rages against foreigners such as Ngu.

Nazareth, the second key character, is deeply disenchanted with the shape of the present. A veteran of the struggle, trained in Moscow, he returns from exile to the new South Africa only to find there is no place for him in the new dispensation. Reminiscing about his days in the MK, he remarks sardonically: "They told us we were going to punish those whiteys. That we were going to take from them"—a promise of retributive and distributive justice betrayed post-1994 by the prioritizing of restorative justice: the majority of the Black population continues to live in economically dire circumstances, separated from the prosperous few, well-hidden behind high security walls. Upon returning from the ANC camps, he finds himself destitute, his sacrifice forgotten. Realizing that he "didn't fight apartheid to be poor," Nazareth becomes a gangster, aiming to recruit Lucky and Zakes to join him on heists and robberies. Unacknowledged, derided even by the younger generation, he deploys his military skills in a life of crime, trying to get illegally what he thinks is rightfully his—if only the redistributive aspirations of the struggle had not been betrayed: in a dialogue with the two young men, a disgruntled Nazareth states "I may be a communist but I believe god helps those who help themselves." In the absence of substantial social and political empowerment, the limits of the narrative about truth and reconciliation become starkly palpable.

On the other side, police officer Swart and the white owners Lucky pushes into bankruptcy engage in some degree of white ululation about their loss of privilege: "This [South Africa] is the only country in the world where we have to take shit in eleven official languages" remarks a Portuguese realtor, his disdain for majority rule discernible in his facial expressions and intonation. Swart grudgingly proposes that the reason "the bad guys go free" has something to do with "who is running the country," but he is unable to have an honest reckoning about what counts as "good" or "bad" in the new dispensation and who its winners and losers are. Partially defanged by the new political order, he rages powerlessly when Lucky gets away with various crimes, though he does not hesitate to deploy the full force of the militarized police in Lucky's pursuit. Lastly, Leah romanticizes deprivation and thinks of Hillbrow as "Sodom and Gomora," a place that exerts a perverse attraction on the rich whites who come as voyeurs to buy drugs. A more blatant instance of social ignorance and moral disconnectedness could hardly have been conjured.[11]

The afterlives of apartheid in the film are most vividly traced on the geography and architecture of the city. The opening sequences focus on Johannesburg's skyline, seeking to reveal its beauty in time-lapse in the changing light. However, spectacular, lyrical long shots of buildings in sunlight are interspersed with naturalistic images of barbed wire, dark stairwells, and leaking pipes—dismal poverty. The juxtaposition of the two styles signals the irreducible distance between lofty hope and the material reality. Throughout the film, Hillbrow is depicted as a place of despair: poor families, taxi drivers, sex workers, drug addicts, gun traffickers, in Lucky's words, all "poor Black people trying to make a living" appear in dilapidated blocks with no electricity, running water, or sewage, amid piles of rubbish, on the soundtrack of gun shots, blearing sirens, and car alarms. The film's crew shot on location and featured locals as extras, with minimal intervention, animated by an idea of authenticity—enhanced by the photographer's expertise in documentary shooting (Marx 2010)—in a way that prosthetically takes the viewer into a world where hope is meager and frustration overwhelming.

Soweto is Hillbrow's other. Ziman uses footage he shot in the township in 1994: as the film begins and Lucky recounts his youthful hopes in sardonic voice-over, we see Black South Africans united in either celebration or protest, while armed forces in Casspirs—the armored vehicles that had become a symbol of apartheid repression in the townships—watch them from the sides of the road. Patrolling Casspirs make appearances at several points in the film, highlighting the temporal continuity of policing practices into the new era. The architecture of the township sits in sharp contrast to the high-rises in the city: small, modest constructions lining dusty red roads, inhabited by people who continue to live precarious lives, sharing pap at the light of gas lamps.

Other sites appear briefly in the film. A squatter camp, Primrose, is the scene of Lucky's being chased by taxi mobsters. Set in the vicinity of a gold mine and made up mostly of shacks built of corrugated iron sheets, it provides yet another image of ongoing human precarity and the legal and political ecology that keeps reproducing it. Places where Black people live contrast sharply with the white suburb, with affluent villas and high-tech security gates, lush gardens, leafy streets, private tennis courts, and expensive cars—images that justify Lucky's observation that Johannesburg was "a city fathered by gold, mothered by money and then commandeered by white men with cruelty and greed." Inside the villas, Black servants continue to care for white families who lunch on the sunlit porches. In the white neighborhood, behind the secured gates and barbed wire, everything goes on as if 1994 had not happened.

In taking the spectator on a panoramic tour of Johannesburg's neighborhoods, the film sheds light on the material infrastructure of apartheid's aftermath: across all sites, we see hopeless Black poverty, and misery. While some Black people did enjoy a degree of social mobility, large swathes of the population live "ungrievable" lives,[12] in the midst of deprivation, corruption, violence, and the AIDS epidemic. As Koleka Putuma writes, apartheid is "a genocide that can still be found in the townships" (2017, 109). For the majority, the "new dawn" never came: on streets littered with rubbish, new forms of violence feed on the ruins of the dream. Practices of state brutality get reproduced beyond what was supposed to be a "clean transition," while affluent suburbs remain isolated islands of privilege. In Ziman's hands, a seemingly typical gangster film uses the city's geography to render visible and problematize the blind spots of hegemonic visions of freedom, empowerment, and reconciliation and to thematize the materiality of disappointment and the conditions that determine the lives of those still not fully integrated in the political contract. The film thus powerfully confirms Ivan Vladislavić's conclusion that "the actual physical structures of apartheid are going to be difficult, if not impossible, to erase, and that we're going to be living within those structures for a very long time" (Warnes 2000, 78–79).

CONCLUSIONS

> I want someone who is going to look at me
> and love me
> the way that white people look at
> and love
> Mandela.
> Someone who is going to hold onto my memory
> the way that white people hold onto Mandela's legacy.
> A lover who will build Robben Island in my backyard
> and convince me that I have a garden
> and fresh air, a rainbow and freedom.
> A TRC kind of lover.
>
> *
>
> And this is one of the many residues of slavery:
> being loved like Mandela. (Putuma 2017, 101)

This powerful indictment of apartheid's memory and its concrete aftermaths is voiced by poet Koleka Putuma in her "1994: A Love Poem." In just a few lines, she captures the limits of the mnemonic doxa—featuring its supreme hero, its promise of freedom, inclusivity, and prosperity—and denounces its deception but also, perhaps most importantly, reveals the visceral political longing it left unmet. Simultaneously, the poet highlights the deep and incontestable connection between resilient oppressive sociopolitical structures and the colonization of a community's mnemonic space by convenient narratives of redemption and reconciliation. Thus, South Africans are shown to live within "segregated temporalities" (Brendese 2013).

The alignment of segregated temporalities and segregated geographies was caringly thematized by the artists included in this chapter, in particular by Kani, Vladislavić, and Ziman. This is one of the most illuminating particularities of the South African case study: it carefully and steadfastly traces the historically incontestable imbrication of hermeneutical and material exclusions—of the field's structure and its afferent doxa—and its effect on the present, the habituses it allows to reproduce over time and the differential horizons of expectations it engenders. A second key particularity is the direct and self-reflective tackling of mnemonic curation and its intolerable blind spots. While Netzer, Porumboiu, and Friang did touch on the collective yearning for consecrated heroes, Afrika, Dangor, and Wicomb help us inhabit the psyche of the masculine resister in order to grasp his emotional and political struggle with what is unassimilable, both to their identity and public hagiographies. In doing so, these refuseniks help us see not only how much is at stake in mnemonic excisions but also how difficult it is to undo them. Thirdly and relatedly, unlike in the other two cases, the importance and value of corrective mnemonic labor is foregrounded as essential to the possibility of articulating alternative political projects: Wicomb's amanuensis and Kani's librarian emerge as avatars of caring refusal in a way that enriches the typology of resistance I sketched in the first part of the book. Their voices emerge as essential in relation to both totalizing hero mythologies *and* white reveries of restored racial orders—so well captured by Vladislavić.

In choosing the South African artists to be featured in this chapter, the array of possibilities was overwhelming. Niq Mhlongo's *Way Back Home* (2013), Zakes Mda's *The Madonna of Excelsior* (2002), Njabulo Ndebele's *The Cry of Winnie Mandela* (2003), Marlene Van Niekerk's *Agaat* (2004),

Damon Galgut's *The Good Doctor* (2003), Zoë Wicomb's *Playing in the Light* (2006), and Nadine Gordimer's *Burger's Daughter* (1979) or *My Son's Story* (1990)—all offer extraordinary insights into the double erasure of multifaceted, dynamic complicities and impure resistances. Films such as Ramadan Suleman's *Fools* (1997) or *Zulu Love Letter* (2004), Oliver Schmitz's *Mapantsula* (1997), Anthony Fabian's *Skin* (2008), Norman Maake's *Homecoming* (2005), and Jans Rautenbach's *Katrina* (1969) would have helped illuminate various aspects of the racial ecology of violence, as well as the occlusions characterizing dominant mnemonic regimes. While accepting the limits of the selection included here, I hope that the caring refuseniks who did make the final cut persuasively advance this book's argument about the need to challenge consoling, official stories and render them more hospitable to competing visions and voices.

CONCLUSION
Heretic Visions, Responsible Futures

WHAT IS POLITICALLY at stake in refusing to "stay with the trouble"—to invoke Donna Haraway's powerful imperative yet again—and in embracing escapist, self-serving mythologies of clean beginnings? What is lost in obscuring the bodies caught between history's "dirty plates"—to recall Zoë Wicomb's powerful imagery? What forms of relationality and solidarity are precluded in the future if we fail to account for how percepticide works on a large scale under conditions of systemic violence? What can we, "ordinary beasts in the swamp called the present," aspire to when ecologies of violence persist, entrenched in ankylosed perceptions, affective registers, and habits, but also institutions, materialities, and practices? And how is our horizon of hope and repertoire of action constricted if we remain stuck with a stubborn yearning for salvific heroes? How can we reboot the political imagination in a way that reconfigures both the past and the future, opening up the space for inclusive, nonalienated forms of sociality?

These are the questions this book has sought to address, simultaneously highlighting the limits of existing frameworks and crossing disciplinary boundaries in search of illumination and inspiration. In tracing the complex and variable social dynamics behind political action under conditions of systemic repression as captured in a series of novels and films, I sought to trouble received paradigms of grappling with complicity and resistance in moral and political philosophy, as well as in large swathes of the transitional justice literature. The starting point was a frustration with individualizing, temporally static accounts that dominate academic and political imaginaries alike and that—inadvertently or not—contribute conceptually and practically to the double erasure. Therefore, first, the book is meant as a modest attempt to expand these fields' ontological perspectives by conceptualizing action—both complicit and resistant—in terms of the agents' relational positionality, which affects the resources their memory can summon, the scope of their imagination, the courage of their hopes, and the direction of their engagement with the world. Trespassing into sociology and history, the contextual analysis of the three countries' spectra of involvement has shown the salience of the conceptual and methodological changes in perspective I proposed and opened the path for a more nuanced account of complicity *in* and resistance *to* systemic wrongdoing.

The book's critical analysis of causality, temporality, and agency emerged as an imperative dictated both by what I take the standards of good academic work to be and a certain ethical understanding of responsibility for the ideas researchers contribute to communities' hermeneutical pools, beyond the walls of the university. The work undertaken here sought to avoid scholarly complicity with reductive, impoverishing frameworks of thought, analytically but also politically—a risk social epistemologists, feminists, critical race theorists, and genealogists have long warned us about. In the first part of the book, I showed that historians, anthropologists, sociologists, and theorists have often shared with artists the work of caring refusal. It is therefore important to recognize the exemplarity of such work and its authors' patient, thorough, sustained, and self-reflective practice of engaging with social reality in ways that do not reproduce problematic doxas. As I argued elsewhere (2019), as purveyors of conceptualizations, principles, and critique, scholars contribute hermeneutical resources to public debates, often oblivious to how they tap into a community's political imaginary, sometimes challenging, other times reinforcing it. Researchers' framing of a problematique—conceptually and methodologically—therefore matters epistemically, but also ethically and politically. I suggest that the notion of epistemological care can orient scholars to assume responsibility for how they conceptually carve out "reality" and for the normative assessment thereof, often enunciated from a position of authority. Living up to the idea of hermeneutical care sketched here does not require that specific theoretical and methodological choices be made in relation to the study of violent ecologies and their aftermaths—care is compatible with a variety of approaches. What it does require is a robust commitment to epistemic humility and a high degree of vigilance regarding what is revealed and what is obscured by methodological choices and the effects of those erasures on the terms of the academic—but also public—conversation.

In foregrounding the role artworks can play politically, the book remained firmly grounded in sociological and historical research. The novels and films included here are located within different genres and traditions. Some are innovative stylistically; others resort to classic choices. They have enjoyed variable degrees of success and popularity—domestically and internationality. What they share is their capacity to map the configurations of the spectrum of involvement in the three case studies, highlighting its internal heterogeneity and temporal dynamism. They are also united—I argue—in their capacity to embark spectators and readers on seductive prosthetic journeys into an unfamiliar past, thereby introducing heretic ideational, emotional, and sensorial knowledges. They do so via their interruption of routine political attitudes, affective alignments, and perceptions, decoupling them from official memory and rebooting the political imagination. In unpacking the social determinants of both resistance and complicity; in casting a critical light on the underbelly of resistance movements; in disclosing the deep socio-affective investments in reductive national mythologies and their limited cast of characters; in tracking the reproduction of violent doxas, institutions, and habituses beyond much-celebrated moments of rupture; and in recuperating marginalized knowledges of the past, the creators of the works included here have performed a valuable work of mnemonic care. They have invited us to stretch our political imagination to make space for the unassimilable—be it in relation to doxastic ideas of victimhood, resistance, or complicity—in a way that can catalyze processes of solidary attunement. This work requires our normative and political recognition, irrespectively of the reception they received from the publics they were addressing. As discussed earlier, care is a risky business, fraught with tensions and conflicts and yet, just because care is not always well-received, it is nonetheless valuable.

Some of the works included "echoed" (Medina 2013b) more effectively than others—and this was a function of the economy of international awards and their prestige-conferring power, the context in which the works were released (the domestic and geopolitical situation, their timing), their genre, their canonization and inclusion in school curricula, and the change of generation. Some have more effectively than others subverted their communities' entrenched investment in the double erasure and contributed to the development of a committal public memory, one that did not abstract the past by disconnecting it from the problems of the present. As I explained in the introduction, however, the level of success was only one among several criteria for my selection, alongside theoretical and thematic relevance. Most importantly, this book's inclusion of internationally less well-known works and of works not translated into English will help, first, support these works' seductive and prosthetic force and, second, contribute to a more equitable representation of the relevant artistic fields. This balancing imperative guided me throughout, in ways that I hope will resonate with readers attuned to the discrepancies characterizing the global economy of prestige and knowledge production.

To give some concreteness to this concern, let's consider some examples. In South Africa, a great deal of academic and public attention has been paid to world-renowned writers such as J. M. Coetzee and Nadine Gordimer—both white English-language writers and Nobel Award laureates. Notwithstanding these two authors' relevance for this project, I sought to give due attention to exciting, less well-known voices. In the French case, the discussion of internationally known authors such as Modiano, Duras, and Malle was balanced by the exploration of Friang's and Laurent's writing. Lastly, in the Romanian case, it is only Müller's writings and Porumboiu's and Netzer's films that enjoy some level of international visibility—because of their success in winning international awards. Regardless of the level of celebrity and canonization enjoyed, all artists included in this book have deep knowledge of the context they engaged with—caringly and aesthetically—and all avoided the twin peril of both lamentation and intransigent moralization. In embracing a variety of voices, I hope this book can itself challenge narrow global imaginaries about who counts as a writer or filmmaker.

While I selected my refuseniks from the arts of cinema and the novel, a variety of other artistic media offered equally valuable critical material. South African theater stands out in its powerful and lucid engagement with apartheid and its remainders. John Kani, Maishe Maponya, Winston Ntshona, the Khulumani Support Group, Zakes Mda, Jane Taylor, and the Handspring Puppet Company are just some of the many figures whose work fits the category of caring refusal. Installation art, happenings, and performances by artists such as Ion Grigorescu, László Ujvárossy, Lia Perjovschi, Geta Brătescu, and Mircea Stănescu have shed light on the closed horizon of hope Romanians lived and acted under. In France, Robert Doisneau's pictures of the German occupation transport the viewer into a universe of shortages and fear, while Henri Cartier-Bresson's photos of the liberation often focus a critical lens on the nation's "heroes," their violence, and their scapegoats.

The initiator of an exercise of the type attempted in this book has to acknowledge its parameters, blind spots, or, to be normatively consistent, erasures. In the theoretical chapters, alternative theoretical frameworks presented themselves for grappling with the complexity of the in-between and the mechanisms through which encounters with artworks could disrupt ankylotic remembering. In each case study, a wealth of artistic material presented itself to the author, whose genres, prosthetic and seductive qualities offered multiple and rich interpretive possibilities. Making the choices that constitute the backbone of this project set me on a specific course, foreclosing strategies that may have more effectively propelled the argument forward. My hope is that the book opens up a new perspective on how we might troubleshoot our mnemonic imagination in view of articulating and pursuing politically—with great care—heretic visions for less heroic yet more welcoming and more responsible futures. As pressure mounts on affluent, western democracy to deal with its violent ecologies and their histories, Titian's injunction, so central to Manea's incisive understanding of political temporalities, needs restating: "Ex praeterito praesens prudenter agit ni futura actione deturpet" (From the example of the past, mankind today acts prudently, to avoid endangering the future).

Notes

Introduction

1. Quinney (2007, 48) remarks that both in French (*rhinocéros*) and English, the plural of *rhinoceros* is identical to the singular. This feature symbolizes, as I explain later, the social relationalities underpinning ideological mobilization: one never becomes a rhinoceros in isolation.

2. For an account of his work as a journalist in Bucharest in the 1930s, see Lupaș (2014).

3. For some recent critical accounts of this aspect, see Meister (2010); Forti and Hanafi (2014); Shotwell (2016); Robbins (2017); and Rothberg (2019).

4. In this sense, my project is different from Bruce Robbins's reflection in *The Beneficiary* (2017): while his project is driven by a strong normative thrust and delineates ethical prescriptions, I am more interested in tracing critically the sociology and politics of complicity and of its misremembrance.

5. For recent work on other artforms in relation to political memory, see, for example, Asavei (2019); Garnsey (2019); and Rothberg (2019).

6. Unless otherwise specified, the translation of passages and titles from French and Romanian is mine.

7. Entrenched exclusionary imaginaries are ever-changing and so are the forms of violence they underpin. Excluding complex complicities and impure resistances from official memory enables systemic forms of violence to continue unchallenged

and evolve in new, sometimes unexpected directions, as we shall see from the analysis of the case studies.

8. French people who joined the Nazi secret police, the Gestapo.

9. Members of the Légion des volontaires français contre le bolchévisme ([LVF] Legion of French Volunteers against Bolshevism)—a collaborationist militia not officially connected to the Vichy government, whose members volunteered to fight against the Soviet Union in the East.

10. The novel's meandering trajectory to publication is recounted in Manea (2013).

11. The concept was theorized by Diana Taylor (1997) in relation to the most recent Argentine dictatorship.

12. The armed branch of the African National Congress.

CHAPTER 1

1. For the multidirectionality of memory, see Rothberg's (2009) classic.

2. In this sense, Debarati Sanyal's (2015) conceptualization of public memory's silences as themselves a form of complicity at the level of historical engagement is highly illuminating.

3. For a discussion of the politicization of categories, see Jeffery and Candea (2006); Fassin and Rechtman (2009); Govier (2015); and Maguire (2017).

4. Or, as we shall see in the case of France, its projection on a group of vulnerable citizens—women—who serve as scapegoat.

5. See Kutz (2000, 2007); Gardner (2007); May (2010); Ciurria (2011); and Lepora and Goodin (2013).

6. For example, while Kutz (2000) emphasizes participatory intent, Lepora and Goodin (2013) argue that knowledge of the wrongdoing and knowledge of the fact that one's actions contribute to wrongdoing are sufficient. For disagreements over causation, see Gardner (2007); and Kutz (2007).

7. Michael Rothberg's excellent recent book *The Implicated Subject* (2019) also focuses on demystifying the liberal paradigm of responsibility, going beyond the victim–perpetrator dyad, and thinking through complicity in a structurally complex manner, synchronically and diachronically. Unlike Rothberg, with his focus on the privileged, often distant, implicated subject, however, I seek to sketch a diverse cartography of the spectrum of involvement—one that shows its heterogeneity and temporal dynamism and that, as we shall see, also includes impure resistances as figures of implicatedness.

8. Several critics have problematized this blind spot. See, for example, Nagy (2008); K. Andrieu (2010); Gready and Robins (2014); Mullen (2015); and Evans (2016).

9. Whistleblowers and environmental crusaders are more recent additions to the panoply.

10. Analyzing apartheid, Sanders (2002) proposes two senses of complicity. First, he discusses the inescapable form of complicity that is inherent in sociality. Apartheid destroys this social form of complicity by separating people—setting them *apart*. He distinguishes this from more discrete acts of complicity, for which individuals can be held accountable. In what follows, I argue that there are also some forms of sociability that we can be held responsible for because they can cumulatively and insidiously contribute to catastrophic wrongdoing.

11. "Les agents sociaux ne sont pas simplement des particules mues par des forces physiques, ce sont aussi des agents connaissants qui sont porteurs de structures cognitives" (Social agents are not just particles moved by physical forces, they are also knowing agents endowed with cognitive structures) (2012, 262).

12. I am relying here on a vast literature in the philosophy and sociology of hope. For some representative accounts, see Day (1969); Bovens (1999); Pettit (2004); McGeer (2004, 2008); and Govier (2011).

13. To quote Stockdale (2019, 29), "Selves that hope are *relational*: they are socially constituted subjects whose identities, experiences, and opportunities are shaped by the multiple and overlapping relations in which they exist." I discuss the relationship between positionality and the scope of our imagination and hope in Mihai (2016).

14. Collective political action that prima facie appears hopeless can still be motivated by hopes that it will have a certain expressive or inspirational power for others or that it will secure a certain type of posterity (heroic, sacrificial, glorious).

15. See Kissell (1999); Celermajer (2009); and Applebaum (2010).

16. Bourdieu prioritizes the discourses of a specific group of individuals, who operate with a habitus of self-objectification: social scientists working in interdisciplinary research centers. He trusts the structure of scientific inquiry to potentially ensure their insulation against ideological mystification and hopes that, when coupled with active efforts to secure the political and economic independence of research, it can produce the kind of knowledge that is necessary to denaturalize reality. For the details of my critical engagement with Bourdieu's account of social change and its agents, see Mihai (2016b).

17. To give a couple of stark examples of historians who provided mnemonic care, think of the impact of Robert Paxton's book *La France de Vichy* (1973) or Adam Hochschild's *King Leopold's Ghost* (1998). Activists associated with movements such as Rhodes Must Fall and Black Lives Matter are also involved in a collective labor of mnemonic care that focuses on the mystifications of imperial memory.

18. *Délation* refers to (often anonymous) letters sent by "good" citizens to the authorities, informing on their peers' belonging to "undesirable" groups and engaging in illegal activities or violations of discriminatory rules and regulations. Out of the cases covered here, France and Romania stand out for the pervasive practice of délation.

19. For accounts of the benefits of collaboration in Paris in the 1940s, see Halimi (1983); Rousso (1992); Jackson (2003); and Sebba (2016). For profiles of French collabos, see Joly (2011). For a historical approach to complicity in socialist Romania, see L. Vasile, Vasilescu, and Urs (2016). For a critical account of how apartheid's beneficiaries got a free pass from the TRC, see Foster, Haupt, and de Beer (2005). In the chapters that follow, I will thematize these benefits contextually.

20. For a psychosocial account of bystanders, see Edgren (2012).

21. Interviewed by Angelika Klammer, writer Herta Müller (2016b) declared that, to remain a decent human being under authoritarianism, one had to fail miserably in the public domain. This is not something many intellectuals were ready to accept.

22. For a recent publication on inner emigration, see Klapper (2015).

23. For the atomizing effect of fear in France under the occupation, see Joly (2012, 23–24). For normalized fear in authoritarian Romania, see Mihăilescu (1993); Müller (2016b); and I. Pârvulescu (2015). For the effect of permanent fear on Black subjectivities in South Africa, see Subreenduth (2006) and Steyn (2012).

24. For a global selection of testimonies about the various sources of hope and the intersubjective scaffolding that sustain resisters, see Bould (1991).

CHAPTER 2

1. See, for example, Lang (2000); Felman and Laub (2013); and Rothberg (2009).

2. For an undiluted trust in the humanities' power to achieve this, see Spivak (2013).

3. Davide Panagia (2009) has emphasized the role of interruption at the level of sensation via encounters with visual artworks. He argues that such moments of interruption can mark the subject's freedom from all determination, moments when the referential order is suspended and can potentially be reconfigured. Given the account of subjectification I outlined earlier, Panagia's account appears simultaneously too optimistic (regarding the transformative power of sensation) and too thin (in its decoupling sensation from other aspects of subjectification) to support the idea of transformation advanced here.

4. There is a rich and insightful literature in disability studies that dispels myths of full, able-bodied mastery and provides phenomenological accounts of gradual and heterogeneous—yet not always seamless and almost never complete—processes of accommodating oneself to and incorporating auxiliary objects (prostheses) into both one's consciousness and embodiment by individuals who are disabled. See Murray (2004); Davis (2006); Lane (2006); Lundberg, Hagberg, and Bullington (2011); and Salamon (2012).

5. Beausoleil (2015) offers an insightful critique of mastery as the goal of any encounter with difference.

6. For two critical accounts of excess trust in imagination's emancipatory power, see Schiff (2013) and Mihai (2016b).

7. There is a big debate in aesthetics over the authenticity of emotions experienced through fiction. I agree with Moran (1994) and Medina (2013a) that these emotions are real and that it is only the object of the emotion that is fictional. It is not the case that we are imagining a fictional emotion; we are imagining with emotion.

8. Spelman (1990) sees the essence of the apprentice as the readiness for self-transformation in the encounter with alterity.

9. Those that allow for the extension of caring practices beyond the limited space in which it has historically developed.

10. For an account of why care cannot be merely a virtue, see Held (2007). Robinson (1998, 29) also writes, "Care ethics asks not only *why* should I care, but also *how* should I care, and how can I best promote caring personal and social relations among others."

11. Bowden (1997) includes citizenship as a site of practices of care but does not extrapolate beyond issues related to welfare policy.

12. Discussing responses to globalization, Pulcini (2013) describes the subject

who cares for the world while avoiding both heroic individualism and identitarian reification.

13. For an excellent criticism of the mirage of independence, see Drucker (2005).

14. For a sophisticated account of the epistemic friction emerging from victim-artists' disengagement and refusal to provide such alternative visions, see Schaap (2020).

CHAPTER 3

1. For portraits of intellectuals who thrived under the occupation, see Golsan (2006).

2. Joly (2016) speculates that office work was not among the most preferred types of "action" for the virulent anti-Semites.

3. Unsurprisingly, during the postwar legal purges, miliciens received much harder punishments than did miliciennes, once again affirming gendered notions of responsibility (Simonin 2010).

4. Spoliation is an important motivator: denunciations catalyze "economic aryanisation" (Bruttmann 2013).

5. Sebba (2016) offers an insight into the classed experience of women in occupied Paris.

6. For accounts of the collabos' political maneuvering in response to changes on the frontline, see Joly (2011); and Drake (2015).

7. For a complex account of the politics projected on subsequent filmic and theatrical productions on the basis of the novel *Le silence de la mer*, see Bowles (2014). For further contextualization, see Lloyd (2003) and Corbin (2019).

8. For an insightful analysis of both strategies' reductivism, see Atack (1989).

9. For a critique of the ahistoricism, moralism, and gauchism of the film in the post–1968 period, see Atack (1999).

10. For an account of historical debates post–1968, see Nettelbeck (1985).

11. For a critical analysis, see McDonnell (2019).

12. For discussions of these trials, see Chalandon and Nivelle (1998); Jean and Salas (2002); and Golsan (2012).

13. It is only in 2007 that the role colonial troops played in the liberation is recognised by the state, not in small part because of Rachid Bouchareb's 2006 film *Indigènes*.

14. For an illuminating account of the ideological debates around *mode rétro* and their historical complexity, see Ory (1981). For the scandal the film caused, see Mihai (2019b); and Corbin (2019).

15. Therefore, I disagree with Charles F. Altman (1976), who sees Lucien as a bundle of directionless energy.

16. See Malle and French (1993).

17. Not translated into English. The title can be roughly translated as *The Duckling*.

18. For accounts of the literary New Right to which Laurent belonged to after the war, see Nettelbeck (1989); Renard (2010); Dambre and Flood (2000); Hewitt (1996); and Bragança (2015a).

19. As Bourdieu argues, "Manliness must be validated by other men, in its reality as actual or potential violence, and certified by recognition of membership of the group of 'real men'" (2001, 52).

20. Translated into English as *The Night Watch*.

21. These features have led Kawakami (2016) to describe Modiano's work as postmodern.

22. I here disagree with Morris's (1996) conclusion that the Troubadour lacks an ethical identity.

23. This, I believe, dramatically distinguishes Modiano's character from another famous double agent in French postwar literature, Sanders in Roger Nimier's *Les épées*.

24. Not translated into English. The title's literal translation is *Like an Orchard before the Winter*.

25. The book was translated into English as *The War*. In my analysis, I rely on the French original.

26. The literal translation of the title is "Ter, the Militiaman."

27. The title refers to a mysterious note found in the traitor's address book and can be roughly translated as "Albert of the Capitals/Capital Cities"—a code name.

28. I therefore disagree with Comfort (2015), who sees Duras introducing this violence merely as an expression of the psychic pain of waiting for her deported husband.

29. For a survey of artworks that tackle the phenomenon of the *tonte*, see Prundeanu (2017).

30. For a discussion of forgetting and trauma, see Buys (2009).

CHAPTER 4

1. For comprehensive accounts of the mix between communism and nationalism in Romania, see Copilaş (2015); and Totok and Macovei (2016).

2. For accounts of the cross-pollination between the Orthodox Church and extreme right-wing movements, see Ciobanu (2017); and C. Vasile (2017).

3. For three portraits of such informers, see Tuzu (2016); L. Vasile (2016); and Vasilescu (2016).

4. See, for example, the victims of the so-called Pitești experiment. For a critical account of their nationalist martyrization, see Ciobanu (2015b).

5. For an analysis of the Romanian artworld under communism, see Preda (2017b).

6. For a discussion of the term "dissident," see Petrescu (2013).

7. See the Gheorghe Ursu case (Stan 2013).

8. The texts of the flyers studied by Floroiu (2015) are symptomatic in this sense.

9. It was only in 2007, due to intense external pressure, that a truth commission about the Romanian participation in the Shoah was established.

10. For critical takes on the report, see Cesereanu (2008); Ciobanu (2009); Abraham (2012); Ciobanu (2011); Tănăsoiu (2007); and Tileagă (2017).

11. For an analysis of the moralist anti-communism of historiography between 1989 and 2012, see Abraham (2012).

12. In literal translation, *The Memorial of Pain.*

13. For a gendered account of how official-memory gatekeepers judged both resisters and colluders, see Stan (2014).

14. The concept was theorized by Diana Taylor (1997) in relation to the most recent Argentine dictatorship.

15. For an account of the scandal her Nobel caused, see Mihai (2019b).

16. For a broader discussion of Manea's work, see Mihai (2019c).

17. *Concurs* was inspired by a real-life incident and the director's own memories of a murder that nobody intervened to stop (*Dan Pița* 2015).

18. In this sense I disagree with Nasta (2013, 49), who argues that the participants lose control of the situation and no longer know who they really are.

19. The analysis of Müller's work is based on the Romanian translations.

20. For a detailed analysis, see Eke (2013).

21. For an account of Müller's love for the Romanian language and some of its artistic traditions, see Drace-Francis (2013).

22. For a more detailed account of resisters' complicitous silences in Müller's work, see Mihai (2020).

23. Reflecting this book's argument about the subsequent colonizations of the hermeneutical space, this is how she also refers to her own father, a former SS officer.

24. This is based on the experience of Müller's (2016b) friend, Rolf Bossert.

25. This episode is based on Müller's friend, Jenny, who, terminally ill and romantically involved with a Securitate officer, came to Berlin to spy and warn her friend to stop speaking publicly about the dictatorship. See Müller (2016b, 134–38).

26. A recent film by Radu Jude (2018) problematizes Romanian troops' participation in the Shoah in the Eastern bloodlands. For an insightful analysis, see Popa (2019).

CHAPTER 5

1. For an insightful account of de Kock's positioning after apartheid, see Gobodo-Madikizela (2003).

2. On the other side, the End the Conscription Campaign benefited from the support of many white women, motivated not by antiapartheid views, but by worries for the lives of their conscripted sons (Cock 1991, 174).

3. See, for example, Asmal, Asmal, and Roberts (1997); Nuttall and Coetzee (1998); Ross (2003); Howarth and Norval (1998); R. Wilson (2001); Posel and Simpson (2002); Gobodo-Madikizela (2008); Gready (2011); and Sitze (2013).

4. For excellent analyses, see Samuelson (2007); Baiada (2008); Negri (2017); and Álvarez (2011).

5. Giffel (2018) persuasively reads Wicomb as recuperating the silenced authorial voices against the postmodern critique as a corrective measure against hegemonic power.

6. This play has been selected by the South African National Department of Education for study in Grade 12.

7. I therefore disagree with Marais's (2002) focus on the discursive order to which Tearle belongs, overlooking his embodied and affective investment in white supremacy.

8. Term coined by Steyn and Foster (2008), discussed below.

9. Peters (2009) identifies a series of typos in the first two editions of the novel that, he argues, point to an alternative, resistant, postcolonial vision of reality—another formal trick that sabotages Tearle's authoritative voice.

10. Marx (2010) sees economic deprivation as central to the film's genre and critical input.

11. De Villiers (2009) suggests this is the director's way of showing awareness of how the film itself may be read as voyeuristic and deflecting such a criticism.

12. See Butler (2006).

References

Abraham, Florin. 2012. "Istoriografie și memorie socială în România după 1989." *Anuarul Institutului de Istorie "George Barițiu," Series HISTORICA* 51: 145–72.

Adebayo, Sakiru. 2020. "White Grief, Black Grievance." Conference paper delivered at the University of Edinburgh, January 31.

Adler, Karen. 1995. "No Words to Say It? Women and the Expectation of Liberation." In *The Liberation of France: Image and Event*, edited by Nancy Wood and H. R. Kedward, 77–89. Oxford: Berg.

Afrika, Tatamkhulu. 2006. *The Innocents*. New York: Seven Stories Press.

Afxentiou, Afxentis, Robin Dunford, and Michael Neu. 2017. *Exploring Complicity: Concept, Cases and Critique*. London: Rowman & Littlefield.

Albu, Mihai. 2008. *Informatorul. Studiu aspura colaborării cu Securitatea*. Bucharest: Polirom.

Alcoff, Linda. 2000. "On Judging Epistemic Credibility: Is Social Identity Relevant?" In *Women of Color and Philosophy: A Critical Reader*, edited by Naomi Zack, 235–62. Hoboken, NJ: JohnWiley.

———. 2015. *The Future of Whiteness*. Cambridge: Polity Press.

Al-Saji, Alia. 2014. "A Phenomenology of Hesitation: Interrupting Racializing Habits of Seeing." In *Living Alterities: Phenomenology, Embodiment, and Race*, edited by Emily S. Lee, 133–72. Albany, NY: State University of New York Press.

Altman, Charles. 1976. "*Lacombe, Lucien*: Laughter as Collaboration." *French Review* 49 (4): 549.

Álvarez, David. 2011. "'Dulcie Longs for the Comfort of the Quotidian': The Place of Everyday Life in Zoë Wicomb's David's Story." *Current Writing: Text and Reception in Southern Africa* 23 (2): 127–36. https://doi.org/10.1080/1 013929X.2011.602907.

Andreescu, Gabriel. 2013. *Cărturari, opozanți si documente. Manipularea Arhivei Securității.* Bucharest: Polirom.

Andrieu, Claire. 2000. "Women in the French Resistance." *French Politics, Culture & Society* 18 (1): 13–27. https://doi.org/10.3167/153763700782378238.

Andrieu, Kora. 2010. "Civilizing Peacebuilding: Transitional Justice, Civil Society, and the Liberal Paradigm." *Security Dialogue* 41 (5): 537–58. https://doi.org/10.1177/0967010610382109.

Applebaum, Barbara. 2010. *Being White, Being Good: White Complicity, White Moral Responsibility, and Social Justice Pedagogy.* Lanham, MD: Lexington Books.

Asavei, Maria Alina. 2017. "'Call the Witness': Romani Holocaust Related Art in Austria and Marika Schmiedt's Will to Memory." *Memory Studies*, November 19. https://doi.org/10.1177/1750698017741929.

———. 2019. "The Art and Politics of Imagination: Remembering Mass Violence against Women." *Critical Review of International Social and Political Philosophy* 22 (5): 618–36. https://doi.org/10.1080/13698230.2019.1565704.

Asmal, Kader, Louise Asmal, and Ronald Suresh Roberts. 1997. *Reconciliation through Truth: A Reckoning of Apartheid's Criminal Governance.* Claremont, South Africa: David Philip Publishers.

Assouline, Pierre. 1985. *L'epuration des intellectuels.* Mémoire du siècle. Brussels: Editions Complexe.

Atack, Margaret. 1989. *Literature and the French Resistance: Cultural Politics and Narrative Forms, 1940–1950.* Manchester: Manchester University Press.

———. 1999. "May 68 in French Fiction and Film: Rethinking Society, Rethinking Representation." In *Nation/History: Repenser la France*, 102–22. Oxford: Oxford University Press. www.oxfordscholarship.com/view/10.1093/acprof:oso/9780198715153.001.0001/acprof-9780198715153-chapter-7.

———. 2016. "Performing the Nation in the Mode Rétro." *Journal of War & Culture Studies* 9 (4): 335–47. https://doi.org/10.1080/17526272.2016.1226545.

Atack, Margaret, and Christopher Lloyd. 2012. "Introduction." In *Framing Narratives of the Second World War and Occupation in France, 1939–2009: New Readings*, 1–15. Manchester: Manchester University Press.

Avram, Andrei. n.d. "Rezistența anticomunistă pe teritoriul României." *Historia.* www.historia.ro/sectiune/general/articol/rezistenta-anticomunista-pe-teritoriul -romaniei.

Azéma, Jean-Pierre. 1979. *De Munich à la Libération, 1983–1944.* Paris: Le Seuil.

Baalen, Sebastian van. 2014. "The Microdynamics of Conflict Escalation: The Case of ANC-IFP Fighting in South Africa in 1990." *Pax et Bellum Journal* 1 (1): 14–20.

Bădică, Simina. 2010. "The Black Hole Paradigm. Exhibiting Communism in Post-Communist Romania." In *History of Communism in Europe*, edited by IICCMER, 1:83–101. Bucharest: Zeta Books.

Baiada, Christa. 2008. "On Women, Bodies, and Nation: Feminist Critique and Revision in Zoë Wicomb's David's Story." *African Studies* 67 (1): 33–47. https://doi.org/10.1080/00020180801943081.

Beausoleil, Emily. 2015. "Mastery of Knowledge or Meeting of Subjects? The Epistemic Effects of Two Forms of Political Voice." *Contemporary Political Theory* 15 (1): 16–37. https://doi.org/10.1057/cpt.2015.22.

Benedik, Stefan. 2018. "Non-Committal Memory: The Ambivalent Inclusion of Romani Suffering under National Socialism in Hegemonic Cultural Memory." *Memory Studies*, December 17. https://doi.org/10.1177/1750698018818220.

Bennett, Jill. 2005. *Empathic Vision: Affect, Trauma, and Contemporary Art.* Stanford, CA: Stanford University Press.

Biko, Steve. 1987. *I Write What I Like: A Selection of His Writings.* Oxford: Heinemann.

Bilbija, Ksenija, Jo Ellen Fair, Cynthia E. Milton, and Leigh A. Payne, eds. 2005. *The Art of Truth-Telling about Authoritarian Rule.* Madison: University of Wisconsin Press.

Binckes, Robin. 2018. *Vlakplaas: Apartheid Death Squads, 1979–1994.* South Yorkshire, UK: Pen & Sword.

Bisschoff, Lizelle, and Stefanie van de Peer. 2013. *Art and Trauma in Africa: Representations of Reconciliation in Music, Visual Arts, Literature and Film.* London: Tauris Academic Studies.

Bleiker, Roland. 2009. *Aesthetics and World Politics.* London: Palgrave.

Bloomberg, Charles. 1990. *Christian-Nationalism and the Rise of the Afrikaner Broederbond, in South Africa, 1918–48.* Edited by Saul Dubow. London: Palgrave Macmillan.

Boia, Lucian. 2016. *Strania istorie a comunismului românesc.* Bucharest: Humanitas.

Booth, W. James. 2008. "The Color of Memory: Reading Race with Ralph Ellison." *Political Theory* 36 (5): 683–707. https://doi.org/10.1177/0090591708321034.

Bordeleau, Francine. 1985. "La passion selon Duras." *Nuit Blanche* 18: 50–52.

Bosomitu, Ştefan, Mihai Burcea, and Cristina Diac, eds. 2012. *Spectrele lui Dej: Încursiuni în biografia şi regimul unui dictator.* Iasi: Polirom.

Bould, Geoffrey. 1991. *Conscience Be My Guide.* London: Zed Books.

Bourdieu, Pierre. 1977. *Outline of a Theory of Practice*. Cambridge: Cambridge University Press.

———. 1990. *The Logic of Practice*. Stanford, CA: Stanford University Press.

———. 2000. *Pascalian Meditations*. Stanford, CA: Stanford University Press.

———. 2001. *Masculine Domination*. Cambridge: Polity.

———. 2010. *Distinction*. London: Routledge.

———. 2012. *Sur l'État. Cours au Collège de France*. Paris: Raisons d'agir/Seuil.

Bovens, Luc. 1999. "The Value of Hope." *Philosophy and Phenomenological Research* 59 (3): 667–81. https://doi.org/10.2307/2653787.

Bowden, Peta. 1997. *Caring: Gender-Sensitive Ethics*. London: Routledge.

Bowles, Brett. 2014. "Résistance Oblige? Historiography, Memory, and the Evolution of *Le Silence de la mer*, 1942–2012." *French Politics, Culture and Society* 32 (1): 68–100.

Bragança, Manuel. 2015a. "Moving Beyond the Rhetoric of Provocation: The French and World War II in the Novels of the Hussards (1949–1954)." *Journal of War & Culture Studies* 8 (3): 228–39. https://doi.org/10.1179/17526280 15Y.0000000015

———. 2015b. "'Un Village Français': Les clefs d'un succès." *The Conversation*, September 20. http://theconversation.com/un-village-francais-les-clefs-dun-succes-46367.

Brendese, P. J. 2013. *The Power of Memory in Democratic Politics*. Rochester, NY: University of Rochester Press.

Brossat, Alain. 1993. *Les tondues, un carnaval moche*. Levallois-Perret, France: Manya.

Broun, Kenneth S. 2012. *Saving Nelson Mandela: The Rivonia Trial and the Fate of South Africa*. Oxford: Oxford University Press.

Brown, Julian. 2016. *The Road to Soweto: Resistance and the Uprising of 16 June 1976*. Martlesham, UK: Boydell & Brewer.

Bruttmann, Tal. 2013. "La délation, un instrument au service de 'l'aryanisation'?" *Archives Juives* 46 (1): 35–44.

Bucur, Maria. 2008. "Gendering Dissent: Of Bodies and Minds, Survival and Opposition Under Communism." *Oxford Slavonic Papers* 7: 204–23.

Bull, Anna Cento, and Hans Lauge Hansen. 2016. "On Agonistic Memory." *Memory Studies* 9 (4): 390–404. https://doi.org/10.1177/1750698015615935.

Burrin, Philippe. 1996. *Living with Defeat: France under the German Occupation, 1940–1944*. London: Arnold.

Burton, Mary. 2010. "The Black Sash Story: Protest and Service Recorded in the Archives." *English Academy Review* 27 (2): 129–33. https://doi.org/10.1080/101 31752.2010.514992.

Butaud, Nadia. 2008. *Patrick Modiano*. Paris: Textuel.

Butler, Judith. 2006. *Precarious Life: The Powers of Mourning and Violence*. New York, NY: Verso.

Buys, Anthea. 2009. "*Hiroshima Mon Amour* and the Necessity of Oblivion." *English Studies in Africa* 52 (1): 50–60. https://doi.org/10.1080/00138390903172526.

Calhoun, Cheshire. 2008. "Hope Matters." Conference paper delivered at Vanderbilt University, 28 March.

Campbell, Joseph. 2004. *The Hero with a Thousand Faces*. Introduction by Clarissa Pinkola Estés. Commemorative ed. Bollingen series 17. Princeton, NJ: Princeton University Press.

Capdevila, Luc. 1998. "Le mythe du guerrier et la construction sociale d'un 'éternel masculin' après la guerre." *Revue française de psychanalyse* 62 (2): 607–24. https://doi.org/10.3917/rfp.g1998.62n2.0607.

———. 2001a. "Identités masculines et féminines pendant et après la guerre." In *1939–1945: Combats de femmes*, edited by Évelyne Morin-Rotureau, 199–220. Paris: Autrement.

———. 2001b. "The Quest for Masculinity in a Defeated France, 1940–1945." *Contemporary European History* 10 (3): 423–45. https://doi.org/10.1017/S0960777301003058.

———. 2002. "L'identité masculine et les fatigues de la guerre (1914–1945)." *Vingtième siècle* 75 (3): 97–108. https://doi.org/10.3917/ving.075.0097.

Cazenave, Jennifer. 2011. "La voix off au féminin: *Hiroshima mon amour* et *Aurélia Steiner*." *Cahiers de Narratologie* 20, July 13. https://doi.org/10.4000/narratologie.6365.

Celermajer, Danielle. 2009. *The Sins of the Nation and the Ritual of Apologies*. Cambridge: Cambridge University Press.

———. 2018. *The Prevention of Torture: An Ecological Approach*. Cambridge: University Press.

Cépède, Michel. 1961. *Agriculture et alimentation en France durant la IIe Guerre mondiale*. Paris: Éditions M.-Th. Génin.

Cesereanu, Ruxandra. 2008. "The Final Report on the Holocaust and the Final Report on the Communist Dictatorship in Romania." *East European Politics and Societies* 22 (2): 270–81. https://doi.org/10.1177/0888325408315764.

Chalandon, Sorj, and Pascale Nivelle. 1998. *Crimes contre l'humanité: Barbie, Touvier, Bousquet, Papon*. Paris: Plon.

Cieutat, Michel. 2005. "*Lacombe, Lucien*, ou l'ordinaire des contradictions." *Positif: Revue Mensuelle de Cinéma* 538: 89–91.

Ciobanu, Monica. 2009. "Criminalising the Past and Reconstructing Collective Memory: The Romanian Truth Commission." *Europe-Asia Studies* 61 (2): 313–36. https://doi.org/10.1080/09668130802630870.

———. 2011. "Rewriting and Remembering Romanian Communism: Some Controversial Issues." *Nationalities Papers* 39 (2) 205–21. https://doi.org/10.1 080/00905992.2010.549472.

———. 2014. "Reconstructing the History of Early Communism and Armed Resistance in Romania." *Europe-Asia Studies* 66 (9): 1452–81. https://doi.org/1 0.1080/09668136.2014.956440.

———. 2015a. "The Challenge of Competing Pasts." In *Post-Communist Transitional Justice Lessons from Twenty-Five Years of Experience*, 148–66. Cambridge: Cambridge University Press.

———. 2015b. "Pitești: A Project in Reeducation and Its Post-1989 Interpretation in Romania." *Nationalities Papers* 43 (4): 615–33. https://doi.org/10.1080/009 05992.2014.984288.

———. 2017. "Remembering the Gulag: Religious Representations and Practices." In *Justice, Memory and Redress in Romania: New Insights*, edited by Lavinia Stan and Lucian Turcescu, 214–34. Newcastle: Cambridge Scholars Publishing.

Ciurria, Michelle. 2011. "Complicity and Criminal Liability in Rwanda: A Situationist Critique." *Res Publica* 17 (4): 411–19. https://doi.org/10.1007/s11158-011-9157-z.

Cloete, Michael. 2019. "Steve Biko: Black Consciousness and the African Other—The Struggle for the Political." *Angelaki* 24 (2): 104–15. https://doi.or g/10.1080/0969725X.2019.1574083.

Cock, Jacklyn. 1991. *Colonels and Cadres: War and Gender in South Africa*. Cape Town: Oxford University Press.

Cohen, Stanley. 2000. *States of Denial: Knowing About Atrocities and Suffering*. Cambridge: Polity Press.

Coleman, Max. 1998. *A Crime Against Humanity: Analysing the Repression of the Apartheid State*. Johannesburg: Human Rights Commission.

Comfort, Kathy. 2015. "Relieving Pain in Marguerite Duras's 'La Douleur' and 'Albert Des Capitales.'" *Neohelicon* 42 (2): 551–69. https://doi.org/10.1007/ s11059-015-0305-x.

Comisia Prezidențială pentru Analiza Dictaturii Comuniste din România. 2006. "Raport Final." Bucharest. https://archive.org/details/ComisiaPrezidentiala-PentruAnalizaDictaturiiComunisteDinRomania-Raport.

Conradi, Elisabeth. 2015. "Redoing Care: Societal Transformation through Critical Practice." *Ethics and Social Welfare* 9 (2): 113–29. https://doi.org/10.1080/ 17496535.2015.1005553.

Cooke, Dervila. 2005. *Present Pasts: Patrick Modiano's (Auto)Biographical Fictions*. Amsterdam: Rodopi.

Coombes, Annie E. 2011. "Witnessing History/Embodying Testimony: Gender and Memory in Post-Apartheid South Africa." *Journal of the Royal Anthropological Institute* 17: S92–112.

Copilaş, Emanuel. 2015. *Natiunea socialistă. Politica identităţii in Epoca de Aur.* Bucharest: Polirom.

Corbin, Christophe. 2019. *Revisiting the French Resistance in Cinema, Literature, Bande Dessinée, and Television (1942–2012).* Lanham, MD: Lexington Books.

Corobca, Liliana. 2015. "Reacţii la cenzura comunistă." In *Nesupunere şi contestare în România comunistă*, edited by Clara Mareş and Constantin Vasilescu. Bucharest: Polirom.

———. 2016a. *Controlul cărţii: Cenzura literaturii în regimul comunist din România.* Bucharest: Cartea Romaneasca.

———. 2016b. "Profilul Cenzorilor din Direcţia Generală pentru Presă şi Tipărituri." In *Traversând comunismul. Convieţuire, conformism, compromis*, edited by Lucian Vasile, Constantin Vasilescu, and Alina Urs, 21–46. Bucharest: Polirom.

Craig, Siobhan S. 2005. "Tu n'as Rien vu à Hiroshima: Desire, Spectatorship and the Vaporized Subject in *Hiroshima Mon Amour*." *Quarterly Review of Film and Video* 22 (1): 25–35. https://doi.org/10.1080/10509200590449895.

Crawford, Neta C. 2007. "Individual and Collective Moral Responsibility for Systemic Military Atrocity." *Journal of Political Philosophy* 15 (2): 187–212. https://doi.org/10.1111/j.1467-9760.2007.00278.x.

Dambre, Marc, and Christopher Flood. 2000. "The Politics of Provocation in the Hussards." *South Central Review* 17 (4): 61–71. https://doi.org/10.2307/3190167.

Dan Piţa. 2015. http://aarc.ro//cineasti/cineast/dan-pita.

Dangor, Achmat. 2003. *Bitter Fruit.* London: Atlantic.

Dass, Minesh. 2011. "'Amanuensis' and 'Steatopygia': The Complexity of 'Telling the Tale' in Zoë Wicomb's *David's Story*." *English in Africa* 38 (2): 45-60. DOI: 10.4314/eia.v38i2.3

Davis, Lennard J. 2006. "Constructing Normalcy." In *The Disability Studies Reader*, edited by Lennard J. Davis, 3–16. New York: Routledge.

Day, J. P. 1969. "Hope." *American Philosophical Quarterly* 6 (2): 89–102.

Deletant, Dennis. 1995. *Ceauşescu and the Securitate: Coercion and Dissent in Romania, 1965–1989.* London: M. E. Sharpe.

Desai, Ashwin. 2015. "Indian South Africans and the Black Consciousness Movement under Apartheid." *Diaspora Studies* 8 (1): 37–50. https://doi.org/10.1080/09739572.2014.957972.

Desgranges, Jean-Marie. 1948. *Les crimes masqués du résistantialisme.* Paris: Éditions de l'Élan.

Diamond, Hanna. 1999. *Women and the Second World War in France, 1939–48: Choices and Constraints.* Women and Men in History. Harlow: Longman.

Dingler, Catrin. 2015. "Disenchanted Subjects? On the Experience of Subjectivity in Care Relations." *Ethics and Social Welfare* 9 (2): 209–15. https://doi.org/10.1080/17496535.2015.1023059.

Disch, Lisa. 1996. *Hannah Arendt and the Limits of Philosophy: With a New Preface.* Ithaca, NY: Cornell University Press.

Dlamini, Jacob. 2015. *Askari: A Story of Collaboration and Betrayal in the Anti-Apartheid Struggle.* London: Hurst.

Dobrincu, Dorin. 2006. "Rezistenta armată anticomunistă în sud-estul Munților Apuseni (I)." *Revista 22*, December 22. https://revista22.ro/istorie/rezistenta-armata-anticomunista-in-sud-estul-muntilor-apuseni-i.

———. 2007a. "Rezistența armată anticomunistă din Munții Făgăraș—Versantul nordic. Grupul carpatic făgărășan/Grupul Ion Gavrilă (1949/1950–1955/1956)." *Anuarul Institutului de Istorie G. Barițiu» din Cluj-Napoca* XLVI: 433–502.

———. 2007b. "Rezistenta armată anticomunistă în sud-estul Munților Apuseni (II)." *Revista 22*, January 3. www.revista22.ro/rezistenta-armata-anticomunista-in-sudestul-muntilor-apuseni-ii-3340.html.

Dotson, Kristie. 2011. "Tracking Epistemic Violence, Tracking Practices of Silencing." *Hypatia* 26 (2): 236–57. https://doi.org/10.1111/j.1527-2001.2011.01177.x.

———. 2012. "A Cautionary Tale: On Limiting Epistemic Oppression." *Frontiers: A Journal of Women Studies* 33 (1): 24–47. https://doi.org/10.5250/fronjwomestud.33.1.0024.

———. 2014. "Conceptualizing Epistemic Oppression." *Social Epistemology* 28 (2): 1–24. https://doi.org/10.1080/02691728.2013.782585.

Drace-Francis, Alex. 2013. "Beyond the Land of Green Plums: Romanian Culture and Language in Herta Müller's Work." In *Herta Müller*, edited by Brigid Haines and Lyn Marven, 32–49. Oxford: Oxford University Press.

Drake, David. 2015. *Paris at War, 1939–1944.* Cambridge, MA: Belknap Press of Harvard University Press.

Drucker, Johanna. 2005. *Sweet Dreams.* New York: Columbia University Press.

Dube, Siphiwe Ignatius. 2011. "Transitional Justice Beyond the Normative: Towards a Literary Theory of Political Transitions." *International Journal of Transitional Justice* 5 (2): 177–97. https://doi.org/10.1093/ijtj/ijr004.

Dubow, Saul. 1992. "Afrikaner Nationalism, Apartheid and the Conceptualization of Race." *Journal of African History* 33 (2): 209–37.

———. 2014. *Apartheid, 1948–1994.* Oxford: Oxford University Press.

Dunton, Chris. 2004. "Tatamkhulu Afrika: The Testing of Masculinity." *Research in African Literatures* 35 (1): 148–61. DOI:10.1353/ral.2004.0010.

Duras, Marguerite. 1959. *Hiroshima, mon amour.* Directed by Alain Resnais. Paris: Pathé Films.

Duras, Marguerite. 2011. *La douleur.* Paris: Folioplus Classiques.

Eddy, Beverley Driver. 2013. "A Mutilated Fox Fur: Examining the Contexts of Herta Müller's Imagery in *Der Fuchs War Damals Schon Der Jäger*." In *Herta Müller*, edited by Brigid Haines and Lyn Marven, 84–98. Oxford: Oxford University Press.

Edgren, Henrik, ed. 2012. *Looking at the Onlookers and Bystanders: Interdisciplinary Approaches to the Causes and Consequences of Passivity*. Vol. 13. Stockholm: Living History Forum.

Eke, Norbert Otto. 2013. "'Macht Nichts, Macht Nichts, Sagte Ich Mir, Macht Nichts': Herta Müller's Romanian Novels." In *Herta Müller*, edited by Brigid Haines and Lyn Marven, 99–117. Oxford: Oxford University Press.

Ellis, Stephen. 2013. *External Mission. The ANC in Exile, 1960–1990*. Oxford: Oxford University Press.

Engster, Daniel, and Maurice Hamington. 2015. *Care Ethics and Political Theory*. Oxford: Oxford University Press.

Enloe, Cynthia H. 1990. *Bananas, Beaches, and Bases: Making Feminist Sense of International Politics*. Berkeley, CA: University of California Press.

Evans, Matthew. 2016. "Structural Violence, Socioeconomic Rights, and Transformative Justice." *Journal of Human Rights* 15 (1): 1–20. https://doi.org/10.10 80/14754835.2015.1032223.

Everatt, David. 2009. *The Origins of Non-Racialism: White Opposition to Apartheid in the 1950s*. Johannesburg: Wits University Press.

Fageot, Christelle. 2008. *La Milice en Vaucluse, 1943–1945*. Mazan: Études comtadines. https//catalog.hathitrust.org/Record/005964692.

Fanon, Frantz. 2008. *Black Skin, White Masks*. New York: Grove Press.

Fassin, Didier, and Richard Rechtman. 2009. *The Empire of Trauma: An Inquiry into the Condition of Victimhood*. Translated by Rachel Gomme. Princeton, NJ: Princeton University Press.

Felman, Shoshana, and Dori Laub. 2013. *Testimony: Crises of Witnessing in Literature, Psychoanalysis and History*. New York: Routledge.

Filippi, Natacha. 2016. "Institutional Violence and the Law in Apartheid South Africa." *Journal of Colonialism and Colonial History* 17 (3). https://doi. org/10.1353/cch.2016.0038.

Fletcher, Angus. 1999. "The Place of Despair and Hope." *Social Research*, 521–29.

Floroiu, Mihai. 2015. "Forme de opoziție politică in anii '80: Scrisori, inscripții și manifeste anti-ceaușiste." In *Nesupunere și contestare în România comunistă*, edited by Clara Mareș and Constantin Vasilescu, 207–34. Bucharest: Polirom.

Flower, John. 2007. *Patrick Modiano*. Faux Titre 305. Amsterdam: Rodopi.

———. 2014. "A Continuing Preoccupation with the Occupation." *French Cultural Studies* 25 (3–4): 299–308. https://doi.org/10.1177/0957155814534144.

Fobi, Brian Tangang. 2014. "The Engineers of History: Hendrik Verwoerd, George Wallace and the Power of Historical Memory." PhD diss., Yale University.

Fogg, Shannon L. 2009. *The Politics of Everyday Life in Vichy France: Foreigners, Undesirables, and Strangers.* Cambridge: Cambridge University Press.

Forti, Simona, and Zakiya Hanafi. 2014. *The New Demons: Rethinking Power and Evil Today.* Palo Alto, CA: Stanford University Press.

Foster, Don, Paul Haupt, and Marésa de Beer. 2005. *The Theatre of Violence: Narratives of Protagonists in the South African Conflict.* Cape Town: HSRC Press.

Foucault, Michel, Pascal Bonitzer, and Serge Toubiana. 2000. "Anti-Rétro." In *Cahiers Du Cinéma: Volume Four, 1973–1978: History, Ideology, Cultural Struggle. An Anthology from* Cahiers Du Cinéma*, Nos 248–292, September 1973–September 1978,* edited by Jim Hillier, David Wilson, Bérénice Reynaud, and Nick Browne, 159–72. New York: Psychology Press.

Franco, Zeno E., Kathy Blau, and Philip G. Zimbardo. 2011. "Heroism: A Conceptual Analysis and Differentiation Between Heroic Action and Altruism." *Review of General Psychology* 15 (2): 99–113. https://doi.org/10.1037/a0022672.

Franco, Zeno E., and Philip G. Zimbardo. 2006. "The Banality of Heroism." *Greater Good*, September 1. https://greatergood.berkeley.edu/article/item/the_banality_of_heroism.

Frenkel, Ronit. 2008. "Performing Race, Reconsidering History: Achmat Dangor's Recent Fiction." *Research in African Literatures* 39 (1): 149–65.

Friang, Brigitte. 1978. *Comme un verger avant l'hiver.* Paris: Julliard.

Gacon, Stéphane. 2002. *L'Amnistie. De la Commune à la guerre d'Algérie.* Paris: Le Seuil.

Gardner, John. 2007. "Complicity and Causality." *Criminal Law and Philosophy* 1 (2): 127–41. https://doi.org/10.1007/s11572-006-9018-6.

Garnsey, Eliza. 2019. *The Justice of Visual Art: Creative State-Building in Times of Political Transition.* Cambridge: Cambridge University Press.

Giffel, Kaelie. 2018. "Historical Violence and Modernist Forms in Zoë Wicomb's *David's Story.*" *Twentieth Century Literature* 64 (1): 53–78. https://doi.org/10.1215/0041462X-4387701.

Gilligan, Carol. 1982. *In a Different Voice.* Cambridge, MA: Harvard University Press.

Gilzmer, Mechtild, Christine Levisse-Touzé, and Stefan Martens, eds. 2003. *Les femmes dans la Résistance en France.* Paris: Tallandier.

Gobodo-Madikizela, Pumla. 2003. *A Human Being Died That Night: A South African Woman Confronts the Legacy of Apartheid.* Boston, MA: Houghton Mifflin.

———. 2008. "Transforming Trauma in the Aftermath of Gross Human Rights

Abuses: Making Public Spaces Intimate through the South African Truth and Reconciliation Commission." In *Social Psychology of Intergroup Reconciliation*, edited by Thomas E. Malloy and Jeffrey D. Fisher, 57–75. Oxford: Oxford University Press.

———. 2020. "Witnessing Trauma: A Call to Reparative Humanism." Conference paper delivered at the University of Edinburgh, January 31.

Golsan, Richard Joseph. 1998. "Author, Identity and the Voice of History in Patrick Modiano's *La Ronde de Nuit and Les Boulevards de Ceinture.*" In *Paradigms of Memory: The Occupation and Other Hi/Stories in the Novels of Patrick Modiano*, edited by Martine Guyot-Bender and William VanderWolk, 137–44. Currents in Comparative Romance Languages and Literatures 64. New York, NY: Peter Lang.

———. 2000. *Vichy's Afterlife: History and Counterhistory in Postwar France.* Lincoln, NE: University of Nebraska Press.

———. 2006. *French Writers and the Politics of Complicity: Crises of Democracy in the 1940s and 1990s.* Baltimore, MD: Johns Hopkins University Press.

———. 2012. *The Papon Affair: Memory and Justice on Trial.* New York, NY: Routledge.

———. 2017. *The Vichy Past in France Today.* Lanham, MD: Lexington Books.

Gorrara, Claire. 1998. *Women's Representations of the Occupation in Post-'68 France.* London: Palgrave. https://doi.org/10.1007/978-1-349-26461-2.

Govier, Trudy. 2011. "Hope and Its Opposites." *Journal of Social Philosophy* 42 (3): 239–53. https://doi.org/10.1111/j.1467-9833.2011.01532.x.

———. 2015. *Victims and Victimhood.* Peterborough, Ontario: Broadview Press.

Gqola, Pumla. 2001a. "Contradictory Locations: Blackwomen and the Discourse of the Black Consciousness Movement (BCM) in South Africa." *Meridians* 2 (1): 130–52.

———. 2001b. "Defining People: Analysing Power, Language and Representation in Metaphors of the New South Africa." *Transformation* 47: 94–106.

———. 2009. "'The Difficult Task of Normalizing Freedom': Spectacular Masculinities, Ndebele's Literary / Cultural Commentary and Post-Apartheid Life." *English in Africa* 36 (1): 61–76. DOI: 10.4314/eia.v36i1.42868.

———. 2016. "Intimate Foreigners or Violent Neighbours? Thinking Masculinity and Post-Apartheid Xenophobic Violence through Film." *Agenda* 30 (2): 64–74. https://doi.org/10.1080/10130950.2016.1215625.

Graham, Shane. 2007. "Memory, Memorialization, and the Transformation of Johannesburg: Ivan Vladislavić's *The Restless Supermarket* and *Propaganda by Monuments.*" *Modern Fiction Studies* 53 (1): 70–96. https://doi.org/10.1353/mfs.2007.0024.

———. 2009. *South African Literature after the Truth Commission: Mapping Loss.* New York: Palgrave Macmillan.

Gready, Paul. 2007. "Medical Complicity in Human Rights Abuses: A Case Study of District Surgeons in Apartheid South Africa." *Journal of Human Rights* 6 (4): 415–32. https://doi.org/10.1080/14754830701677303.

———. 2011. *The Era of Transitional Justice: The Aftermath of the Truth and Reconciliation Commission in South Africa and Beyond.* Transitional Justice. London: Routledge.

Gready, Paul, and Simon Robins. 2014. "From Transitional to Transformative Justice: A New Agenda for Practice." *International Journal of Transitional Justice* 8 (3): 339–61. https://doi.org/10.1093/ijtj/iju013.

Greco, Mauro. 2019. *Responsabilidades y resistencias. Memorias de vecinos de la dictadura.* Córdoba, Argentina: EDUVIM.

Grégoire, Vincent. 2007. "Sous le signe du gamma: Le rôle de la Milice de Vichy dans la littérature de l'immédiate après-guerre." *Symposium: A Quarterly Journal in Modern Literatures* 61 (2): 117–36. https://doi.org/10.3200/SYMP.61.2.117-136.

———. 2018. "Aimer en toute infidélité: L'analyse d'un adultère hors-norme dans *Hiroshima mon amour.*" *Romance Notes* 58 (1): 17–27. https://doi.org/10.1353/rmc.2018.0002.

Grosescu, Raluca. 2017. "Judging Communist Crimes in Romania: Transnational and Global Influences." *International Journal of Transitional Justice* 11 (3): 505–24. https://doi.org/10.1093/ijtj/ijx016.

Grosescu, Raluca, and Raluca Ursachi. 2009. *Justiția penală de tranziție. De la Nurnberg la postcomunismul românesc.* Iasi: Polirom.

Guynn, William. 2016. *Unspeakable Histories: Film and the Experience of Catastrophe.* New York: Columbia University Press.

Hachten, William A., and C. Anthony Giffard. 1984. *The Press and Apartheid: Repression and Propaganda in South Africa.* London: Macmillan.

Hadfield, Leslie. 2013. "Challenging the Status Quo: Young Women and Men in Black Consciousness Community Work, 1970s South Africa." *Journal of African History* 54 (2): 247–67. DOI:10.1017/S0021853713000261

Hadj-Moussa, R., and M. Nijhawan. 2014. *Suffering, Art, and Aesthetics.* New York: Palgrave Macmillan.

Halimi, André. 1983. *La délation sous l'occupation.* Paris: Editions AMoreau.

Hamel, Yan. 2005. "Mémoires et déchirements: La représentation de la Seconde Guerre mondiale dans le roman français (1945–2001)." Montréal: Université de Montréal.

Haraway, Donna J. 2016. *Staying with the Trouble: Making Kin in the Chthulucene.* Durham, NC: Duke University Press.

Harris, Verne. 2011. "Madiba, Memory and the Work of Justice." Presented at the Alan Paton Centre & Struggle Archives, University of KwaZulu Natal, Pietermaritzburg. http://paton.ukzn.ac.za/Files/ALAN%20PATON%20 LECTURE%202011.pdf.

Hawthorne, Melanie, and Richard Joseph Golsan. 1997. "Introduction." In *Gender and Fascism in Modern France*, edited by Richard Joseph Golsan and Melanie Hawthorne, 1–11. Hanover, NH: University Press of New England.

Held, Virginia. 2007. *The Ethics of Care: Personal, Political, and Global*. Oxford: Oxford University Press.

Hemer, Oscar. 2012. *Fiction and Truth in Transition: Writing the Present Past in South Africa and Argentina*. Münster, Germany: LIT Verlag Münster.

Hewitt, Nicholas. 1996. *Literature and the Right in Postwar France: The Story of the "Hussards."* Berg French Studies. Oxford: Berg.

Hill Collins, Patricia. 2009. *Black Feminist Thought: Knowledge, Consciousness, and the Politics of Empowerment*. New York: Routledge.

Hiralal, Kalpana. 2015. "Narratives and Testimonies of Women Detainees in the Anti-Apartheid Struggle." *Agenda* 29 (4): 34–44. https://doi.org/10.1080/1013 0950.2015.1104883.

Hirsch, Alexander. 2013. *Theorizing Post-Conflict Reconciliation: Agonism, Restitution and Repair*. London: Routledge.

Hochschild, Adam. 1998. *King Leopold's Ghost: A Story of Greed, Terror, and Heroism in Colonial Africa*. New York, NY: Houghton Mifflin.

Hooker, Juliet. 2017. "Black Protest / White Grievance: On the Problem of White Political Imaginations Not Shaped by Loss." *South Atlantic Quarterly* 116 (3): 483–504. https://doi.org/10.1215/00382876-3961450.

Howarth, David R., and Aletta J. Norval. 1998. *South Africa in Transition: New Theoretical Perspectives*. Basingstoke, UK: Macmillan.

Hugo, Pierre. 1998. "'The Politics of Untruth': Afrikaner Academics for Apartheid." *Politikon* 25 (1): 31–55. https://doi.org/10.1080/02589349808705052.

Hutchison, Emma. 2010. "Unsettling Stories: Jeanette Winterson and the Cultivation of Political Contingency." *Global Society* 24 (3): 351–68. https://doi.org /10.1080/13600826.2010.485561.

Hutchison, Yvette. 2013. *South African Performance and Archives of Memory*. Manchester: Manchester University Press.

Ieta, Rodica. 2010. "The New Romanian Cinema: A Realism of Impressions." *Film Criticism* 34 (2/3): 22–36.

Jackson, Julian. 2003. *France: The Dark Years, 1940–1944*. Oxford: Oxford University Press.

Jaladieu, Corinne. 2003. "Les résistantes dans les prisons de Vichy." In *Les femmes dans la Résistance en France*, edited by Mechtild Gilzmer, Christine Levisse-Touzé, and Stefan Martens, 256–82. Paris: Tallandier.

Jansen, Anemari. 2015. *Eugene de Kock: Assassin for the State.* Cape Town: Tafelberg.

Jean, Jean-Paul, and Denis Salas. 2002. *Barbie, Touvier, Papon: Des procès pour la mémoire.* Paris: Autrement.

Jeffery, Laura, and Matei Candea. 2006. "The Politics of Victimhood." *History & Anthropology* 17 (4): 287–96. https://doi.org/10.1080/02757200600914037.

Jennings, Éric. 2002. "Discours corporatiste, propagande nataliste, et contrôle social sous Vichy." *Revue d'histoire moderne et contemporaine* 49–4 (4): 101. https://doi.org/10.3917/rhmc.494.0101.

John, Eileen. 1998. "Reading Fiction and Conceptual Knowledge: Philosophical Thought in Literary Context." *Journal of Aesthetics & Art Criticism* 56 (4): 331–48.

———. 2005. "Art and Knowledge." In *The Routledge Companion to Aesthetics*, edited by Berys Gaut and Dominic McIver Lopes, 417–39. London: Routledge.

Joly, Laurent. 2007. "La délation antisémite sous l'Occupation." *Vingtième Siècle. Revue d'histoire* 4 (96): 137–49. https://doi.org/10.3917/ving.096.0137.

———. 2011. *Les Collabos. Treize portraits d'après les archives des services secrets de Vichy, des Renseignements Généraux et de l'Épuration.* Paris: Éditions Les Échappés.

———. 2012. "D'une guerre l'autre. L'Action française et les Juifs, de l'Union sacrée à la Révolution nationale (1914–1944)." *Revue d'histoire moderne et contemporaine* (59–4): 97–124. https://doi.org/10.3917/rhmc.594.0097.

———. 2013. "Contextes sociaux de la dénonciation des Juifs sous l'Occupation." *Archives Juives* 46 (1): 12–34. https://doi.org/10.3917/aj.461.0012.

———. 2015. "Fascisme et antisémitisme dans la France des années 1930: Une irrésistible convergence?" *Revue d'histoire moderne et contemporaine* (62–2/3): 115–36. https://doi.org/10.3917/rhmc.622.0115.

———. 2016. "Postuler un emploi auprès du commissariat général aux Questions juives (1941–1944). Antisémitisme d'État et crise de recrutement dans la fonction publique des années noires." *Revue d'histoire moderne et contemporaine* (63–3): 163–85. https://doi.org/10.3917/rhmc.633.0163.

———. 2017. *Dénoncer les Juifs sous l'Occupation: Paris, 1940–1944.* Collection "Seconde Guerre mondiale". Paris: CNRS Editions.

Joly, Laurent, and Françoise Passera. 2016. "Se souvenir, accuser, se justifier: Les premiers témoignages sur la France et les Français des années noires (1944–1949)." *Guerres mondiales et conflits contemporains* (263): 5–34. https://doi.org/10.3917/gmcc.263.0005.

Juckes, Tim J. 1995. *Opposition in South Africa: The Leadership of Z. K. Matthews, Nelson Mandela, and Stephen Biko.* Westport, CT: Praeger.

Jude, Radu. 2018. *"Îmi este indiferent dacă în istorie vom intra ca barbari."* Directed by Radu Jude. Bucharest: Micro Film.

Kani, John. 2008. *Nothing but the Truth.* Directed by John Kani. Paris: Odélion Films.

Kaplan, Alice. 2000. *The Collaborator.* Chicago: Chicago University Press.

Kawakami, Akane. 2016. *Patrick Modiano.* Modern French Writers. Liverpool, UK: Liverpool University Press.

Keightley, Emily, and Michael Pickering. 2012. *The Mnemonic Imagination. Remembering as Creative Practice.* Basingstoke, UK: Palgrave Macmillan.

Kelly, Michael. 1995. "The Reconstruction of Masculinity at the Liberation." In *The Liberation of France: Image and Event,* edited by H. R. Kedward and Nancy Wood, 117–28. Berg French Studies. Oxford: Berg.

Keyser, L. 1975. "Three Faces of Evil: Fascism in Recent Movies." *Journal of Popular Film and Television* 4 (1): 21–31.

Kissell, Judith. 1999. "Complicity in Thought and Language: Toleration of Wrong." *Journal of Medical Humanities* 20 (1): 49–60. https://doi.org/10.1023/A:1022938600602.

Klapp, Orrin Edgar. 1948. "The Creation of Popular Heroes." *American Journal of Sociology* 54 (2): 135–41.

———. 1949. "Hero Worship." *American Sociological Review* 14 (5): 53.

———. 1954. "Heroes, Villains and Fools, As Agents of Social Control." *American Sociological Review* 19 (5): 56.

———. 1964. *Symbolic Leaders: Public Dramas and Public Men.* Chicago: Aldine.

Klapper, John. 2015. *Nonconformist Writing in Nazi Germany: The Literature of Inner Emigration.* Cologne: Boydell & Brewer.

Kligman, Gail. 1998. *The Politics of Duplicity.* Berkeley, CA: University of California Press.

Koggel, Christine M., and Joan Orme. 2013. *Care Ethics: New Theories and Applications.* London: Routledge.

Kutz, Christopher. 2000. *Complicity: Ethics and Law for a Collective Age.* Cambridge Studies in Philosophy and Law. Cambridge: Cambridge University Press.

———. 2007. "Causeless Complicity." *Criminal Law and Philosophy* 1 (3): 289–305. https://doi.org/10.1007/s11572-006-9026-6.

Landsberg, Alison. 2004. *Prosthetic Memory: The Transformation of American Remembrance in the Age of Mass Culture.* New York, NY: Columbia University Press.

Lane, Harlan. 2006. "Construction of Deafness." In *The Disability Studies Reader*, edited by Lennard J. Davis, 79–92. New York, NY: Taylor & Francis.

Lang, Berel. 2000. *Holocaust Representation: Art Within the Limits of History and Ethics*. Baltimore, MD: John Hopkins University Press.

Lara, Maria Pía. 1998. *Moral Textures: Feminist Narratives in the Public Sphere*. Cambridge: Polity Press.

———. 2007. *Narrating Evil: A Postmetaphysical Theory of Reflective Judgment*. New York, NY: Columbia University Press.

Laurent, Jacques. 1975. *Le petit canard*. Seville: Imprenta Sevillana.

Leebaw, Bronwyn. 2011. *Judging State-Sponsored Violence, Imagining Political Change*. Cambridge: Cambridge University Press.

Lehman, Daniel. 2011. "'When We Remembered Zion:' The Oscar, the Tsotsi, and the Contender." *English in Africa* 38 (3): 113–29.

Lepora, Chiara, and Robert E. Goodin. 2013. *On Complicity and Compromise*. Oxford: Oxford University Press.

Lloyd, Christopher. 2003. *Collaboration and Resistance in Occupied France: Representing Treason and Sacrifice*. Basingstoke, UK: Palgrave Macmillan.

Lodge, Tom. 2011. *Sharpeville: An Apartheid Massacre and Its Consequences*. Oxford: Oxford University Press.

Lorde, Audre. 1993. *Poetry Is Not a Luxury*. Osnabrück, Germany: Druck- & Verlagscooperative.

Lovinescu, Monica. 2010. *Jurnal esenţial*. Bucharest: Humanitas.

Lowenstein, Adam. 2005. *Shocking Representation: Historical Trauma, National Cinema, and the Modern Horror Film*. New York, NY: Columbia University Press.

Lugones, María. 1987. "Playfulness, 'World'-Travelling and Loving Perception." *Hypatia* 2 (2): 3–19.

Lundberg, Mari, Kerstin Hagberg, and Jennifer Bullington. 2011. "My Prosthesis as a Part of Me: A Qualitative Analysis of Living with an Osseointegrated Prosthetic Limb." *Prosthetics and Orthotics International* 35 (2): 207–14. https://doi.org/10.1177/0309364611409795.

Lupaş, Maria. 2014. "Early Resistance to Fascism in Eugène Ionesco's Interwar Romanian Journalism." *Journal of Modern Literature* 37 (3): 74–91. https://doi.org/10.2979/jmodelite.37.3.74.

Madala, Tholakele H. 2000. "Rule under Apartheid and the Fledgling Democracy in Post-Apartheid South Africa: The Role of the Judiciary." *North Carolina Journal of International Law and Commercial Regulation* 26: 743–66.

Magadla, Siphokazi. 2015. "Women Combatants and the Liberation Movements in South Africa." *African Security Review* 24 (4): 390–402. https://doi.org/10.1080/10246029.2015.1088645.

Magaziner, Daniel R. 2011. "Pieces of a (Wo)Man: Feminism, Gender and Adulthood in Black Consciousness, 1968–1977." *Journal of Southern African Studies* 37 (1): 45–61.https://doi.org/10.1080/03057070.2011.552542.

Maguire, Geoffrey. 2017. *The Politics of Postmemory: Violence and Victimhood in Contemporary Argentine Culture.* Palgrave Macmillan Memory Studies. Cham, Switzerland: Palgrave Macmillan.

Malle, Louis and Patrick Modiano. 1974. *Lacombe, Lucien.* Directed by Louis Malle. Paris: Cinema International Corporation.

Malle, Louis, and Philip French. 1993. *Conversations avec Louis Malle.* Paris: Denoël.

Mamdani, Mahmood. 2015. "Settler Colonialism: Then and Now." *Critical Inquiry* 41 (3): 596–614. https://doi.org/10.1086/680088.

Manea, Norman. 2013. *Despre clovni.* Iasi: Polirom.

———. 2015. *Plicul negru.* Bucharest: Polirom.

Marais, Mike. 2002. "Visions of Excess: Closure, Irony, and the Thought of Community in Ivan Vladislavic's *The Restless Supermarket.*" *English in Africa* 29 (2): 101–17.

Marcot, François. 2006. *Dictionnaire historique de la Résistance: Résistance intérieure et France libre.* Paris: Laffont.

Marcu, Ionuţ Mircea. 2016. "Forme şi instrumente de control politico-ideologic al istoriografiei in România comunistă." In *Traversând comunismul. Convieţuire, conformism, compromis,* edited by Lucian Vasile, Constantin Vasilescu, and Alina Urs, 67–89. Bucharest: Polirom.

Mareş, Clara. 2012. "Intelectualii. Cotidian şi identitate publică in timpul regimului Gheorghiu-Dej." In *Spectrele lui Dej: Incursiuni în biografia şi regimul unui dictator,* 337–58. Iasi: Polirom.

Mareş, Clara, and Constantin Vasilescu, eds. 2015. *Nesupunere şi contestare în România comunistă.* Bucharest: Polirom.

Marx, Lesley. 2010. "At the End of the Rainbow: Jerusalema and the South African Gangster Film." *Safundi* 11 (3): 261–78. https://doi.org/10.1080/17533171003787388.

May, Larry. 2010. "Complicity and the Rwandan Genocide." *Res Publica* 16 (2): 135–52. https://doi.org/10.1007/s11158-010-9112-4.

McDonald, Peter D. 2009. *The Literature Police: Apartheid Censorship and Its Cultural Consequences.* Oxford: Oxford University Press.

McDonnell, Hugh. 2019. "François Mitterrand and the Emergent Grey Zone of Vichy France." *French Politics, Culture & Society* 37 (2): 87–109.

McGeer, Victoria. 2004. "The Art of Good Hope." *ANNALS of the American Academy of Political and Social Science* 592 (1): 100–127. https://doi.org/10.1177/0002716203261781.

———. 2008. "Trust, Hope and Empowerment." *Australasian Journal of Philosophy* 86 (2): 237–54. https://doi.org/10.1080/00048400801886413.

Medina, José. 2013a. "An Enactivist Approach to the Imagination: Embodied Enactments and 'Fictional Emotions.'" *American Philosophical Quarterly* 50 (3): 317–35.

———. 2013b. *The Epistemology of Resistance: Gender and Racial Oppression, Epistemic Injustice, and Resistant Imaginations.* Oxford: Oxford University Press.

Meister, Robert. 2010. *After Evil: A Politics of Human Rights.* New York: Columbia University Press.

Mihai, Mihaela. 2014. "Denouncing Historical 'Misfortunes': From Passive Injustice to Reflective Spectatorship." *Political Theory* 42 (4): 443–67. https://doi.org/10.1177/0090591714544706.

———. 2016a. *Negative Emotions and Transitional Justice.* New York: Columbia University Press.

———. 2016b. "Theorizing Change: Between Reflective Judgment and the Inertia of Political Habitus." *European Journal of Political Theory* 15 (1): 22–42. https://doi.org/10.1177/1474885114537634.

———. 2018. "Epistemic Marginalisation and the Seductive Power of Art." *Contemporary Political Theory* 17 (1): 395–416. https://doi.org/10.1057/s41296-017-0186-z.

———. 2019a. "Engaging Vulnerabilities: An Outline for a Responsive and Responsible Theory." *Journal of Social Philosophy* 51 (4): 583–607. https://doi.org/10.1111/josp.12316.

———. 2019b. "The 'Affairs' of Political Memory: Hermeneutical Dissidence from National Myth-Making." *Angelaki* 24 (4): 52–69. https://doi.org/10.1080/0969725X.2019.1635825.

———. 2019c. "The Caring Refusenik: A Portrait." *Constellations* 26 (1): 148–62. https://doi.org/10.1111/1467-8675.12384.

———. 2020. "The Hero's Silences: Vulnerability, Complicity, Ambivalence." *Critical Review of International Social and Political Philosophy* 24 (3): 1–22. https://doi.org/10.1080/13698230.2020.1796332.

Mihăilescu, Ioan. 1993. "Mental Stereotypes in the First Years of Post-Totalitarian Romania." *Government and Opposition* 28 (3): 315–24. https://doi.org/10.1111/j.1477-7053.1993.tb01318.x.

Miller, Ana. 2008. "The Past in the Present: Personal and Collective Trauma in Achmat Dangor's *Bitter Fruit.*" *Studies in the Novel* 40 (1): 146–60.

Miller, Kim. 2009. "Moms with Guns: Women's Political Agency in Anti-Apartheid Visual Culture." *African Arts* 42 (2): 68–75. https://doi.org/10.1162/afar.2009.42.2.68.

Miller, Zinaida. 2008. "Effects of Invisibility: In Search of the 'Economic' in Transitional Justice." *The International Journal of Transitional Justice* 2: 266–91. https://doi.org/10.1093/ijtj/ijn022.

Mills, Charles W. 1998. *Blackness Visible: Essays on Philosophy and Race*. Ithaca, NY: Cornell University Press.

———. 2007. "White Ignorance." In *Race and Epistemologies of Ignorance*, edited by Shannon Sullivan and Nancy Tuana, 11–38. Albany, NY: SUNY Press.

———. 2014. "White Time: The Chronic Injustice of Ideal Theory." *Du Bois Review: Social Science Research on Race* 11 (1): 27–42. https://doi.org/10.1017/S1742058X14000022.

Milne, Tom. 1974. "*Lacombe, Lucien*." *Sight and Sound* 43 (3): 176.

Milton, Cynthia E. 2014. *Art from a Fractured Past: Memory and Truth-Telling in Post-Shining Path Peru*. Durham, NC: Duke University Press.

Modiano, Patrick. 1968. *La place de l'Étoile*. Paris: Gallimard.

———. 1969. *La Ronde de nuit*. Paris: Gallimard.

———. 1972. *Les boulevards de ceinture*. Paris: Gallimard.

———. 2015a. *The Night Watch*. In *The Occupation Trilogy*, 117–214. London: Bloomsbury.

———. 2015b. *The Occupation Trilogy*. London: Bloomsbury.

Mohanty, Chandra Talpade. 2003. *Feminism without Borders. Decolonizing Theory, Practicing Solidarity*. Durham, NC: Duke University Press.

Moon, Claire. 2006. "Narrating Political Reconciliation: Truth and Reconciliation in South Africa." *Social & Legal Studies* 15 (2): 257–75. https://doi.org/10.1177/0964663906063582.

Moran, Richard. 1994. "The Expression of Feeling in Imagination." *Philosophical Review* 103 (1): 75–106. https://doi.org/10.2307/2185873.

More, Mabogo Percy. 2018. *Biko*. Cape Town: HSRC Press.

Morris, Alan. 1992. *Collaboration and Resistance Reviewed: Writers and the "Mode Rétro" in Post-Gaullist France*. Berg French Studies. New York: Berg.

———. 1996. *Patrick Modiano*. New Directions in European Writing. Oxford: Berg.

Mosse, George L. (George Lachmann). 1990. *Fallen Soldiers: Reshaping the Memory of the World Wars*. New York: Oxford University Press.

Motlhabi, Mokgethi. 1984. *The Theory and Practice of Black Resistance to Apartheid: A Social-Ethical Analysis*. Johannesburg: Skotaville.

Mrovlje, Maša. 2017. "Judging Violent Resistances: Camus's Artistic Sensibility and the Grey Zone of Rebellion." *Law, Culture and the Humanities*, July 14. https://doi.org/10.1177/1743872117721421.

———. 2019. "Beyond Nussbaum's Ethics of Reading: Camus, Arendt, and the Political Significance of Narrative Imagination." *European Legacy* 24 (2): 162–80. https://doi.org/10.1080/10848770.2018.1540514.

———. 2020. "The Horizon of Betrayal: Contesting Ideals of Heroic Solidarity in Resistance Movements." Unpublished manuscript.

Msimang, Sisonke. 2018. "All Is Not Forgiven: South Africa and the Scars of Apartheid." *Foreign Affairs* 97 (1): 28–34.

Mullen, Matthew. 2015. "Reassessing the Focus of Transitional Justice: The Need to Move Structural and Cultural Violence to the Centre." *Cambridge Review of International Affairs* 28 (3): 462–79. https://doi.org/10.1080/09557571.2012. 734778.

Müller, Herta. 2014. *Astăzi mai bine nu m-aș fi întâlnit cu mine însămi.* Bucharest: Humanitas.

———. 2016a. *Animalul inimii.* Bucharest: Humanitas.

———. 2016b. *Patria mea era un sâmbure de măr.* Bucharest: Humanitas.

———. 2017. *Regele se-nclină și ucide.* Bucharest: Humanitas.

Murray, C. D. 2004. "An Interpretative Phenomenological Analysis of the Embodiment of Artificial Limbs." *Disability and Rehabilitation* 26 (16): 963–73. https://doi.org/10.1080/09638280410001696764.

Nagy, Rosemary. 2008. "Transitional Justice as Global Project: Critical Reflections." *Third World Quarterly* 29 (2): 275–89. https://doi. org/10.1080/01436590701806848.

Nasta, Dominique. 2012. "Continuity, Change and Renewal in Romanian Auteur Films: From *Reconstruction* (1969) to *If I Want to Whistle, I Whistle* (2010)." *Film International* 10 (April): 34–56. https://doi.org/10.1386/fiin.10.1.34_1.

———. 2013. *Contemporary Romanian Cinema: The History of an Unexpected Miracle.* New York, NY: Columbia University Press.

Ndebele, Njabulo S. 1998. "Memory, Metaphor and the Triumph of Narrative." In *Negotiating the Past: The Making of Memory in South Africa,* edited by Sarah Nuttall and Carli Coetzee, 19–28. Cape Town: Oxford University Press.

Negri, Alexandra. 2017. "Gendered Inclusions and Exclusions in Zoë Wicomb's David's Story." *Current Writing: Text and Reception in Southern Africa* 29 (2): 89–99. https://doi.org/10.1080/1013929X.2017.1347422.

Németi, Beáta. 2016. "Structurile teritoriale ale Direcţiei Generale a Presei şi Tipăriturilor (1949–1977). Studii de caz." PhD diss., University of Oradea, Romania.

Nettelbeck, Colin. 1985. "Getting the Story Right: Narratives of World War II in Post–1968 France." *Journal of European Studies* 15 (2): 77–116. https://doi. org/10.1177/004724418501500201.

———. 1989. "The Chameleon Rearguard of Cultural Tradition: The Case of Jacques Laurent." In *The Culture of Reconstruction—European Literature, Thought and Film, 1945–50,* edited by Nicholas Hewitt, 153–71. Basingstoke, UK: Palgrave Macmillan.

Nettelbeck, Colin, and Penelope A. Hueston. 1986. *Patrick Modiano, pièces d'identité: Écrire l'entretemps*. Archives des lettres modernes 220. Paris: Lettres Modernes.

Netzer, Călin Peter. 2009. *Medalia de Onoare*. Directed by Călin Peter Netzer. Cologne: Pandora Film.

Neubauer, John, and Borbála Zsuzsanna Török. 2009. *The Exile and Return of Writers from East-Central Europe: A Compendium*. Berlin: Walter de Gruyter.

Norval, Aletta J. 1998. "Memory, Identity and the (Im)Possibility of Reconciliation: The Work of the Truth and Reconciliation Commission in South Africa." *Constellations* 5 (2): 250–65. https://doi.org/10.1111/1467-8675.00091.

Nuttall, Sarah, and Carli Coetzee, eds. 1998. *Negotiating the Past: The Making of Memory in South Africa*. Cape Town: Oxford University Press.

O'Brien, Kevin A. 2010. *The South African Intelligence Services: From Apartheid to Democracy, 1948–2005*. London: Routledge.

Office of the President of South Africa. 1995. *Promotion of National Unity and Reconciliation Act*. www.fas.org/irp/world/rsa/act95_034.htm.

Oprea, Marius. 2008. *Bastionul Cruzimii. O istorie a Securității (1948–1964)*. Bucharest: Polirom.

Origgi, Gloria. 2012. "Epistemic Injustice and Epistemic Trust." *Social Epistemology* 26 (2): 221–35. https://doi.org/10.1080/02691728.2011.652213.

Ory, Pascal. 1981. "Comme de l'an quarante. Dix années de 'rétro satanas.'" *Le Debat* 16 (9): 109–17.

Panagia, Davide. 2009. *The Political Life of Sensation*. Durham, NC: Duke University Press.

Pankhurst, Donna. 2008. *Gendered Peace: Women's Struggles for Post-War Justice and Reconciliation*. London: Routledge.

Pârvulescu, Constantin. 2013. "Post-Heroic Revolution." In *A Companion to the Historical Film*, edited by Constantin Pârvulescu and Robert A. Rosenstone, 365–83. John Wiley. https://doi.org/10.1002/9781118322673.ch18.

Pârvulescu, Ioana. 2015. *Și eu am trăit în comunism*. Bucharest: Humanitas.

Pauw, Jacques. 2017a. *Into the Heart of Darkness: Confessions of Apartheid's Assassins*. Cape Town: Jonathan Ball.

———. 2017b. *Into the Heart of the Whore: The Story of Apartheid's Death Squads*. Cape Town: Jonathan Ball.

Paxton, Robert O. 1973. *La France de Vichy, 1940–1944*. L'Univers historique. Paris: Editions du Seuil.

———. 2001. *Vichy France: Old Guard and New Order 1940–1944*. New York, NY: Columbia University Press.

Peabody, Bruce, and Krista Jenkins. 2017. *Public Opinion and Heroism*. Oxford: Oxford University Press.

Peters, J. C. 2009. "The Missing 'i': Corrigenda in Ivan Vladislavic's Second Edition of *The Restless Supermarket*." *English in Africa* 36 (2): 45–63.

Petrescu, Cristina. 2013. *From Robin Hood to Don Quixote: Resistance and Dissent in Communist Romania*. Bucharest: Editura Enciclopedică. www.academia.edu/6722852/From_Robin_Hood_to_Don_Quixote_Resistance_and_Dissent_in_Communist_Romania.

Petrescu, Cristina, and Dragos Petrescu. 2007. "Resistance and Dissent under Communism: The Case of Romania." *Totalitarismus Und Demokratie* 4 (2): 323–46.

Pettit, Phillip. 2004. "Hope and Its Place in Mind." *Annals of the American Academy of Political and Social Science* 592: 152–65. https://doi.org/10.1177/00027162 03261798.

Pfeifer, Moritz. 2018. "Truth-Detectors: Romania's Struggle with Literal Meaning." *eefb: East European Film Bulletin* (blog). January 6. https://eefb.org/retrospectives/a-linguistic-reading-of-corneliu-porumboius-1208-east-of-bucharest-a-fost-sau-n-a-fost-2006/.

Pityana, N. Barney. 1991. *Bounds of Possibility: The Legacy of Steve Biko and Black Consciousness*. Cape Town: David Philip Zed.

Pleşa, Liviu. 2015. "Formele de manifestare a nemulţumirii populaţiei din judeţiul Alba în anii '80." In *Nesupunere şi contestare în România comunistă*, edited by Clara Mareş and Constantin Vasilescu, 235–83. Bucharest: Polirom.

Pleşu, Andrei. 2010. "Rezistenţa prin cultură." *Dilema Veche*, October 14. http://dilemaveche.ro/sectiune/situatiunea/articol/rezistenta-prin-cultura.

Pohlhaus, Gaile. 2012. "Relational Knowing and Epistemic Injustice: Toward a Theory of Willful Hermeneutical Ignorance." *Hypatia* 27 (4): 715–35. https://doi.org/10.1111/j.1527-2001.2011.01222.x.

Pollard, Miranda. 1998. *Reign of Virtue: Mobilizing Gender in Vichy France*. Chicago: University of Chicago Press.

Popa, Diana. 2019. "Hopeless Didacticism: Archival Sources and Spectatorial Address in 'I Do Not Care If We Go Down in History as Barbarians'." *Law, Culture and the Humanities*. https://doi.org/10.1177/1743872119880313.

Popescu, Delia. 2017. "Pain and Politics in Victim Testimonials." In *Justice, Memory and Redress in Romania: New Insights*, edited by Lavinia Stan and Lucian Turcescu, 257–81. Newcastle: Cambridge Scholars Publishing.

Porumboiu, Corneliu. 2006. *A fost sau n-a fost?* London: Palisades Tartan.

———. 2007. "Corneliu Porumboiu: Nu cred în istorie cu majuscule, ci doar în istorii personale." Interview by Andrei Creţulescu. LiterNet (website). January 26. https://atelier.liternet.ro/articol/4206/Andrei-Cretulescu-Corneliu-Porumboiu/Corneliu-Porumboiu-Nu-cred-in-istorie-cu-majuscule-ci-doar-in-istorii-personale.html.

Posel, Deborah. 1991. *The Making of Apartheid 1948–1961: Conflict and Compromise*. New York, NY: Oxford University Press.

———. 2001. "What's in a Name? Racial Categorisations under Apartheid and Their Afterlife." *Transformation* 47: 50–74.

Posel, Deborah, and Graeme Simpson. 2002. *Commissioning the Past: Understanding South Africa's Truth and Reconciliation Commission*. Johannesburg: Witwatersrand University Press.

Potra, Carmen-Elena. 2015. "Revoltele ţărănesti din judeţul Bihor în vara anului 1949." In *Nesupunere şi contestare în România comunistă*, edited by Clara Mareş and Constantin Vasilescu, 19–42. Bucharest: Polirom.

Preda, Caterina. 2017a. *Art and Politics under Modern Dictatorships*. Basingstoke, UK: Palgrave Macmillan.

———. 2017b. "Art Must Be Politicized: Official Art in Romania." In *Art and Politics under Modern Dictatorships*, 141–209. Cham: Palgrave Macmillan. https://doi.org/10.1007/978-3-319-57270-3_4.

Propst, Lisa. 2017. "Reconciliation and the 'Self-in-Community' in Post-Transitional South African Fiction." *Journal of Commonwealth Literature* 52 (1): 84–98. https://doi.org/10.1177/0021989415592944.

Prundeanu, Andreea Mica. 2017. "Cutting Delilah's Hair: Sentimental Collaborators and the Politics of Female Sexuality in WWI/II France." PhD diss., Michigan State University. https://search.proquest.com/docview/1853452251/abstract/AoDFDA2091AC4824PQ/1.

Pulcini, Elena. 2013. *Care of the World: Fear, Responsibility and Justice in the Global Age*. Studies in Global Justice. Dordrecht: Springer.

Pusca, Anca. 2011. "Restaging the 1989 Revolution: The Romanian New Wave." *Cambridge Review of International Affairs* 24 (4): 573–92. https://doi.org/10.1080/09557571.2011.558888.

Putuma, Koleka. 2017. *Collective Amnesia*. Cape Town: uHlanga.

Quinney, Anne Holloway. 2007. "Excess and Identity: The Franco-Romanian Ionesco Combats Rhinoceritis." *South Central Review* 24 (3): 36–52. https://doi.org/10.1353/scr.2007.0044.

Ramphele, Mamphela. 1991. "The Dynamics of Gender within Black Consciousness Organisations: A Personal View." In *Bounds of Possibility: The Legacy of Steve Biko and Black Consciousness*, edited by B. Pityana, M. Ramphele, M. Mpumlwana, and L. Lixinski. Cape Town: D. Philip.

Reinhardt, Mark, Holly Edwards, John Stomberg, and Erina Dugganne. 2007. *Beautiful Suffering: Photography and the Traffic in Pain*. Williamstown, MA: Williams College Museum of Art.

Renard, Paul. 2010. "La littérature et le cinéma à la hussarde." *Roman 20–50* 49 (1): 147–56. https://doi.org/10.3917/r2050.049.0147.

Robbins, Bruce. 2017. *The Beneficiary*. Durham, NC: Duke University Press.

Robinson, Fiona. 1998. *Globalising Care: Ethics, Feminist Theory, and International Relations*. Feminist Theory and Politics. Boulder, CO: Westview.

———. 2011. "Stop Talking and Listen: Discourse Ethics and Feminist Care Ethics in International Political Theory." *Millennium: Journal of International Studies* 39 (3): 845–60. https://doi.org/10.1177/0305829811401176.

Ross, Fiona C. 2003. *Bearing Witness: Women and the Truth and Reconciliation Commission in South Africa*. Anthropology, Culture, and Society. London: Pluto Press.

Rothberg, Michael. 2009. *Multidirectional Memory: Remembering the Holocaust in the Age of Decolonization*. Palo Alto, CA: Stanford University Press.

———. 2019. *The Implicated Subject: Beyond Victims and Perpetrators*. Palo Alto, CA: Stanford University Press.

Rousso, Henry. 1987. *Le syndrome de Vichy*. Paris: Éditions du Seuil.

———. 1992. *Les années noires: Vivre sous l'Occupation*. Paris: Gallimard.

Roux, Baptiste. 1999. *Figures de l'Occupation dans l'œuvre de Patrick Modiano*. Paris: L'Harmattan.

Royer, Michelle. 2019. *The Cinema of Marguerite Duras: Multisensoriality and Female Subjectivity*. Edinburgh: Edinburgh University Press.

Ruddick, Sara. 1995. *Maternal Thinking: Toward a Politics of Peace*. Boston, MA: Beacon Press.

Rush, Peter D., and Olivera Simić, eds. 2014. *The Arts of Transitional Justice*. New York, NY: Springer. http://link.springer.com/10.1007/978-1-4614-8385-4.

Rusu, Mihai Stelian. 2017. "Transitional Politics of Memory: Political Strategies of Managing the Past in Post-Communist Romania." *Europe-Asia Studies* 69 (8): 1257–79. https://doi.org/10.1080/09668136.2017.1380783.

Salamon, Gayle. 2012. "The Phenomenology of Rheumatology: Disability, Merleau-Ponty, and the Fallacy of Maximal Grip." *Hypatia* 27 (2): 243–60. https://doi.org/10.1111/j.1527-2001.2012.01266.x.

Samuelson, Meg. 2007. "The Disfigured Body of the Female Guerrilla: (De)Militarization, Sexual Violence, and Redomestication in Zoë Wicomb's *David's Story*." *Signs* 32 (4): 833–56. https://doi.org/10.1086/512491.

Sanders, Mark. 2002. *Complicities: The Intellectual and Apartheid*. Durham, NC: Duke University Press.

Sansico, Virginie. 2002. *La justice du pire. Les cours martiales sous Vichy*. Paris: Payot.

Sanyal, Debarati. 2015. *Memory and Complicity: Migrations of Holocaust Remembrance*. New York, NY: Fordham University Press.

Sarnecki, Judith Holland. 2006. "Double Take: Louis Malle's Competing Versions of France under Nazi Occupation." *Women in French Studies*, 13–38. DOI:10.1353/wfs.2006.0045.

Schaap, Andrew. 2004. "Assuming Responsibility in the Hope of Reconciliation." *Borderlands* 3 (1). https://minerva-access.unimelb.edu.au/bitstream/handle/11343/34109/66535_Schaap_Assuming%20responsibility.pdf?sequence=1&isAllowed=y.

———. 2008. "Reconciliation as Ideology and Politics." *Constellations* 15 (2): 249–64. https://doi.org/10.1111/j.1467-8675.2008.00488.x.

———. 2020. "Do You Not See the Reason for Yourself? Political Withdrawal and the Experience of Epistemic Friction." *Political Studies* 68 (3): 565–81. https://doi.org/10.1177/0032321719873865.

Schiff, Jade Larissa. 2013. "The Varieties of Thoughtlessness and the Limits of Thinking." *European Journal of Political Theory* 12 (2): 99–115. https://doi.org/10.1177/1474885111430616.

———. 2014. *Burdens of Political Responsibility: Narrative and the Cultivation of Responsiveness.* Cambridge: Cambridge University Press.

Schwartz, Paula. 1995. "Résistance et différence des sexes: Bilan et perspectives." *Clio* 1 (April). https://doi.org/10.4000/clio.516.

———. 1999. "The Politics of Food and Gender in Occupied Paris." *Modern & Contemporary France* 7 (1): 35–45. https://doi.org/10.1080/09639489908456468.

Sebba, Anne. 2016. *Les Parisiennes: How the Women of Paris Lived, Loved and Died in the 1940s.* London: Weidenfeld & Nicolson.

Şerban, Alexandru Leo. 2010. "Romanian Cinema: From Modernity to Neo-Realism." *Film Criticism* 34 (2/3): 2–21.

Sevenhuijsen, Selma. 2003. *Citizenship and the Ethics of Care: Feminist Considerations on Justice, Morality, and Politics.* London: Routledge.

Shotwell, Alexis. 2016. *Against Purity: Living Ethically in Compromised Times.* Minneapolis, MN: University of Minnesota Press.

Simić, Olivera, and Kathleen Daly. 2011. "'One Pair of Shoes, One Life': Steps towards Accountability for Genocide in Srebrenica." *International Journal of Transitional Justice* 5 (3): 477–91. https://doi.org/10.1093/ijtj/ijr020.

Simonin, Anne. 2010. "La femme invisible: La collaboratrice politique." *Histoire@Politique* 9 (February): 96–96.

Sineux, Michel. 1974. "Le Hasard, le chagrin, la nécéssité, la pitié sur Lacombe Lucien)." *Positif* 0: 25.

Singerman, Alan J. 2007. "Histoire et ambiguïté: Un nouveau regard sur Lacombe Lucien." *French Review: Journal of the American Association of Teachers of French* 80 (5): 1058–68.

Sitze, Adam. 2013. *The Impossible Machine.* Ann Arbor: University of Michigan Press. https://www.press.umich.edu/243251/impossible_machine.

Smuts, Aaron. 2014. "Painful Art and the Limits of Well-Being." In *Suffering*

Art Gladly, 123–52. London: Palgrave Macmillan. https://doi.org/10.1057 /9781137313713_7.

Sontag, Susan. 1963. "Simone Weil." *New York Review of Books*, February 1. www.nybooks.com/articles/1963/02/01/simone-weil/.

Spelman, Elizabeth. 1990. *Inessential Woman: Problems of Exclusion in Feminist Thought*. London: The Women's Press.

Spivak, Gayatri Chakravorty. 2013. *An Aesthetic Education in the Era of Globalization*. Cambridge, MA: Harvard University Press.

Stan, Lavinia. 2004. "Spies, Files and Lies: Explaining the Failure of Access to Securitate Files." *Communist and Post-Communist Studies* 37 (3): 341–59.

———. 2012. "Witch-Hunt or Moral Rebirth? Romanian Parliamentary Debates on Lustration." *East European Politics and Societies* 26 (2): 274–95.

———. 2013. *Transitional Justice in Post-Communist Romania: The Politics of Memory*. Cambridge: Cambridge University Press.

———. 2014. "Women as Anti-Communist Dissidents and Secret Police Collaborators." In *Genre and the (Post)Communist Woman. Analyzing Transformations of the Central and Eastern European Female Idea*, edited by Florentina Andreescu and Michael Shapiro, 80–97. London: Routledge.

Stan, Lavinia, and Lucian Turcescu. 2005. "The Devil's Confessors: Priests, Communists, Spies, and Informers." *East European Politics and Societies* 19 (4): 655–85. https://doi.org/10.1177/0888325404272454.

———. 2017. *Justice, Memory and Redress in Romania: New Insights*. Newcastle: Cambridge Scholars Publishing.

Stensöta, Helena Olofsdotter. 2015. "Public Ethics of Care—A *General* Public Ethics." *Ethics and Social Welfare* 9 (2): 183–200. https://doi.org/10.1080/174 96535.2015.1005551.

Steyn, Melissa. 2012. "The Ignorance Contract: Recollections of Apartheid Childhoods and the Construction of Epistemologies of Ignorance." *Identities* 19 (1): 8–25. https://doi.org/10.1080/1070289X.2012.672840.

Steyn, Melissa, and Don Foster. 2008. "Repertoires for Talking White: Resistant Whiteness in Post-Apartheid South Africa." *Ethnic & Racial Studies* 31 (1): 25–51. https://doi.org/10.1080/01419870701538851.

Stockdale, Katie. 2019. "Social and Political Dimensions of Hope." *Journal of Social Philosophy* 50 (1): 28–44. https://doi.org/10.1111/josp.12270.

Stone-Mediatore, S. 2003. *Reading Across Borders: Storytelling and Knowledges of Resistance*. New York: Palgrave.

Strauss, Helene. 2008. "Listening Otherwise: The Semiotics of the Voice in Achmat Dangor's *Bitter Fruit*." *Wasafiri* 23 (1): 51–56. https://doi. org/10.1080/02690050701778165.

Subreenduth, Sharon. 2006. "'Why, Why Are We Not Allowed Even . . . ?': A

De/Colonizing Narrative of Complicity and Resistance in Post/Apartheid South Africa." *International Journal of Qualitative Studies in Education* 19 (5): 617–38. https://doi.org/10.1080/09518390600886403.

Tănăsoiu, Cosmina. 2007. "The Tismaneanu Report: Romania Revisits Its Past." *Problems of Post-Communism* 54 (4): 60–69. https://doi.org/10.2753/PPC1075-8216540405.

Taylor, Diana. 1997. *Disappearing Acts: Spectacles of Gender and Nationalism in Argentina's "Dirty War."* Durham, NC: Duke University Press.

Thaler, Mathias. 2014. "Political Imagination and the Crime of Crimes: Coming to Terms with 'Genocide' and 'Genocide Blindness.'" *Contemporary Political Theory* 13 (4): 358–79. https://doi.org/10.1057/cpt.2013.48.

Thomson, David. 2014. "One of the 20th Century's Most Powerful Films Is Being Forgotten." *New Republic*, November 30. https://newrepublic.com/article/120155/remembering-hiroshima-mon-amour-manny-farber-and-stanley-kauffmann.

Tileagă, Cristian. 2017. "Conceptions of Memory and Historical Redress." In *Justice, Memory and Redress in Romania: New Insights*, 2–23. Newcastle: Cambridge Scholars Publishing.

Totok, William, and Elena-Irina Macovei. 2016. *Între mit și bagatelizare. Despre reconsiderarea critică a trecutului, Ion Gavrilă Ogoranu și rezistența anticomunistă din Rromânia.* Bucharest: Polirom.

Tronto, Joan C. 1995. "Care as a Basis for Radical Political Judgments." *Hypatia* 10 (2): 141–49.

———. 1996. "Care as a Political Concept." In *Revisioning the Political*, edited by Nancy J. Hirschmann and Christine DiStefano, 139–56. Boulder, CO: Westview.

———. 2013. *Caring Democracy: Markets, Equality, and Justice.* New York, NY: New York University Press.

Tronto, Joan C., and Berenice Fisher. 1990. "Toward a Feminist Theory of Caring." In *Circles of Care*, edited by E. Abel and M. Nelson, 36–54. Albany, NY: SUNY Press.

Tutu, Desmond. 1998. *Report of the South African Truth and Reconciliation Commission.* Cape Town: Juta.

Tuzu, Andreea Iustina. 2016. "Nicoleta Valeria-Grossu în slujba Serviciului Special de Informații și a Securității. Reconsiderări biografice." In *Traversând comunismul. Conviețuire, conformism, compromis*, edited by Lucian Vasile, Constantin Vasilescu, and Alina Urs, 125–62. Bucharest: Polirom.

Unterhalter, Elaine. 2000. "The Work of the Nation: Heroic Masculinity in South African Autobiographical Writing of the Anti-Apartheid Struggle." *European Journal of Development Research* 12 (2): 157–78.

Urban Walker, Margaret. 2006. *Moral Repair*. New York, NY: Cambridge University Press.

———. 2007. *Moral Understandings: A Feminist Study in Ethics*. 2nd ed. Studies in Feminist Philosophy. New York, NY: Oxford University Press.

Uricaru, Ioana. 2012. "Follow the Money." In *A Companion to Eastern European Cinemas*, 427–52. Hoboken, NJ: John Wiley. https://doi.org/10.1002/9781118294376.ch22.

Urs, Alina. 2015. "Răzvrătire in parohia Titan: Povestea preotului Costică Maftei." In *Nesupunere și contestare în România comunistă*, edited by Clara Mareș and Constantin Vasilescu, 155–81. Bucharest: Polirom.

Van Zyl-Hermann, Danelle. 2018. "Make Afrikaners Great Again! National Populism, Democracy and the New White Minority Politics in Post-Apartheid South Africa." *Ethnic and Racial Studies* 41 (15): 2673–92. https://doi.org/10.1080/01419870.2017.1413202.

Vasile, Cristian. 2017. "Coming to Terms with the Controversial Past of the Orthodox Church." In *Justice, Memory and Redress in Romania: New Insights*, edited by Lavinia Stan and Lucian Turcescu, 235–56. Newcastle: Cambridge Scholars Publishing.

Vasile, Lucian. 2016. "Legendă și dilemă istorică. Biografia agentului dublu Mihail Țanțu." In *Traversând comunismul. Conviețuire, conformism, compromis*, edited by Lucian Vasile, Constantin Vasilescu, and Alina Urs, 163–214. Bucharest: Polirom.

Vasile, Lucian. 2015. "Spre adevărata libertate. Grupul Mihai Roth și deturnarea vasului 'Cernavodă'." In *Nesupunere și contestare în România comunistă*, edited by Clara Mareș and Constantin Vasilescu, 121–53. Bucharest: Polirom.

Vasile, Lucian, Constantin Vasilescu, and Alina Urs, eds. 2016. *Traversând comunismul. Conviețuire, conformism, compromis*. Bucharest: Polirom.

Vasilescu, Constantin. 2015. "La limita răbdării și dincolo de ea. Grupul Ninei Dombrovschi și 'atentatul' de la magazinul Textila." In *Nesupunere și contestare în România comunistă*, edited by Clara Mareș and Constantin Vasilescu, 83–120. Bucharest: Polirom.

———. 2016. "Împovăratul drum al delațiunii sau apăsătoarea biografie a unui intelectual: Paul „Popescu" Găleșanu." In *Traversând comunismul. Conviețuire, conformism, compromis*, edited by Lucian Vasile, Constantin Vasilescu, and Alina Urs, 215–80. Bucharest: Polirom.

Veillon, Dominique. 2003. "Les femmes anonymes dans la Résistance." In *Les femmes dans la Résistance en France*, edited by Mechtild Gilzmer, Christine Levisse-Touzé, and Stefan Martens, 89–105. Paris: Tallandier.

Verwey, Cornel, and Michael Quayle. 2012. "Whiteness, Racism, and Afrikaner

Identity in Post-Apartheid South Africa." *African Affairs* 111 (445): 551–75. https://doi.org/10.1093/afraf/ads056.

Vice, Samantha. 2010. "How Do I Live in This Strange Place?" *Journal of Social Philosophy* 41 (3): 323–42. https://doi.org/10.1111/j.1467-9833.2010.01496.x.

Villiers, Dawid W. de. 2009. "After the Revolution: "Jerusalema" and the Entrepreneurial Present." *South African Theatre Journal* 23 (1): 8–22. https://doi.org/10.1080/10137548.2009.9687899.

Virgili, Fabrice. 2002. *Shorn Women: Gender and Punishment in Liberation France*. English ed. Oxford: Berg.

Vladislavić, Ivan. 2012. *The Restless Supermarket*. London: & other stories.

Vlies, Andrew van der. 2017. *Present Imperfect: Contemporary South African Writing*. Oxford: Oxford University Press.

Walker, Lawrence J., Jeremy A. Frimer, and William L. Dunlop. 2010. "Varieties of Moral Personality: Beyond the Banality of Heroism." *Journal of Personality* 78 (3): 907–42. https://doi.org/10.1111/j.1467-6494.2010.00637.x.

Walsh, Moira. 1974. "*Lacombe, Lucien.*" *America* 131 (12): 234.

Warnes, Christopher. 2000. "The Making and Unmaking of History in Ivan Vladislavic's *Propaganda by Monuments and Other Stories.*" *Modern Fiction Studies* 46: 67–89. DOI: 10.1353/mfs.2000.0013.

Weitz, Margaret Collins. 1995. *Sisters in the Resistance: How Women Fought to Free France, 1940–1945*. Hoboken, NJ: John Wiley.

Welsh, David. 2010. *The Rise and Fall of Apartheid*. Johannesburg: Jonathan Ball.

Wicomb, Zoë. 2001a. "Afterword." In *David's Story*, 215–54. New York, NY: The Feminist Press at CUNY.

———. 2001b. *David's Story*. New York, NY: The Feminist Press at CUNY.

Wieviorka, Olivier. 2010. *La mémoire désunie*. Paris: Éditions du Seuil.

———. 2016. *The French Resistance*. Translated by Jane Marie Todd. Cambridge, MA: The Belknap Press of Harvard University Press.

Wildschut, Glenda, and Pat M. Mayers. 2018. "Conflict, Complicity, and Challenges: Reflections on the South African Truth and Reconciliation Commission Health Sector Hearing." *Journal of Nursing Scholarship* 51 (3): 299–307. https://doi.org/10.1111/jnu.12438.

Wilson, Catherine. 1983. "Literature and Knowledge." *Philosophy* 58 (226): 489–96.

Wilson, Richard. 2001. *The Politics of Truth and Reconciliation in South Africa: Legitimizing the Post-Apartheid State*. Cambridge Studies in Law and Society. Cambridge: Cambridge University Press.

Winters, Joseph Richard. 2016. *Hope Draped in Black: Race, Melancholy, and the Agony of Progress*. Durham, NC: Duke University Press.

Worden, Nigel. 2012. *The Making of Modern South Africa: Conquest, Apartheid, Democracy*. 5th ed. Historical Association Studies. Hoboken, NJ: John Wiley.

Young, James O. 2001. *Art and Knowledge*. New York: Routledge.

Zerubavel, Eviatar. 2006. *The Elephant in the Room: Silence and Denial in Everyday Life*. Oxford: Oxford University Press.

———. 2010. "The Social Sound of Silence: Towards a Sociology of Denial." In *Shadows of War: A Social History of Silence in the Twentieth Century*, edited by Efrat Ben-Ze'ev, Eviatar Zerubavel, and Jay Winter, 32–44. Cambridge: Cambridge University Press. https://doi.org/10.1017/CBO9780511676178.

———. 2012. *Time Maps: Collective Memory and the Social Shape of the Past*. Chicago: University of Chicago Press.

Ziman, Ralph. 2008. *Gangster's Paradise: Jerusalema*. Directed by Ralph Ziman. London: United International Pictures.

Zimbardo, Philip G., James N. Breckenridge, and Fathali M. Moghaddam. 2013. "'Exclusive' and 'Inclusive' Visions of Heroism and Democracy." *Current Psychology* 32 (3): 221–33. https://doi.org/10.1007/s12144-013-9178-1.

Zolkos, Magdalena. 2008. "The Time That Was Broken, the Home That Was Razed: Deconstructing Slavenka Drakulić's Storytelling About Yugoslav War Crimes." *International Journal of Transitional Justice* 2 (2): 214–26. https://doi.org/10.1093/ijtj/ijn006.

Index

Cultural Memory | in the Present

The authorized representative in the EU for product safety and compliance is:
Mare Nostrum Group
B.V Doelen 72
4831 GR Breda
The Netherlands

www.ingramcontent.com/pod-product-compliance
Lightning Source LLC
Chambersburg PA
CBHW020500270326
41926CB00008B/683

* 9 7 8 1 5 0 3 6 3 0 1 2 3 *